# Retooling the Mind Factory

## Education in a Lean State

# Dedication

To Henry and Doreen Sears, who taught me from the outset that learning should be fun and fulfilling.

# Retooling the Mind Factory
# Education in a Lean State

by Alan Sears
*University of Windsor*

Garamond Press
Aurora, Ontario

© The author, 2003

No part of this book may be reproduced or transmitted in any form, by any means, electronic or mechanical, without permission of the publisher, except by a reviewer who may quote brief passages in a review.

*Printed and bound in Canada*

*Published 2003 in Canada by Garamond Press Ltd,*
*63 Mahogany Court, Aurora, Ontario L4G 6M8*

*Cover illustration: Demolition of Newmarket High School,*
*Ontario, Fall 2000. Photo courtesy Ron Pilfrey, Newmarket Historical Society*

National Library of Canada Cataloguing in Publication

Sears, Alan, 1954-
   Retooling the mind factory : education in a lean state / Alan Sears.

Includes bibliographical references and index.
ISBN 1-55193-044-7

   1. Education and state—Ontario. 2. Educational change—Ontario.
3. Ontario—Social policy. I. Title.

LC91.2.O6S42 2003         379.713         C2003-901287-5

*Garamond Press gratefully acknowledges the support of the Department of Canadian Heritage, Government of Canada, and the support of the Ontario Media Development Corporation of the Government of Ontario.*

# Contents

**Introduction: Education in a Lean State** ................................................. 1
    "The System is Broken" : Legitimizing Education Change ................... 3
    A Revolution in Common Sense ................................................. 6
    Cultural Revolution and Citizenship ........................................... 10
    Social Policy of the Lean State ................................................. 13
    Education Reform for a Lean World ........................................... 20
    The Critique of Liberal Education ............................................. 23
    Theoretical Foundations ......................................................... 23
    Method of Historical Sociology ................................................. 25
    Notes ......................................................................................... 28

**Chapter 1: The Embrace of the State** ................................................. 31
    Entering the State ................................................................... 32
    Education Before the Welfare State ........................................... 37
    The Broad Welfare State and Educational Expansion ..................... 44
    Elementary Schools: Engaging the Individual ............................... 46
    Secondary Schools: There's a Place for Us ................................. 48
    Post-Secondary Education: Increasing Access ............................. 50
    Access to Universities ............................................................. 51
    A New Point of Access: Colleges and Polytechnics ..................... 54
    The End of Growth? ............................................................... 56
    Notes ......................................................................................... 58

**Chapter 2: Education for an Information Age?** ................................... 59
    Skills for the Information Age? ................................................. 59
    Skills and Lean Production ..................................................... 61
    New Kinds of Problem-Solving? ............................................... 62
    Standards Not Skills ............................................................... 65
    Streaming and Labour Market Polarization ............................... 67
    The Ideology of Training ......................................................... 69
    Lean Discipline ....................................................................... 71
    The Vocationalist Ethos ........................................................... 72
    Skills Planning in a "Free" Market ........................................... 75
    Undermining the Culture of Citizenship ..................................... 76
    Developing a Market Orientation ............................................. 78
    Notes ......................................................................................... 83

## Chapter 3: Education for the Nation .................................................. 85
Educational Optimism and the Broad Welfare State ........................... 86
Seeing Like a State7 ............................................................................ 89
Making National Culture .................................................................... 94
Science and National Culture .............................................................. 97
Culture in a Lean State ...................................................................... 100
The Culture Industries After National Culture ................................. 103
Science After History? ...................................................................... 107
Innovation Culture ............................................................................ 113
Science As Innovation Culture .......................................................... 115
The Culture of Entrepreneurship ...................................................... 117
Conclusion ........................................................................................ 119
Notes ................................................................................................. 121

## Chapter 4: Education, Citizenship and Inequality ...................... 123
Introduction: Education for Equity? ................................................. 123
W.E.B Du Bois on Education for Freedom ...................................... 124
Education and the Contradictions of Citizenship ............................ 128
Equity and Education Reform .......................................................... 131
Education and Racialization ............................................................. 133
Official Multiculturalism: The Highest Stage of Liberalism ............. 141
Post-Liberal Education: Standards and Racialization ....................... 149
Notes ................................................................................................. 154

## Chapter 5: Education: Gender and Sexuality ............................. 155
Education and Gender Equity .......................................................... 156
Gender in a Lean World ................................................................... 157
Gender and the Broad Welfare State ................................................ 158
Masculinity in Mass Production ....................................................... 160
Domestic Femininity ........................................................................ 162
Childhood and School in the Welfare State ..................................... 168
Shifting Gender Relations ................................................................ 169
Gender and Post-Liberal Education .................................................. 179
A Note on Schooling for Sexuality ................................................... 185
Notes ................................................................................................. 189

## Chapter 6: Children of the Market .............................................. 191
Childhood in a Lean World .............................................................. 192
Continuous Improvement ................................................................ 194
Inequality and Polarization ............................................................... 198
Fear the Children .............................................................................. 199
The Market Orientation ................................................................... 207
Closing Extra-Economic Space ........................................................ 209
Commodifying Education Space ...................................................... 210
Teaching Enterprise Culture ............................................................. 211

Knowledge As a Commodity ............................................................. 215
Market Mechanisms in Education ................................................... 220
Towards Lean Education .................................................................. 225
Notes .................................................................................................. 229

## Chapter 7: Learning Freedom .................................................. 231
Fighting Back .................................................................................... 233
Teachers on the Front Line ............................................................ 234
Teacher-Bashing and Education Reform ...................................... 236
Mobilizing Against the Harris Agenda ......................................... 239
Fightbacks by Other Education Workers, High School Students
and Parents ....................................................................................... 242
Fightbacks in the Post-Secondary Sector .................................... 243
Towards Education for Freedom ................................................... 246
Brecht on Teaching and Learning ................................................. 247
Mind and Body ................................................................................. 250
Making the Familiar Strange ......................................................... 251
Art and Science Together ............................................................... 253
Social Movements and Ways of Knowing ................................... 254
Is Brecht Useful? .............................................................................. 255
Active Learning For a Change ....................................................... 257
Notes .................................................................................................. 258

## Bibliography ................................................................................... 259

## Index .................................................................................................. 279

## Acknowledgments

I appreciate the assistance of the following people who read parts of the manuscript or gave me feedback during the process of developing this book: Lillian Allen, Anne Brackenbury, Mike Burke, Christina Burr, David Camfield, Sue Ferguson, Anne Forrest, Jacqueline Murray, Joanne Naiman, Colin Mooers, John Shields, Christina Simmons and Jyotika Virdi.

I would particularly like to thank Ken LeClair and David McNally who read through the whole manuscript and provided important feedback. Thanks for moving to Windsor, Ken. Terry Wotherspoon provided a very helpful review that guided an extensive rewrite. Lesley Cameron did a very helpful edit. Peter Saunders from Garamond Press has been encouraging and helpful. Thank you particularly for keeping the dissident press alive!

Earlier versions of parts of this book have been published in other forms and are reprinted here with permission. Parts of the Introduction appeared in different form as "The 'Lean' State and Capitalist Restructuring: Towards a Theoretical Account," Studies in Political Economy 59: 91-114 (1999). Parts of Chapter 2 appeared in different form as "Education for a Lean World" in Mike Burke, Colin Mooers and John Shields (editors), Restructuring and Resistance: Canadian Public Policy in an Age of Global Capitalism (Halifax: Fernwood Publishing 1999). Thanks to Studies in Political Economy and Fernwood for kind permission to reprint.

# Introduction

# Education in a Lean State

Education reform was a headline issue for much of Mike Harris's term as Premier of Ontario between 1995 and 2002. The Conservative Party, headed by Mike Harris, won the 1995 election in Ontario, sweeping aside the New Democratic Party (NDP) government of Bob Rae. The Harris government made education reform a central priority from the beginning of its mandate. There was nothing unique about this priority. Ontario was just one of many jurisdictions across Canada, and in many other countries around the world, implementing broadly similar education reform policies around the same time.

Mike Harris left politics in 2002 and the Conservative government chose a new premier. There is no doubt that Harris left behind a dramatically transformed education system – a transformation that was hotly contested not only as it was happening, but also for some time afterwards; it required serious battles with teachers, students, school board trustees and parents.

In this book, I analyze the logic of the Harris government's education reform agenda. It is, of course, tempting for those of us who have fought against the Harris government to argue that the transformation has no logic; to see it as the irrational product of an unusually ideological provincial government. It is difficult to believe that all this turbulence and damage has been inflicted deliberately.

It is important not to simply treat the Harris education reform agenda as a temporary aberration that will end when a different government is elected. Indeed, key elements of the education reform agenda in Ontario, such as dramatic hikes in tuition fees for post-secondary education, were introduced by the social democratic NDP government that preceded Harris. Contemporary education reform is not the property of a single political current or a particular jurisdiction. It is not a quirk or a blip.

Education reform does have a logic, even if at times it seems bizarre to those of us who work and study in the schools, colleges and universities. I will analyze this logic through the lens of Marxist approaches to the state, labour processes and culture. Specifically, I will relate education reform to a broad-ranging strategy that aims to recast the relations of citizenship in the light of the process of capitalist restructuring that has been underway since the 1970s. This broad-ranging strategy is often referred to as "neo-liberalism," indicating a renewed approach to the "free market" strategies of the 19th century associated with classical liberalism.

One of the central goals of these neo-liberal strategies is to put citizenship on a crash diet. Citizenship gained some heft during the period of the broad welfare state beginning just after World War II. Membership in the nation began to have its privileges as citizens gained access to certain benefits and services, ranging from education and social assistance to pensions and unemployment insurance. This heftier version of citizenship is now portrayed as so much fat by neo-liberals seeking to introduce what I refer to here as a "lean" state.

The lean state is an emerging regime of social policy designed to further the process of capitalist restructuring that began in response to a profitability squeeze dating back to the 1970s. The most important feature of this restructuring process has been the development of lean production methods in the workplace. Lean production is a set of management strategies to eliminate the waste in work processes by increasing flexibility, reducing the core workforce to an absolute minimum by driving up productivity and contracting-out significant chunks of work. These methods, which are explained in more detail below, were first developed in automobile factories and are now spreading across the spectrum of private and public sector workplaces.

The social policy of the lean state aims to secure the conditions for the spread of lean production methods. Lean production requires a more polarized workforce, with large sections of the population working in lower pay sectors offering little or no security, including contracted-out feeder plants and large swaths of the growing service sector. The social programs of the broad welfare state provided a limited degree of security and generated certain legitimate expectations that impeded the polarization of the workforce. Employers and allied policy-makers have come to see the heftier model of citizenship associated with the welfare state as an obstacle to the spread of lean production methods.

The new lean state is not, however, simply a reduction in the scope of state power. The "free" market requires the state to force people into market relations and regulate their activities there. Social programs are being slashed at the same time as policing and immigration controls are being dramatically increased. The lean state aims to orient the population towards the market, in part by suppressing any non-market alternatives for survival. The emerging social policy of the lean state is to force us onto the market in two ways: through seeking jobs on the labour market, which means selling our capacity to work to employers; and through the purchase of market goods and services to survive.[1]

The program of the lean state also requires education reform. The system of liberal education that developed over the past century focused largely on the development of citizens. Thus, the education reform agenda aims to shift the focus of schools, colleges and universities so that they focus on preparing people for the relations of the market rather than those of citizenship. The logic of the Harris government's agenda has been to develop a more entrepreneurial and consumerist orientation throughout the education system. Education reform is part of the neo-liberal transformation of citizenship. The mind factory is being retooled to bring it more in line with state of the art production systems that have developed in other fields of work.

This book is, therefore, not only about schools. Instead, I examine education reform in relation to a broad process of cultural and economic change. This gives the book a rather sweeping scope that I believe is required to make my case. That is, that education reform is one aspect of a broad-ranging neo-liberal agenda that aims to push the market deeper into every aspect of our lives by eliminating or shrinking non-market alternatives. This Introduction lays out this argument in detail. I begin by showing that advocates of education reform have had to make the case that the current system is not working. This sets the ground for an examination of Mike Harris's "common sense revolution," a claim that drastic change was required to redesign government policies that fit a changing world. Lean production methods are a crucial component of this changing world. A broader social and cultural change is now required to consolidate the emerging order built on the spread of lean production methods. The social policy of the lean state is designed to effect the required cultural and social change, recasting the relations of citizenship. In subsequent chapters I will look in detail at the ways that education reform fits with the goals of the lean state.

## "The System is Broken"[2]: Legitimizing Education Change
The education reform agenda began with John Snobelen's rather bold yet simple claim that the current system does not work. On 12 Septem-

ber 1995, the first Education Minister in Ontario's Conservative government told education officials that "If we really want to fundamentally change the issue in training and ... education we'll have to first make sure we've communicated brilliantly the breakdown in the process we currently experience. That's not easy. We need to invent a crisis. That's not just an act of courage. There's some skill involved." (Cited in Kuehn 1995b:12. See also *The Toronto Star*, 13 September 1995). The Ontario Tories are not alone in employing this theme. The Thatcher government's first successful election campaign in Britain included posters proclaiming "Education isn't working" (Centre for Contemporary Cultural Studies [CCCS] 1981:191). One of the first challenges for those who would restructure education is to convince people that the education system is indeed "broken."

According to the Ontario government, the education system is broken because it has not kept up with the pace of social and technological change. A 1996 discussion paper on high-school reform included the heading: "The world has been changing faster than our high schools have." The first dimension discussed under that heading is technological change. "Computer technology is transforming employment opportunities and requirements, and the way we share knowledge. Most high schools have not kept up. Most school boards have bought computer equipment, but many teachers have not had opportunities to learn how to use it effectively" (Ontario Ministry of Education and Training [OMET] 1996a:2). Note that the major obstacle to change here seems to be teachers, who have not had the opportunity to retool themselves.

But technological change is not the only source of pressure for school reform. The discussion paper also suggested that there had been a cultural shift. "Student populations have become more diverse; high schools have struggled to ensure that every student has an opportunity to learn and excel. School safety is an issue today. Teachers and students face the real and perceived risk of violence" (OMET 1996a:2).

The paper presented education reform as a necessary response to social, economic and cultural changes. It concluded with the statement, "There is a pervasive sense that 'the system' is not keeping up with change, and that it is time for fundamental reform" (OMET 1996a:2). The education reform agenda is presented here in technocratic rather than political terms, as a necessary response to social change. This paints opponents of education reform as politicized and ideological, clinging to old ways in the face of a changing world. British education reformers similarly cloaked themselves in the guise of technical rationality; the claim that the need to increase efficiency can be treated impartially, separate from any considerations of politics or social justice (Avis 1996a:109).

A wide variety of changes have been invoked to justify restructuring. These include: technological change, global competition, the changing labour market, cultural changes and the place of young people in society. Education reformers draw on management theories to compare the school to an out-of-date "black smoke" factory that has failed to keep up due to bureaucracy, rigidity and inefficiency (Arnold 1996:231). Educators are presented as active opponents of sensible change. Elyse Allan, President of The Toronto Board of Trade, announced her organization's new report on education with the statement, "Postsecondary institutions have resisted change more than any other sector" (Canada News Wire 1998:1).

The argument that external changes are driving education reform cloaks the restructuring agenda in technocratic neutrality. The report of the Ontario Government's Advisory Panel on Future Direction for Postsecondary Education stated that, "[i]n many areas we have been marking time, and in a fast-moving and highly competitive world, that means we have been slipping back" (OMET 1996b:13).

The report positions reform as the practical response to a changing world. "We must not, however, be prisoners of our past. There is much that is worthy of praise along the road we have travelled, but there is much that needs to change of the way ahead. Boldness tempered by wisdom is needed in charting our future course. Pragmatism, not ideology, will best guide our journey" (OMET 1996b:13). This is a bold statement of technical rationality. Educational restructuring is presented as a practical response to this epoch of rapid change. Ideology has no part in this debate. Once educational restructuring is elevated to this fact-like status, it is more difficult to challenge it politically. The argument that education reform is a necessary and ideologically neutral response to a changing world has developed as a strategy in the face of ongoing resistance. Richard Johnson documented the long struggle of the pioneering right-wing Thatcher government in Britain to pull together an education reform strategy that the public would buy. "It took twenty years of campaigning, ten years of government and three election victories to develop a practice adequate to New Right purposes at all" (Johnson 1991:31). The Harris government in Ontario could draw upon the previous experience of neo-liberal governments such as Thatcher's Conservatives in Britain.

The Ontario education reform agenda has been founded on a technocratic strategy that avoided some of the ideological flashpoints that have drawn fire elsewhere, such as an early shift towards privatization by pushing for a full voucher system in which parents would be given a certain sum of money towards their children's education to be used for tuition fees at public or private schools. Even so, it has not been easy for the education reformers to proclaim this crisis. There has been important opposition to the education reform agenda in Ontario.

Indeed, militant and activist resistance to education reforms has often won the support of public opinion. For example, the illegal two-week general strike by Ontario teachers in 1997 actually gained public support as it progressed, despite the vilification of teachers by the government and the massive inconvenience caused by the work disruption (*The Globe and Mail* 1999:A7). Indeed, the lowest point of popularity for the Harris government in its first term was around the time of that teacher's strike (Campbell 1999: A13, Ibbitson 2001:A11). The crisis argument does not win support automatically, but it does lend education reform an air of inevitability that makes sustained opposition difficult.

## A Revolution in Common Sense

In this book, I try to challenge the technocratic claims of inevitability that are attached to the contemporary education reform agenda. I argue that education reform is a profoundly political project linked to a broader neo-liberal agenda for restructuring. This agenda is so broad that its proponents describe it as a revolution. The Conservative platform for the 1995 campaign that first elected the Harris government in Ontario was called the Common Sense Revolution.

Education reform is a key feature in the neo-liberal agenda to achieve a revolution in common sense, though I am using those words rather differently than the Tories do. Antonio Gramsci (1971:323-28), an Italian Marxist theorist from the period between the two world wars, used the term "common sense" to describe the everyday conceptions about the world that tend to be shared among people in similar social positions at a particular moment in time. These ideas take on a fact-like solidity as they are widely shared and therefore seldom challenged. The Harris government in Ontario, like other neo-liberal administrations, is attempting to accomplish a revolution in common sense, shifting the taken-for-granted assumptions and expectations that are widespread among the population.

The education system contributes to the development of particular forms of common sense. Students learn a world view through the educational system. The methods of liberal education that developed over the twentieth century tended to teach particular ways of seeing and of locating oneself in the world.[3] Education reform aims to supplant the methods of liberal education with new post-liberal approaches that will develop different ways of seeing and a new understanding of our place in the world.

The Conservatives are attempting to foment a revolution in common sense in order to extend and deepen the current process of capitalist restructuring. The economic downturn of the 1970s signalled a global profitability squeeze that forced corporations to change the ways they do business at every level.[4] This process of restructuring to restore profitability cannot be confined to the level of the enterprise alone. Wider changes in policies, attitudes and expectations are required to solidify these new ways of doing business, which I refer to in this text as the regime of lean production.[5]

Lean production is a set of management strategies to boost work by eliminating "waste" and creating a more flexible workplace. These strategies were developed through a process of improvisation and generalization between employers beginning with the economic downturn of the 1970s. The 1980s and 1990s saw increasing numbers of corporations undertake restructuring along lean production lines in order to restore profitability.

Lean production is based on three key principles: the elimination of "waste" associated with older mass production methods; the introduction of new forms of workplace organization and labour discipline; and the polarization of the workforce. These strategies do not represent a single magic formula that can be employed successfully to restructure any workplace by enhancing productivity and immobilizing worker resistance (Rainnie and Kraithman 1992:49). Individual employers have selected from among these strategies and used them with varying degrees of success in the face of different levels of resistance.

The elimination of "waste" is the first principle of lean production and the basis of the lean imagery in contemporary workplace restructuring. This has meant cutting the "fat" in the form of various buffers built into older mass production systems to protect against breakdown in the whole interconnected process of production due to a problem in one area. These buffers included the stocking of parts in various locations, the use of relief workers and the variation of the speed of the line (Clarke 1992:19-20). In contrast, lean production is based on "just in time" delivery of parts and minimal staffing levels with little or no cover (see Rinehart, Robertson, Huxley and Wareham 1994:153). These methods originated in manufacturing and have crept into areas such as service, caregiving and office work as older labour-intensive methods are replaced by lean production.

The deployment of information technologies is one of the crucial dimensions in the elimination of "waste." New information technologies have been used to increase productivity across the whole spectrum of workplaces, generally strengthening trends towards deskilling jobs to minimize the specific preparation required and increase the interchangeability of workers (see Walker 1989). Further, computer-based information technologies have been used to spread mass production techniques to previously labour-intensive areas, including the service industries, health care, office work and white-collar occupations (see Gershuny and Miles 1983). These technological changes are complemented by the regime of "continuous improvement," which attempts to enlist everyone in the workplace in "waste" elimination. Continuous improvement requires a flexible workforce that can expand, contract or move between tasks as required (Burrow, Gilbert and Pollert 1992: 4-5).[6]

The introduction of new forms of workplace organization and labour discipline is the second principle of lean production. Employers in lean production systems often try to enlist workers into this process of continuous improvement through teamwork mechanisms (see Robertson, Rinehart, Huxley and the CAW Research Group on CAMI 1992). One of the aims of this strategy is remake workplace culture (see Wells 1997). Garrahan and Stewart (1992:94, 116, 138) argue that the more "participatory" workplace culture in lean production systems does not increase workers' control over production, but rather contributes to new forms of identification with management goals of quality, productivity and flexibility.

The emphasis on teamwork in some lean production systems should not be taken as an indicator of kinder, gentler labour relations. Lean production has generally combined attempts at fostering co-operation and the co-optation of workers' knowledge with the intensification of pressure and compulsion. Mike Parker and Jane Slaughter (1994) refer to this aspect of lean production as "management by stress". The stress comes from the speed of the line, the apparently ever-present threat of lay-offs, the minimal employment levels and the intolerance of delay built into "just in time." Stress in the immediate workplace is reinforced by a broader social and economic context marked by the mobility of capital and the declining circumstances of the jobless and the poor.

The third principle of lean production is the increased polarization of the workforce. Indeed, one of the greatest sources of stress that operates as a pressure on the whole working class is the increased polarization of the workforce to enhance flexibility and reduce upward pressure on wages. The Economic Council of Canada (1990) described this in blunt terms as the division between "good" jobs (better pay, benefits and security, more likely to be full-time) and "bad" jobs (lower pay, fewer benefits and little security, more likely to be part-time, temporary or contractual). Women, immigrants, people of colour and people with lower levels of formal education are most likely to end up in the secondary labour market of 'bad' jobs. In Canada, there has been a sharp increase since the 1970s in the number of people working part-time, on temporary contracts or in certain forms of self-employment, all of whom now constitute between 28 and 34 per cent of the workforce (Shields 1996:57-58).

The automotive industry has been the real pioneer in the development of lean production, beginning in Japan. The use of the "subcontracting periphery" has played an important part in the Japanese model of lean production and is used increasingly in the North American context (see Elger and Smith 1994:44). The automotive industry is increasingly divided between assembly plants with unionized workers who have relatively secure, higher paid jobs and the largely non-union parts sector where pay is lower and employment less stable.[7] The parts sector offers the main automobile manufacturers cheaper labour and promotes experiments in enhancing productivity among competing smaller shops. A similar periphery has now been developed across the economy including, for example, the public sector where workers in various community-based agencies or contracted-out services tend to have lower pay, less security and less control over work processes than do government employees.

The generalization of the regime of lean production requires a revolution in common sense. Fredric Jameson (1991:xiv) describes this changes as a "cultural revolution," "coordinating new forms of practice and social and mental habits … with the new forms of economic production and organization thrown up by the modification of capitalism." The Conservatives have therefore ironically proclaimed themselves revolutionaries rising up against the status quo. Education reform is a crucial component of this cultural revolution.

## Cultural Revolution and Citizenship

One of the central goals of the neo-liberal cultural revolution is to redraw the boundaries of citizenship. The parameters of citizenship expanded dramatically with the development of the broad welfare state – one of the defining features of which has been "social citizenship" (Marshall 1950) – in the period after World War II. Social citizenship includes the development of a system of benefits (for example, pensions, social assistance and unemployment insurance) and services (for example, health, education and parks) that provides a limited (and often stigmatized) alternative to the market for the satisfaction of needs (Esping-Andersen 1989:20-27). One of the key features of the welfare state was the establishment of social minima, using programs and benefits to provide at least a specified minimum level of income, housing, health and education (see Guest 1980:3-4). The neo-liberal agenda is to narrow the bounds of citizenship by reducing or eliminating these minima so that we have no alternative to the market to meet our needs.

The goal of narrowing the bounds of citizenship requires changes in the education system. Ontario first introduced compulsory schooling in 1871 and, since then, the imperatives of citizenship-formation have largely driven the expansion of public education. A central goal of public education has been to form citizens. In school, the young person develops a self in relation to the state.

David Lloyd and Paul Thomas (1998) argue that schooling provides an anticipation of citizenship and a rehearsal of students' eventual relations with the state. The very structure of the classroom itself is inflected with the character of citizenship relations. Students in a classroom, like citizens, are at once *collectivized* into a learning community and highly *individuated* by a competitive grading system that means we pass or fail alone. This learning community is in fact an illusory one in that the important ties are not the horizontal ones between students but the vertical ones between student and teacher. The classroom is a particular kind of community that forms only through attending to the teacher. Students' relations to each other are mediated through the teacher, who is supposedly disinterested and equidistant from all. Similarly, as citizens we are highly individuated and form a national community only through the vertical relationship with the state, not through horizontal relations with our fellow citizens. The teacher, then, serves as the embodiment of the state in the classroom, backed up by a hierarchy of authority and a set of rules and regulations.

The neo-liberal agenda for education reform seeks to reorient schooling so that the individual develops a self in relation to the market rather than the state. Social citizenship was a strategy of inclusion that brought at least some parts of the working class into the nation as defined by the state.[8] The welfare state expanded as workers developed new capacities to fight back against employers and governments – for example, by forming unions. Social citizenship offered sections of the working-class membership in the nation, partly as a way of confining working-class militancy and limiting class struggles to the highly regulated realm of collective bargaining.[9]

The inclusiveness of social citizenship was always partial. Women, who often qualified for social programs on the basis of their position in the household and not in the workplace, were generally relegated to a second tier of services that combined lower benefits with greater stigma (see Fraser 1989:149-52; and Scott 1996:7-8). The centrality of national identity to social citizenship meant that people of colour, immigrants and refugees were constructed as minorities and granted only some or none of the rights of social citizenship (see Bannerji 1995:7-15; and Harris 1995:5-6). Aboriginal peoples were almost completely excluded from the rights of social citizenship – any access to those rights was made contingent on the loss of aboriginal status and dropping historic claims against the Canadian state (see Warburton1997:125-7 and Purich 1986). The people of Quebec and francophones outside Quebec were deprived of their national rights (see Welch 1997:122-27). Gay men and lesbians were excluded from full participation by a range of measures to police sexuality and regulate "deviance" (see Kinsman 1996:157-200). One of the major themes of political struggles during the welfare state era were various excluded groups' demands for full social citizenship rights.

The partial inclusion strategies of the broad welfare state worked well to accomplish a certain degree of social peace and a framework for capitalist profitability during the period of the long economic boom that extended roughly from the 1940s to the 1960s. The welfare state provided a framework of entitlements and expectations that tied sections of the working class into the system most of the time. However, the profitability squeeze of the 1970s forced employers and governments to seek out new strategies.

Employers and business leaders increasingly identified social citizenship and the social policy of the broad welfare state as an obstacle to the further generalization of lean production.

The broad welfare state inhibited the spread of lean production as it contributed to the development of labour market rigidities in the form of high wages, limited wage differentials, social program entitlements and labour market regulations (see Neilsen 1991:4). The entitlements and expectations associated with social citizenship were a barrier to "management by stress" strategies associated with lean production.

The expansion of lean production has thus required an attack on the framework of entitlements and expectations associated with social citizenship and the broad welfare state. This requires a cultural revolution parallel in some ways to the one that historically made labour-power (the capacity to work) into a commodity (something bought and sold on the market). In the eighteenth and nineteenth centuries in England, labour-power was made into a commodity through a long process of struggle that drove peasants off the land, severing direct producers from the means of production (the tools, resources and processes required to transform nature to meet our wants and needs) and depriving them of access to the means of subsistence (the goods and services we want and need to survive). In England, this meant that capitalism had to destroy the old moral economy that included a particular structure of entitlements and expectations (Thompson 1993a).[10]

The state was centrally involved in the destruction of the old moral economy. Corrigan and Sayer (1985) describe this transformation of expectations and relationships as a "cultural revolution." This required both the destruction of the old structure of expectations and entitlements and the creation of a new one, compatible with capitalist market relations. The process combined elements of violent repression with strategies to organize consent and the incorporation of the working class into capitalist society (see Corrigan and Sayer 1985:114-15).

Neo-liberal strategies now seek to use the state in a similar manner, to destroy the structure of expectations and entitlements that developed through the broad welfare state. This does not simply require the reduction of state power. The "free" market is not produced by the elimination of the state, but rather by the mobilization of state power to reduce barriers to commodification.

The welfare state is therefore being restructured rather than dismantled (Jessop 1991:104) and the direction of this restructuring has been shaped in important ways by the move to lean production. A new social policy framework, the "lean state," is being put in place to supplant the broad welfare state (Sears 1999). The disentitlement and deregulation that mark the social policy of the lean state strip away the protective clothing of citizenship and leave individuals fully exposed to market conditions. We are to be left with no alternative but to sell our capacity to work on the market in order to meet our needs by buying consumer goods on the market.

The destruction of the moral economy of the welfare state requires education reform. The education system has previously been oriented towards the formation of citizens prepared to take their place in the nation. It is now to be reoriented towards the formation of self-commodifying individuals, prepared to take their place in the market as sellers of their own capacity to work (labour-power) and buyers of goods and services.

## Social Policy of the Lean State

The lean state is a reorientation of social policy to create the grounds for the extension of lean production. The capitalist state has always played an important role in generalizing innovative or "vanguard" forms of production (Corrigan, Ramsey and Sayer 1980:19). As Gramsci (1971:294-313) argued in his path-breaking discussion of Americanism and Fordism, the generalization of new forms of production has broader implications for the culture of the population,. The social policy of the lean state contributes to the spread of lean production by forming the flexible worker and generalizing the lean ethos.

The lean state involves a shift in social policy to promote the formation of flexible workers. Flexibility was not new at the end of the twentieth century. Belinda Leach argues that, "flexibility has been inherent in much of women's work, but was perceived as more unusual in men's" (Leach 1993:65) The spread of lean production expands the proportion of the workforce involved in flexible work. Women have been pushed into flexible work (in large part due to the pressures of combining paid and domestic labour) as they have entered paid employment in larger numbers. At the same time, more men are being pushed into this kind of work, particularly immigrants and younger workers.[11] The formation of the flexible worker is promoted by creating conditions favourable to increased working-class polarization and by bringing lean production methods into the state itself.

The increased polarization of the working class is a crucial feature of lean production methods. Contracting out, temporary employment and part-time work have created a growing pool of non-union "flexible" workers. This pool provides a cheap labour sector and may also create a downward pressure on the expectations of unionized workers, particularly in conditions of chronically high unemployment. The strategy of polarization permits employers to reap the benefits of cheaper labour and new labour processes while avoiding full confrontation with workers in core areas of the labour movement, who may be more able and willing to defend their pay and conditions.[12]

The social programs of the broad welfare state act as a brake on the process of working class polarization. René Morisette, John Myles and Garnett Picot (1995:23-24) argue that earnings polarized less rapidly in Canada than in the United States throughout the 1980s as a result of the income maintenance offered by more stable Canadian social programs. The social policy of the lean state in Canada aims to narrow the gap with the United States by increasing the differentiation of the working class. At the core of this strategy are moves to increase the compulsion to work and reduce incomes at the lower end by dramatically diminishing alternatives to the wage for subsistence. This strategy requires the destruction of any sense of entitlement built up through the period of the broad welfare state.

The sharp reduction of benefit levels for people receiving welfare or social assistance is crucial to this. Benefit slashing is accompanied by eligibility restrictions, such as narrower definitions of disability. The stigma associated with receiving these diminished benefits is being increased through mechanisms such as welfare cops to detect "fraud," snitch lines and the requirement for electronic fingerprinting to receive cheques. At the same time, the compulsion to work is bolstered through workfare programs that force assistance recipients to do certain jobs (see Moscovitch 1997:80-91; Shragge 1997:17-34; and Wright 1995:A1, A18).

The sharp reduction in alternatives to taking any job under any conditions forces people into cheaper labour pools. At the same time, labour market deregulation increases the capacity of employers to dictate pay and conditions. This deregulation has taken the form of loosening employment standards and health and safety regulations while sharply cutting enforcement mechanisms.[13] Legislation to weaken trade unions is another important part of labour market deregulation.[14]

The net result of these policies is to drive the most vulnerable literally on to the streets and figuratively out of society. The strategy of (partial) inclusion associated with social citizenship is being replaced by a new politics of exclusion aimed at the poor, refugees, immigrants and vulnerable people with particular needs. The politics of exclusion naturalize the differentiation of the working class by blaming the conditions of the excluded on their own characteristics. The important French strike wave of November–December 1995 – which mobilized public and private sector workers as well as students to stop the introduction of new neo-liberal social policies in many areas, including education – took up the theme of opposition to the new politics of exclusion (see Jeffrey 1996 and Krishnan 1996). An ability to challenge the politics of exclusion will be an important feature in any movement that challenges the agenda of the lean state.

Developing the flexible worker also required the deployment of lean production methods within the state.[15] This attack on a highly standardized sector of the working class allows the state to use its own labour force as a model for new forms of industrial relations. Public sector unions have played a crucial role in the Canadian labour movement over the past twenty-five years, making this modelling all the more significant (see Panitch and Swartz 1993). More widespread lean production in the state also has important implications for the gendering of the flexible workforce, as the state has been a crucial site of "good" jobs for women (Armstrong 1995:390).

The lean state has employed new technologies in various ways, ranging from electronic fingerprinting scanners to identify social assistance recipients to talk of a "virtual university" located on the Internet (see Brehl 1996; and Sarick 1996). Information-based technologies have been particularly important because they have allowed for the spread of mass production techniques to new areas, including various kinds of service and office work (Dominelli and Hoogvelt 1996:78-81; Gershuny and Miles, 1983:188-95).

Eliminating "waste" and increasing public sector productivity is the watchword of the lean state and has included everything from slashing various boards and commissions to the proposed elimination of one year of secondary school education. The lean methods of Total Quality Management have played a key role in the restructuring of Canadian health care systems (Armstrong and Armstrong 1996:121-33); and the focus on waste elimination is central to the Ontario Government's new business plans. "Ministries are continuing to generate new efficiencies, to set and meet performance standards and to work toward better accountability to the public for the money they spend – in short, to do better for less" (Ontario 1996:2).

Finally, an all-out offensive in the form of hard-line bargaining and mass layoffs has been launched against the public sector workforce to increase flexibility by breaking down job categories, privatization and contracting out. The aim is to reduce the core state sector to an absolute minimum, surrounded by a large private, community or workfare sector to provide personnel and services on a cheaper and more flexible basis.[16] This flexible sector would include everything from consultants and private arts producers to community-based health and social services.

The lean state draws not only on the cheaper labour pools described above, but also on pools of unpaid labour. Most importantly, the domestic labour performed primarily by women in the home is being dramatically intensified – for example, by new practices that turn patients out of hospitals much more quickly than in the past (Armstrong and Armstrong 1996:3; Connelly and MacDonald 1996). A second pool of unpaid labour that figures in the lean state strategy is that of volunteers (Shields and Evans 1998:88-103). The right wing, from Reagan on, has presented volunteerism and philanthropy as alternatives to a decent infrastructure of state services. Stiff competition for jobs places enormous pressure on people to volunteer to gain credentials for employment.

The creation of the flexible worker is complemented by the ethos of the lean person. The lean person is driven to maintain herself or himself at peak levels of fitness and generally organizes her or his life around lean principles, avoiding waste and dependence. The lean person is also a risk-taker, who adapts as the security of the insurance state is replaced by a high-stakes game of chance in the lottery state (Neary and Taylor 1998).

Gramsci's suggestive discussion of "Americanism and Fordism" argued that new forms of moral regulation were required to develop workers suitable to the conditions of mass production. He focused particularly on issues of sexuality. "The truth is that the new type of man demanded by the rationalisation of production and work cannot be developed until the sexual instinct has been suitably regulated and until it too has been rationalised" (Gramsci 1971:297). Corrigan and Sayer argued that the economic side of mass production needed to be complemented by a cultural side, organized partly through the state (Corrigan and Sayer 1985:4-5).

The lean ethos, then, is the cultural side of the regime of lean production. It draws heavily on the spread of working-class consumerism since World War II. Sections of the working class pushed up their living standards and won certain social rights as they unionized and fought for improved conditions. Working-class households now meet more of their needs and desires through the marketplace and postmodernists of various stripes have studied the impact of this.[17] There are also important contributions arguing for a historical materialist approach to understanding consumerism.[18] The increased importance of market consumption has created new (and highly contradictory) forms of inclusion in capitalist society that have, to some extent, superseded social citizenship.

The rise of working-class consumerism has given new life to what are in many ways very old right wing ideas about "self-reliance." Purchasing this new "common sense" depends on both a longer-term historical process of commodification and the contemporary balance of forces (management on the offensive, the labour movement generally defensive). In other words, we can take seriously the impact of consumerism without arguing that the working class has fully accepted capitalist relations.[19] The marketplace may provide the means for some to satisfy certain wants and needs, but it also creates widespread privation and insecurity.

Increased working-class consumerism prepared the ground for an ethos of the lean person that revolves around market discipline. Grahame Thompson (1990:3) argues that the market serves the new right agenda as "a source of *discipline* rather than freedom." Market discipline is introduced most directly through user pay, the principle of having individual service-users pay fees towards the costs of services. The extension of user pay in Canada has included a dramatic increase in post-secondary tuition fees, the introduction of user fees for such programs as drug benefits, and increases in transit fares and park admission fees.

People will be further subjected to market discipline to fill the gap as services contract. The combination of transit fare increases and service reduction, for example, will drive people to privatized transportation (primarily the automobile). Corporations are jockeying to seek a place in this expanded market. Shoppers Drug Mart drugstores distributed a brochure that stated: "With recent and future cutbacks to our national health care system, it is becoming more important for each and every one of us to take more responsibility for our own health."[20]

With the spread of market discipline, the shopping relationship is becoming the model for state-citizen relations. Those services that remain within the state purview are increasingly run on a commercial model while many other services are privatized. Privatization has been an important part of the turn to the lean state on a global scale, with the Thatcher government in Britain serving as an important trendsetter. The Klein government in Alberta was the Canadian privatization pacesetter in the 1990s, though it was preceded by the efforts of the Mulroney federal government (Laxer 1995; McBride and Shields 1993:58-59).

Privatization should not be seen as simply a reduction in the breadth of state activity, but rather as an active policy of extending market discipline (Thompson 1990:135-39). The aim is not simply to raise a bit of cash by selling off assets, but also to submit employees and service users to market discipline in such areas as wages, working conditions and prices. In lean rhetoric the language of self-reliance is really about dependence on the market to meet needs and desires. Any (limited) sense of entitlement working class people might have developed through the period of the broad welfare state (for example, full access to decent health care) is being broken in part by shifting services onto the market. The only entitlement for the lean person is what flows from having cold, hard cash (or a good line of credit).

Market discipline in capitalist societies has always been complemented by a coercive discipline organized through the state. The shift to the lean state involves a major reorientation in the direction of coercive discipline. This was certainly one of the classic arguments made about Thatcherism in Britain.[21] State disciplinary activities reinforce market discipline by visibly suppressing forms of "deviant" conduct that threaten the norms of commodity exchange. These activities also direct the very real insecurities that people feel in conditions of high unemployment and lean production against portions of the population constructed as wrongdoers.

The development of "boot camps" for young offenders is a marker of the shift to lean discipline.[22] In 1997, a campaign by the Toronto Transit Commission against people who do not pay fares combines the themes of discipline and user pay. A subway poster explained the crackdown in the following terms. "Every year we are losing over $12 million to Fare Evasion.... We have made a pact that Fare Evaders will pay the price so that you don't have to."

Thus the crackdown on offenders claims to reduce the burden for good, law-abiding riders who pay their fares. This crackdown has particular racialized dimensions, as the offenders are often presumed to be immigrants and refugees. Indeed, there is a harsh racist dynamic to the lean disciplinary regime that is reflected clearly in the toughening of immigration controls. Tightening immigration controls shows that we are not seeing a simple shrinking of the state in the face of globalization (Basok 1996:133). The aim is not necessarily to reduce the numbers who immigrate, but rather to increase their vulnerability and to permit states more discretion in selecting among them.[23]

However, the racist aspects of the lean disciplinary regime go well beyond immigration controls. The Harris government in Ontario eliminated equity legislation and cut back on funding to the human rights commission. At the same time, the turn towards harsher punishment will mean the intensification of racist policing and the criminalization of people of colour.[24] The racist aspects of the lean agenda take us back to the politics of exclusion discussed above. The aim of these politics is not necessarily to literally exclude from the country, but rather to exclude designated groups from full participation in society so as to increase their vulnerability and susceptibility to low-paid work.

The direction of moral regulation in the era of the lean state has been highly contradictory.[25] On the one hand, there has been an element of moral deregulation associated with the extension of amoral market relations deeper into everyday life. On the other hand, there has been a distinct increase in surveillance and harsh punishment. The harsh disciplinary regime is a reminder that the state is playing an active role in promoting the ethos of the lean person, rather than simply removing itself from the realm of social policy.

This lean ethos is gendered in important ways. The ideology of self-reliance has been turned specifically against women, particularly those receiving social assistance who are castigated as "dependent." Linda Gordon argues, "The anti-dependence ideology then penalizes those who care for the inevitably dependent – the young, the sick – who are, of course, disproportionately unpaid women and low-paid service workers" (Gordon 1990:177) Domestic labour is being devalued at the same time as it is being intensified, and true worth is measured only in terms of market location.

Earlier forms of mass production that developed through the twentieth century were certainly gendered. Atina Grossmann argues that there was a particular gendered dimension to the rationalization process discussed by Gramsci. Rather than breaking down gender roles, "rationalization tightened, indeed, institutionalized, the modern sexual division of labour" (Grossman 1995:5-6) Women became the "quintessential rationalized workers," working hard for very little or no money and reconciling the demands of work, family and sexuality. At the same time, conceptions of masculinity were mobilized to develop an ethos in male-dominated workplaces that equated manliness with the ability to withstand the harsh conditions of factory life and provide for a family (Lewchuk 1993).

The shift from mass production to lean production, and the increased employment in the service sector, have been associated with a massive increase in the proportion of women in paid employment. This has in some ways undercut aspects of the gendered division of labour associated with mass production throughout much of the twentieth century. But it has also given rise to a reconfigured division of labour which features job segregation,[26] polarization in hours of work[27] and the challenge, faced primarily by women, of combining paid employment with intensified domestic labour. The forms of dominant masculinity are also shifting.

The lean state draws on and reinforces this gendered division of labour. As discussed above, current policies that seek to reduce employment in the state sector hit those areas where women have made their most important breakthroughs to "good" jobs. Attacks on social programs create an intensification of domestic labour and increase the barriers keeping women from full-time, secure jobs. The aim of the neo-liberal right is not to drive women out of paid employment, but rather to intensify paid and domestic labour while using forms of vulnerability to gain a cheaper, more flexible workforce.

## Education Reform for a Lean World

The right-wing education reform agenda replaces the methods of liberal education with a new post-liberal approach aligned with the policies of the lean state. The post-liberal educational system is charged less with making citizens and more with training consumers and preparing workers for the "real world" of stiff competition for places in an increasingly polarized workforce offering fewer secure jobs and a more "contingent" future. This requires substantial changes in curriculum, motivated more by the requirement for particular forms of moral character than a specific set of skills. Students are to be prepared for life without a net, or at least for a world with an Internet rather than a social safety net.

The limited sense of entitlement associated with social citizenship is to be undone – the education reform agenda will restructure schools, colleges and universities so that they prepare students for a lean world. There are three dimensions to this shift. First, the education system is being commercialized through: the introduction of various forms of corporate sponsorship; the use of real or fictitious market mechanisms in the allocation of resources; and an intensification of user pay in the form of drastic tuition hikes at the post-secondary level. The decommodified spaces of education are being eroded as part of the elimination of any spaces outside of market relations.

Second, the education system is being organized to substantially increase the opportunity for students to fail. This is being done in the name of standards. New report cards, province-wide standardized testing, souped-up homework requirements and the elimination of important forms of out-of-classroom support will create an insurmountable barrier into which many students will crash. They will end their school careers by spinning out into a job market that is significantly smaller for people who have not completed secondary education. This will increase the insecurity of all students, introducing at ever-younger ages the "management by stress" ethos.

Finally, the post-liberal education system is replacing the centrality of citizenship with an entrepreneurial ethos. Those subjects and disciplines that the government sees as having market value (such as computer science and engineering) are being rewarded as opposed to those that are not (such as the liberal and performing arts). Students are encouraged to think about the market throughout their educational career – for example, they are encourage to keep a portfolio from the earliest grades that relates their educational experience to their career goals. These changes are documented in detail later in the text.

This post-liberal education reform agenda requires significant changes in the education workforce. Workers in education, particularly the full-time teachers and professors, stand out as an "unlean" sector. Teaching is a labour-intensive process not easily amenable to technological acceleration. Jobs in the education sector have been relatively secure, offering a fairly high degree of autonomy and little in the way of strict performance standards. The current organization of schooling requires that teachers have the discretion to organize their own work process inside the classroom where they alone face their students.

The policy-makers behind the lean state want to transform the labour process of teaching more radically, employing new technologies, competition, multi-skilling and workforce differentiation to intensify teaching labour. The introduction of Taylorized methods[28] into an area where craft norms have been largely maintained is an important part of the lean project in education. The increased use of contingent labour fits well with this plan. At the same time, the conditions of non-teaching workers in educational institutions (clerical workers, housekeepers, groundskeepers, food services workers) are to be radically transformed by downsizing and contracting out. The aim will be to meet the "best practices" in other sectors, eliminating any unique characteristics that might be associated with work in educational settings.

Unlean education workers are bad role models for the individuals to be forged in the post-liberal educational system. Further, many education workers are imbued with an ethos built around aspects of citizenship, including elements of universality, an emphasis on the importance of ideas and various degrees of "student-centredness" deriving from liberal educational practices. This was, of course, connected to the creation of a sophisticated form of discipline that focused on the internalization of regimes of self-regulation. This form of discipline is now being cast aside in favour of one that combines the drive and insecurity of market competition with the thrall of consumer society.

Resistance to education reform is not, therefore, simply the last gasp of a sad collection of cranks, naïfs, nostalgics and fat cats. It is a crucial mobilization in opposition to the broad agenda of the lean state. Unionized education workers are the primary obstacle to this refashioning of the education ethos. They have been central to the struggle against the Ontario Conservative government, fighting back vigorously against changes in the education sector and playing an important role in the citywide Days of Action organized by the labour movement in partnership with social movements. In defending their own conditions of work, they challenge the ability of the government to restructure education. Students have been the other crucial cornerstone of resistance. These struggles will determine the extent to which the education system will be restructured over the next few years. This book aims to contribute to that resistance by mapping out the dynamics of liberal and post-liberal education in relation to changes in work, social policy and the cultural realm.

## The Critique of Liberal Education

One note of caution is necessary before we continue. I firmly believe that it is important to defend certain aspects of liberal education against the onslaught of the right-wing education reform agenda. We must be careful, however, not to forget that this is not the end of a golden age for progressive education. Liberal education is deeply and irreparably grounded in the perspective of the bourgeois, European, heterosexual, able-bodied man. His culture and his science are seen as the only instruments that make the world knowable. Others' indigenous ways of knowing are marginalized in liberal education.

Further, liberal education does not prepare students to take power. On the contrary, it prepares them to be ruled. In this book, I develop a detailed critique of liberal education, even as I argue that it is superior in certain aspects to the emerging post-liberal approach. I look at the links between liberal education and the nation-state, class exploitation, racialization, sexism and heterosexism. Education for real freedom must occur outside of the straightjacket of liberal education.

## Theoretical Foundations

This book began as an investigation of the relationship between the emergence of lean production and the Harris government's education reform agenda. The innovative Marxist work of Bowles and Gintis (1976) argued that there has been a close correspondence between the development of schooling and changes in the labour market throughout the history of capitalist schooling. Their argument hinges on the correspondence between the rise of Fordist production methods and the development of specific forms of public education that slotted students into the hierarchy of work relations by preparing them for particular normative environments matching their assigned occupational destiny (Bowles and Gintis 1976:11-13, 131-32). I make a case for "correspondence" (that is, a relationship between capitalist restructuring and education reform) in a rather different way that emphasizes the mediation of the state and moves away from the structuralism of Bowles and Gintis.

This focus on the state was inspired by the work of Carnoy and Levin (1985). They argue that education systems have been reformed in response to both changes in the labour market and the development of citizenship relations. These two exist in tension as the workplace is authoritarian and hierarchical while the concept of citizenship in a democratic state has egalitarian and participatory aspects. The educational system is shaped by this contradictory relationship between changing labour markets and developing conceptions of citizenship.

The development of conceptions of citizenship and state formation led me in rather different directions from Carnoy and Levin. I have incorporated socialist-feminist and anti-racist work that highlights the limits of citizenship as inclusion and the reproduction of gendered and racialized citizenship, particularly in Chapters 4 and 5, drawing on the works of Bannerji (1995), Du Bois (1986a), Fraser (1989), Gordon (1990) and Young (1995). The important work of Kay and Mott (1982) and Neocleous (1996) on the centrality of methods of administration to conceptions of citizenship helped me understand both the deployment of administration in education and the production of "administrability" through education. I have linked the idea of administration to a conception of "discipline" that draws on Foucault (1977), though I am using the term in a sense he could not endorse as it is firmly anchored here within a Marxist theory of the state.

This general focus on education and administration was sharpened when I read Lloyd and Thomas's wonderful book *Culture and the State* (1998). This book investigates the ways the classroom and cultural education prepare students for a career of being administered by the state. It made me aware of the importance of culture in the formation of citizens; and it led me to pay attention to diverse culturally oriented approaches to the study of education, particularly Apple (1995), Bernstein (1971), Bourdieu and Passeron (1990), Giroux (1981) and Readings (1996). My approach, however, is more state-centred than theirs tend to be and has a somewhat different take on historical materialist approaches to culture.

In short, I ended up with a much more developed analysis of the ways education prepares students for citizenship than I had expected from my initial focus on the implications of lean production for education reform. Preparation for citizenship includes readiness to participate in the worlds of work (both paid and unpaid), as the capitalist citizen is productive and "self-reliant." There are important continuities between the administration of the population by the state and the work-discipline deployed by employers. But this does not mean that there is a seamless fit between the worlds of education and work. I draw on Livingstone's (1999) important argument that the school system produces an oversupply of educated workers whose capacities are underused in the capitalist workplace. The link between education and the workplace will be discussed in detail in Chapter 2.

Finally, I was reminded by reading Giroux (1985) that all the "richness" of this account of culture, work-discipline and administration would ultimately provide a very thin explanation if it did not at the same time capture the centrality of resistance to educational processes. I will argue here that state education has developed through struggles, inside and outside of schools. These struggles cannot be fully resolved, no strategy could fully capture the oppositional impulse, as long as state education centres on submission and preparation for exploitation.

**Method of Historical Sociology**
I use the methods of historical sociology to examine these developments. Abrams (1982:16) defines historical sociology as "the attempt to understand the relationship of personal activity and experience on the one hand and social organization on the other as something that is continuously constructed in time." These methods understand the present as a moment in an ongoing historical process. This dissolves the fixedness of things, opening up possibilities that vanish if we confine our frame of analysis to the picture of the moment.[29] In this sense, this book attempts to approach "the problem of the present as a historical problem" (see Lukács 1971:157). This means not only understanding the present in the context of what has preceded it, but also assuming that the we are living in one moment of an ongoing process of change.

The historical approach to the present opens up a series of problems. First, our historical analysis of the past often relies on accounts of events in which the end point of a particular trajectory is known (see Callinicos 1995:142-44). We use the wisdom of hindsight to connect up events and infer causal connections that might not have been thinkable for participants. Of course, the trajectory of history never ends and so we always encounter present-day developments that press us to rethink the meanings of past events. Callinicos (1995:143) gives the powerful example of the ways in which the downfall of the USSR and the so-called Socialist regimes of Eastern Europe provided a different perspective on the analysis of the 1917 Russian Revolution.

One of the challenges in writing histories of the present is that we do not know the end point of the trajectories we are examining. It is all too easy, for example, to see the present moment as a harbinger of remarkable changes that simply will not develop. Our readings of the present are bound up in our projections into the future. As soon as we try to read historical import into present events, we are caught up in the links between the past, present and future. This is immensely liberating as it allows us to assess the present in the light of other possible futures, but it is also a remarkably risky game in which failure is inevitable as events take unexpected turns.

The policies of the Harris government in Ontario serve as the case study for the arguments in this book. However, this text is not a detailed empirical account of education reform under the Ontario Tories. The focus in this project is on theoretical development. Over time, detailed work is required to assess the explanatory powers of this theoretical approach and to enrich the account with more of the complexity of the real world. The rather bold theoretical generalizations in this work are intended to inform the direction of analysis and activism, but are not the last word on the topic.

I have drawn on a variety of documentary sources to sketch out the directions of education reform in Ontario, including press reports, Ministry of Education documents and other sources on contemporary education debates in Ontario. I have also drawn heavily on theoretical work from Britain and the United States, where the shift to post-liberal education (and the lean state) started earlier and has gone deeper. This work is tilted towards the presentation of the bigger picture, trying to understand the conditions and forces that influence our experience of education reform.

Understanding the present in historical perspective is also a challenge, given the specific kinds of information overload associated with the theoretical reflection on current events. Education reform has been a huge issue in Ontario, leaving a critic buried in breaking news. The problem is not only the quantity of information but also the type. I have relied rather heavily on information at the level of politics and policy, using press coverage, press releases and official reports. This book does not provide a detailed examination of the way these policies are actually working out on the ground.

There has been important work done on education reform that offers a more detailed investigation of specific cases. I believe these complement my work here, which is more focused on theory building. Alison Taylor (2001) investigates the experience of education reform in Alberta through the lens of a rich and supple Gramscian analysis of shifting "settlements" in education. These settlements represent a particular, widely-shared understanding of the tasks and methods of the educational system in the light of a specific balance of class forces and other circumstances.

Contemporary education reform in Alberta is presented as the attempt to develop a new settlement in the light of a crisis undercutting the old one. Taylor's interviews with participants in these processes add a valuable dimension of experience that I am not able to reproduce here.

R.D. Gidney (1999) sets the education reform of Ontario's Harris government in the context of fifty years of education policy in the province. This book is rich with detail and insight. One of the great contributions of Gidney's historical perspective is to caution against any simple assumptions of novelty in the contemporary education reform agenda. The journal *Our Schools/Our Selves* is an irreplaceable resource in the analysis of contemporary education restructuring.

The final challenge of taking a historical approach to the present is that I myself am located inside the processes I am examining. I am a university teacher whose job has been seriously affected by the education reform agenda – by, for example, the impact of higher tuition fees, increased class size, an increasing emphasis on market "relevance" and university planning and restructuring processes. Further, I am an activist who has tried to contribute to the struggles against education reform, walking on teachers' picket lines, contributing to student days of action and helping to build solidarity with striking workers who faced contracting out on my home campus. It can be difficult as documentary sources and personal experience flow together to figure out the relationship between the formal research processes and the learning that takes place through activism. I have been influenced by Dorothy Smith's (1987:157) conception of institutional ethnography, using my own experiences as a "point of entry" to the examination of the broader processes of education reform.

In the next chapter, I begin to use this historical approach to examine the development of liberal education in Ontario. This context is important for understanding the contemporary education reform agenda, which is a reaction against key aspects of liberal education.

## Notes

1. Broad and Antony 2001 show the breadth of this shift in Canadian social policy towards the market in their important collection *Citizens or Consumers*. I think we have to be a bit cautious about the wording "citizens or consumers" in their title, however, as the market orientation of the emerging social policy regime is as much about an entrepreneurial orientation (towards the sale of our own capacity to work) as it is about consumerism. Further, citizenship is not disappearing but is being redefined as a set of obligations, norms and responsibilities. Many of these issues are addressed in the introduction and articles contained in this useful collection.
2. This phrase in included in the Ontario Government's business plan for Education in 1996 (Ontario 1996:75)
3. In fact, liberal education dates back far beyond the 1800s. The form of liberal education changed over time, including a major reorientation to fit with the expansion of state education in the 1800s and early 1900s. See Axelrod (2002) for an excellent account of liberal education that places the contemporary changes in education policy in the context of a broader history.
4. The general contours of this profitability squeeze are discussed in Smith and Taylor (1996).
5. I am in fact synthesizing the themes of "flexibility" and "lean production" described in Elger and Smith (1994) Moody (1997) and Neilsen (1991).
6. Workforce flexibility therefore requires the breaking down of rigid job classifications. For a specific discussion of the way this has worked in a Canadian steel plant, see Storey (1994).
7. The issue of contracting out and the parts sector has become central to North American automotive industry labour relations over the past few years. See, for example, Keenan (1996).
8. The incorporation of previously excluded classes into the nation is discussed in Corrigan and Sayer (1985:115) and Harris (1995:4-6).
9. Clarke (1983:118-21) discusses the ways in which the state develops out of working class struggle and Lebowitz (1995:198-207) contributes an analysis of the state from the perspective of wage-labour.
10. For example, the Old Poor Law (1560–1602) that established certain forms of assistance for the impoverished had to be replaced with the New Poor Law (1834) which established much harsher conditions for relief.
11. Pat Armstrong (1995:369) describes this as "harmonizing down."
12. The most obvious case in Canada is the CAW workers at core auto plants, who have generally been able to defend their pay and features of their working conditions through the era of lean production. In exchange, the union has collaborated closely with management in productivity-enhancing projects including teamwork and new forms of flexibility, primarily through deals at the local level (Yates 1993:244-46).
13. Examples from Ontario are discussed in Mittelstaedt (1996) and Ontario Federation of Labour (1996:8)
14. The major anti-union legislation of the Harris government in Ontario is described in Mittelstaedt (1995)
15. This discussion draws on Bob Jessop's (1991) discussion of the application of post-Fordism within the state sector.
16. Within weeks of the plan being introduced parents in a Picketing school were pushing for a "workfare person" to be deployed to keep the school open for community use after hours after Board of Education cuts had forced it to shut earlier (Galt 1996a:A6).
17. See Angela McRobbie's (1996) review of the "New Times" debate in Britain.
18. For reviews of work in this area, see Cross (1997) and De Grazia, (1993).
19. Wood (1997:9) argues that the postmodern agenda has tended to based on the assumption that consumer capitalism has "permanently 'hegemonized'" the working class.

20. Shoppers Drug Mart specifically positioned its 1998 "Healthwatch" campaign as a response to cutbacks in health care, offering information through the pharmacy as an alternative to receding health services.
21. The classic statements of this analysis are found in Gamble (1988) and Stuart Hall et al. (1978).
22. On Ontario's "boot camps" see Anderson (1997) and Armstrong (1997).
23. See, for example, Mike Berry's (1989:195-96) discussion of the important role in the process of restructuring played by Third World immigration to the developed industrial countries (as opposed to capital exports to third world countries).
24. See Jean Trickey (1997) for a discussion of the racial politics of the Harris government.
25. See Gray Kinsman's (1996:360-65) pioneering discussion of this contradictory development of moral regulation with regard to lesbian and gay rights.
26. Clement and Myles wrote that "[t]he feminization of the labour force means that in modern capitalism the 'worker' has two prototypes rather than one: the male, blue-collar worker of industrial capitalism and the postindustrial, female service worker" (Clement and Myles 1994:243).
27. Women are more likely to work short time (in part-time or temporary jobs) while men are more likely to work full-time jobs with heavy overtime (Leach 1993:76).
28 Frederick Taylor is the early-twentieth-century engineer associated with the development of key mass production methods, which break down the work process into a series of discrete tasks performed in a standardized way. The assembly line is the best example of Taylorism, with the overall job broken into a series of carefully engineered tasks monitored by detailed time and motion studies. One of the goals of lean production is to introduce some of these methods into areas of work that had previously relied on skilled labour of individuals working with a substantial amount of individual discretion.
29. I am drawing here on Marx's (1954:80) discussion of our "reflections on social life" that "take a course directly opposite to that of their actual historical development." We begin at the end of the process, "with the results of the process of development ready to hand before [us]."

# Chapter 1

# The Embrace of the State

The education system turns students into citizens by bringing them into the embrace of the state. Educational growth since the beginning of compulsory education in Ontario has been driven by the expansion of citizenship, both extensively, by incorporating previously excluded layers of the population into the nation, and intensively, by penetrating deeper into the lives of the people. The general trend over time has been for more people to receive more formal education. This growth is not the simple result of an increase in workplace skills requirements (see Chapter 2). Nor is it in any straightforward way the sign of an increasing commitment to developing capacities for democratic participation. Rather, I will argue that educational expansion has been driven by the imperative of bringing citizens into the embrace of the state.

Through schooling, the state reaches out and touches its children, attempting over time to make them into citizens with requisite discipline, character and capacities. Educational growth, has brought a greater proportion of the younger population into the embrace of the state for longer periods of time. This growth has required change, a reorganization of the system to increase its capacity to attract and hold students.

The discussion of educational growth becomes particularly important in the light of the contemporary education reform agenda. These changes seem in some ways to be reversing the longer-term focus on educational growth. Rather than finding new ways to extend the embrace of the state, the policies seem to be creating new barriers to participation through the return of standardized exams, new principles of user pay and an increased emphasis on failure.

In the first section of this chapter, I make the theoretical case that the education system has been shaped around the project of making citizens. I then trace out the ways citizenship was central to the development of the Ontario education system. Specifically, I argue that the education system was reoriented to fit the heftier version of social citizenship associated with the broad welfare state.

## Entering the State

The first volume of W.G. Fleming's (1971a) massive history of education in Ontario is entitled *The Expansion of the Educational System*. It traces out a remarkable story of consistent growth in Ontario's state educational activity since the development of schooling. Yet, this growth trend is not really problematized in Fleming's work which demonstrates a basic assumption that educational expansion is simply progress, the sensible response to increasing social needs. This is not unusual. Osborne states, "Most people see the creation of free public schooling as a sign of enlightened progress and the advance of democracy" (Osborne 1999:7). The growth of the educational system is simply taken for granted as a social good in many accounts.

I will argue here that educational expansion has been driven by the increasing need to incorporate the population into the realm of administration. Schooling produces citizens by habituating students to state administration. The educational system provides a crucial entry point into the regimes of administration that have developed in the capitalist states. Perhaps the most important aspect of schooling from this perspective is that it develops individuals in relation to their state. State education constitutes the person as a citizen, integrating the individual into the state and the state into the individual. This process is, however, deeply grounded in struggle and resistance so that these processes of integration remain partial and contradictory.

Citizenship is a set of ties between an individual and the state (Tilly 1995:8). Schooling provides an important ground for the establishment of those ties. The specific character of citizenship ties has influenced the pattern of development of state education. Most importantly, citizenship constitutes the individual as the subject of rights and the object of administration (Kay and Mott 1982:93). The individual acquires capacities to act as part of the process of incorporation into a system of power.

The great contribution of Foucault (1977:26) was to conceive of discipline as a form of subordination that develops capacities to act. Citizenship is, in this sense, a discipline (or set of disciplines). However, Foucault's (1979) own work strongly opposed any conception of the state as a unique point of power. In contrast, I argue that we need to view the discipline of citizenship precisely as an activity of the capitalist state (see Neocleous 1996:57-58).

The contradictory combination of rights and subordination is present in the most basic of capitalist social relations: the labour contract. Workers are free in the sense that they own and control their own bodies, but they are compelled to alienate themselves by selling their capacity to work in order to survive. Kay and Mott (1982:3) argue that the labour contract entails a specific form of submission of workers to capital, yet "this submission takes place under the sign of freedom and equivalence." Citizenship revolves around this association of freedom with submission.

Citizenship in the capitalist state defines freedom and equality in terms of specific political rights (for example, civil liberties, press freedom, privacy) rather than meaningful democratic control of society. It has been possible over time to develop more inclusive forms of citizenship that do not threaten the power of capital due to the separation of the economic from the political sphere in capitalist societies (see Wood 1995). The most important decisions are made in corporate boardrooms and similar realms that are immune from the limited democratic accountability of the parliamentary system.

Formal education prepares people for this particular combination of freedom and submission. It anticipates the form of all future relations with the state and habituates individuals to being administered. Schooling teaches people to see as citizens. It begins when students are drawn out of their immediate environment into the physical and cultural space of the school. In this space, students learn a new national perspective that is supposed to supersede the specific perspectives of individuals grounded in their own interests and experiences (including those of class and ethnicity). Lloyd and Thomas (1998:132, 147) argue powerfully that cultural education provides a crucial foundation for the development of this disinterested national perspective. I will argue below that both culture and science have provided the grounds for defining an alleged neutral "universal" standpoint: the national perspective.

The "universal" standpoint in education draws on the state's alleged neutrality and its monopoly on the use of forced education.[1] The state alone has the power to compel attendance and the legitimacy to claim to educate in the interests of society as a whole. There is, of course, a tremendous amount of informal learning that goes on throughout society (Livingstone 1999). For example, many of us learn to cook from friends and family, through informal methods that often mean working together and sharing advice from experience. Over time, however, formal education institutions founded on the authority of the state have come to claim a unique position in learning processes so that, at the level of common sense, education is often identified specifically with state schooling. The identification of state schooling as the unique source of education contributes to the development of hegemony, a form of rule that relies on the consent of the ruled.[2]

This means that the hegemonic curriculum developed through the state education system comes to define "knowledge," marginalizing other experiences and ways of knowing the world. This has specific implications for class, gender and ethnic inequality as particular ways of learning and particular kinds of knowledge – most often associated with middle and ruling classes, men and people from particular European backgrounds – acquire official status while others are relegated to the sidelines (Connell 1993:34-42).

Students develop this national standpoint through a process that combines individuation with membership in a collectivity. Balibar (1991:51-52) argues that the citizen can exist neither as an isolated individual nor as an element totally incorporated into a collectivity. Rather, through specific citizenship practices, the person becomes an individual through participation in the collective body. He gives the example of participation in an election, which "singularizes each citizen, responsible for his vote (his choice), at the same time as it unifies the 'moral' body of the citizens" (Balibar 1991:47)

The classroom combines individuation (for example, through competitive grading) with the formation of a collective body. The school class becomes a collectivity, most importantly through the shared activity of paying attention to the teacher (Lloyd and Thomas 1998:20). This collectivity is defined by its relationship to a single authority figure who personifies it rather than by active participation in a democratic process. The teacher becomes an embodiment of blind justice, the disinterested representative of the general standpoint. Formal education prepares citizens for the formal democracy of the capitalist state which is founded on representation rather than active participation (see Balibar 1991:47-49; Lloyd and Thomas 1998:20-22,46-47; Wood 1995:217).

Representative democracy is founded on formal equality, in which all citizens are constituted as equivalents despite real inequities in access to power and resources. The state plays a key role in establishing this formal equality, as "individuals only confront each other as equivalents through the medium of the state which is equidistant from them all" (Kay and Mott 1982:83). The disinterested teacher, equidistant from every student, anticipates both representative democracy and formal equality.

Schooling also habituates students to the everyday routine of administration. Over time, states have developed administrative apparatuses to regulate civil society (Neocleous 1996:164). These apparatuses operate through specific classificatory regimes that organize the population around particular principles (Kay and Mott 1982:107). Many of these classificatory regimes deploy quantification to measure, compare and evaluate the population (see Shaw and Miles 1979). Time-discipline, the detailed measurement of time and the organization of individual activity around its arbitrary rhythms, is an excellent example of administration through quantification (see Thompson 1993b). It is so deeply integrated into the culture that it is taken for granted and is virtually invisible. The school system provides young people with formative experiences of time-discipline and of being classified on the basis of the quantification and measurement of their work.

The focus on time-discipline derives from key features of the capitalist system. Marx (1954:46-47) argues that goods and services exchange on the market according to their value, the quantity of socially necessary labour time they contain. Capitalist relations reduce the specific work of particular individuals to a quantitative measure of socially necessary labour time. The quantification of time is thus central to specifically capitalist relations (Jameson 1991:268).

It is important to emphasize here that administration can only be understood in relation to resistance. The capitalist state itself develops through a process of struggle. Clarke (1983:119) argues, "If there were no class struggle, if the working class were willing to submit passively to their subordination to capitalist social relations, there would be no state." Working class mobilizations create obstacles to capitalist reproduction, which is identified with the reproduction of society so long as capitalist conditions prevail (see Clarke 1983:123-24). State policy-makers attempt to solve social problems, clearing obstacles to social reproduction by regulating capitalism in particular ways. In this sense, administration is a record of encounters with resistance, each innovation representing some attempt to capture or overcome opposition (see Kay and Mott 1982:96).

It follows, then, that if there were no resistance, there would be no compulsory state educational system. State education has been a central feature of administrative regimes since the early days of social policy. The development of state educational systems has been impelled by resistance, both within and outside of educational institutions. Innovations in education can been understood as new administrative methods to try to capture subjectivities so that every student might find herself or himself within the system.

Resistance outside of the educational setting creates a general climate for social change and can lead to important changes in world view that have an impact inside schooling. Many critical histories of education argue that the development of educational systems in the nineteenth century can be understood as a response to social unrest (see Curtis 1988 and 1992; Lloyd and Thomas 1998; Prentice 1977). The struggles that impelled the state towards the development of compulsory schooling did not necessarily revolve around educational issues. There is often a process of displacement between class struggles and social policy formation, so that workers fighting on one ground may incite changes at other sites (see Topalov 1985). State policy-making is an active process in which agents mobilize available resources to solve what appear (from the perspective of the state) to be social problems. This often includes attempts to redefine the problem (for example, from structural unemployment to training shortfalls) (see Dunk, McBride and Nelson 1996).

Participation in education politics does not necessarily take a direct form. Workers' participation in struggles around the form and content of state education, for example, might not be expressed in class terms but rather through ethnic or neighbourhood affiliations (see Katznelson, Gille and Weir 1982). There have been important mobilizations around education by the women's movement, anti-racist organizations and others who have sought to transform schooling as part of a broader project of social justice. We need to be aware of the diverse forms of social struggle that have influenced education policy.

Resistance within educational systems also takes a number of forms and involves a range of players. These range from explicitly political mobilizations by education workers and students to everyday forms of resistance that could be as active as challenging an authority figures or as passive as minimizing participation in classroom activities. Indeed, one of the problems with such a broad continuum of forms of resistance is that it becomes possible to define almost any activity as oppositional (Giroux 1985:291). This leads to an understanding of resistance that is so broad as to be meaningless in understanding education policy.

A general emphasis on resistance in education needs, therefore, to be complemented by rich ethnographic accounts that are historically specific. Perhaps the most important contribution to clarifying conceptions of resistance in education has come through critical ethnographies which shed light on the subject, developing situation-specific understandings that draw on agents' own world views (see Connell 1989, Corrigan 1979, McRobbie 1978, Willis 1977). These ethnographies also demonstrate the complexities of resistance, which can draw on existing systems of power to address forms of powerlessness (Giroux 1985:285-87). Thus, for example, sexism, racism and heterosexism have been part of the repertoire of certain forms of masculinity (and indeed femininity) developed in response to class inequity in school settings. Working class students who find no space for themselves within the school system at times draw on the power of dominant forms of masculinity and femininity to gain regard in the face of devaluation by the schools (see Connell 1989; McRobbie 1978; and Willis 1977).

There are important parallels between our understanding of resistance in the workplace and in the schools (Apple 1995:75-76). Workers develop a range of alternative knowledges and practices in order to fight for some degree of control over even the most engineered "workerproof" labour processes (see Elger 1982). Just as workers approach the workplace in order to meet their own needs for sustenance, once they have been historically deprived of alternatives, so participants in education use institutions to meet their own needs. There is thus a tension between education for the state and education for oneself built into the system that provides a basis for our understanding of resistance.[3]

This is not an ethnographic study on educational resistance. There is specific discussion of certain forms of struggle in and around education, particularly in Chapter 7 but, more importantly, I have tried to found my whole theoretical approach on the centrality of resistance to the development of the educational apparatus of the state. Giroux (1985:289) argues that an analysis of resistance in education is crucial to provide the basis for a "dialectical notion of human agency that rightly portrays domination as a process that is neither static nor complete." It is my intention to make such a conception of agency central to this work.

## Education Before the Welfare State

The broad welfare state was marked by the expansion of social citizenship, as discussed in the Introduction. The educational system was a crucial component in this project, developing skills, forms of self-discipline and an early identification with the nation-state. Indeed, education was a pioneering form of social policy that pre-dated the welfare state as such.

The educational apparatus expanded along with other elements of social policy to produce the broad welfare state.

The broad welfare state was built on the foundation of pioneering forms of social policy developed by state and private agencies throughout the nineteenth and early twentieth centuries. These pioneering efforts served as workshops for social policy experiments. The most successful innovations were generalized by the state either directly, through the provision of services and benefits, or indirectly, through regulation and funding.[4] Other early programs were rejected or marginalized as the welfare state developed. This was a period of groping towards forms of inclusion that would emerge in full form as citizenship in the broad welfare state. The state moved cautiously towards the provision of benefits and services, impelled forward by working class demands for the right to self-reproduction (the time and resources to stay alive and maintain a household) yet ever fearful of undermining the system of privatized reproduction and "personal responsibility."

State education developed alongside public health programs, social casework methods, settlement houses and policing as pioneering instruments of social policy. State schooling was the first universal social program aimed at promoting the inclusion of the working class as members of capitalist society. Previously, working-class households lived largely outside of "society." It was assumed that they did not share a common social or political space with their rulers (see Corrigan and Sayer 1985:114-20).

Social unrest was one of the key factors that galvanized the state to respond to the problem of working-class exclusion. School was seen as a crucial vehicle for inclusion, quite literally diminishing the distance between classes by bringing together the children of the community, and so compulsory education was introduced in Ontario in 1871 (see Prentice 1977:16, 121, 141). In Britain, education was seen as a crucial foundation for the extension of the franchise as a strategy for working-class inclusion after the Chartist challenge (see Lloyd and Thomas 1998:108).

Schooling, then, was an attempt to domesticate the working class, taming its members and bringing them into the "imagined" community organized around the state. I am drawing here on Anderson's (1983:16) conception of the "imagined community" where, "regardless of the actual inequality and exploitation ... the nation is always conceived as a deep, horizontal comradeship." One of the most important aspects of the domestication of the working class was time-discipline (see earlier), the ordering of work and domestic life around scheduled regularity and the principal of using time efficiently (Thompson 1993b [1967]). Compulsory schooling played a crucial role in bringing children and their families into the realm of time-discipline, forcing working-class households to get children to school on time regardless of their own needs or competing pressures.

As I pointed out earlier, time-discipline is now so throughly internalized as to be invisible and that is true of much of the domestication work accomplished within schools, sometimes labelled the "hidden curriculum." Vallance defines the hidden curriculum as "those non-academic but educationally significant consequences of schooling that occur systematically but are not made explicit at any level of the public rationales for education" (Vallance 1983:11). She argues that a great deal of what is now taken as the "hidden curriculum" was overt in the nineteenth century. After that, however, these tasks were simply taken for granted (20-21). The hidden curriculum is not a dirty secret, nor is it accomplished "behind the backs" of educational actors (teacher, administrators, students, parents) in a structurally determined manner.[5] It is simply so thoroughly integrated into common sense that it is not apparent, except in those circumstances where struggles make the familiar strange and equip people to view the world in new ways.

This process of working-class domestication has been at the core of state education. Bruce Curtis argues that the primary aim of state schooling as it developed was not the teaching of specific skills (reading, writing, arithmetic), but rather the development of certain ways of living. "Education was seen as a means for the remaking of popular culture and character, for the transformation of tastes, for the solidification of genial *habits*, for the creation of a popular intelligence capable of appreciating the 'rational merits' of bourgeois society" (Curtis 1988:14). This enforced discipline was contested. Curtis (168) documents a wide range of forms of resistance to state schooling, the most serious of which revolved around the right of children to leave school, especially when threatened with physical punishment.

The drive for state education was not only propelled by the social reform agenda of working class inclusion. There was a tremendous pressure from working class people themselves for access to education, particularly to develop basic literacy (see Seccombe 1993:96-97). Lloyd and Thomas (1998:140-42) argue that state education in Britain represented a convergence of social reformers' desires for the "cultivation" of the working class (from above) with radicals' commitments to working-class self-education (from below) in the context of the defeat of the militant insurgency of the Chartist movement. In other words, educational expansion was driven in part by the channelling of working-class desires for learning through state institutions while eliminating alternatives associated with working-class self-organization.[6]

Schooling therefore developed in a context of struggle. It involved a serious reorganization of relations between the child, the family, the community and the state. It was one of the first approximations of citizenship, a form of discipline that offers membership in society (as defined around the state) through the establishment of a particular configuration of rights, obligations and norms. These early attempts to form children into citizens met with considerable resistance. State policymakers developed ways of dealing with this resistance, both by making schooling desirable and by establishing a disciplinary hierarchy rooted in central authority. This was accomplished over time through a complex process of innovation – for example, the shift away from corporal punishment towards methods of discipline more oriented around positive feedback.

One of the key problems confronting state authorities was the formation of a centralized apparatus with the recognized authority to regulate school facilities that had developed locally. Bruce Curtis (1992) documented the key role played by School Inspectors in the development of a central educational authority in what is now Ontario. Inspectors served as the vehicle for carrying information back to the centre, generalizing the best local practices and bringing regulations to the locality.[7] Curtis argues that Inspectors "increase the power of central authority to know conditions in localities; they increase the power of local authorities to place their own situations in a more general context" (Curtis 1992:198).

The regulation of teachers was a major problem for those who sought to create centralized authority over schooling – normal schools were introduced to develop certain standards and forms of teaching (Prentice 1977:162). The inculcation of particular forms of self-discipline were central to the development of a regulated teaching process in the face of fragmentation into individual classrooms. Teachers were encouraged to sever local class and community ties, acting as external agents working to elevate the common people, despite the fact that their own conditions were far from elevated. "Beginning in the 1830s and 1840s (and continuing virtually uninterrupted to the present day), state officials and the educational elite have engaged in promoting the "ideology of professionalism," inundating teachers with the ideal that they occupy stations above that of common workers (although, all the while, employing them under poor working conditions, low pay, little job security, and authoritarian work relations)" (Smaller 1995:345).

At the same time, the character of the teaching role was changed to make schooling more desirable. As teaching was professionalized and organized bureaucratically, it was also feminized. Women were employed to make teaching maternal and render schooling more acceptable. The embrace of the state then took on a specific gendered character. Women were also seen as a cheaper and more compliant labour force (Curtis 1988:252-56; Danylewycz, Light and Prentice 1987:33-35; David 1980:240-41; Thompson 1997:320). State schooling was cast as an extension of family relations with the state occupying a parental role (Prentice 1977:171).

Schooling made the state the agent for the development of appropriate forms of disciplined behaviour among children, anticipating broader systems of citizenship. Policy-makers took steps to ensure that the way in to the disciplinary apparatus was eased by, for example, maternalizing elementary school teaching. At the same time, as John Holland argues, "[T]he essential component of public education is, of course, compulsion" (Holland 1976:85)

At first, compulsory education was limited to the elementary levels. Pedagogically, the focus was on drill-style teaching of a basic curriculum focused around reading, writing and arithmetic (McDiarmid 1976:156-58). Entrance exams were required for admission to secondary schools, which was geared to the needs of the few students who would continue on to university, teaching (through normal school) or professional work (Prentice 1977:145; Thomas 1976:101). Although the reach of primary schools was already quite broad by the beginning of the twentieth century, secondary schools served only those who were going on to university. Expanding secondary schools required the introduction of new program s oriented to working-class students.

The expansion of secondary education was driven by changes in the conception of citizenship associated with a major reorganization of work along the lines of mass production. Work was reorganized through the spread of industrialization and the development of scientific management methods. The conception of citizenship was changing in response to increased global competition and the drive to war, as well as the great wave of working class activism culminated in the mass strikes of 1919. At the same time, social reformers argued that they were facing a crisis of social reproduction, which they described in terms of "race degeneration" (see Sears 1990). Reformers located this crisis in the urban slums where they attributed a variety of social problems to demoralization, unhygienic living conditions and mass immigration. The expansion of the education system could serve the combined purposes of moral elevation, social harmonization through inclusion and disciplinary preparation for work.

Indeed, the project of the reformers and state policy-makers of this period was largely educational. Reformers saw the working-class family as inadequate for the task of forming potential citizens. Schooling was an important part of the state educational apparatus that was to prepare people for work, domestic labour and citizenship. Schools were a crucial agency through which boys and girls were to be taught appropriate standards of gendered behaviour and prepared to face the world of work. Immigrants were to be assimilated and the poor were to be taught how to live "well" within their means.

One of the challenges of this scheme of educational uplift was to make schooling more practical. This theme is central to the influential report entitled "Education for Industrial Purposes" written by John Seath, the Superintendent of Education for Ontario in 1911. A central focus in that report was the limited offerings that the educational system made available to working-class students. As a result of the lack of appropriate program s, these students were likely to leave school at the end of their compulsory stay (age 14) or even before that (Ontario Department of Education [Ont DE]1911:266). Seath argued for new kinds of vocational education to develop certain forms of skill and discipline, but also to provide a place in the secondary school system for working-class students. "For the pupil who is going to take up some industrial occupation our school system provides no course which he or his parents recognize as bearing adequately on his future, he is without incentive to continue at school" (Ont DE1911:267).

This emphasis on practicality in education also mirrored the orientation of the philanthropic social reform movement towards new forms of practical morality rooted in science. Abstract moralizing would not touch the actual lives of the poor. This meant that they often had a "vocational" view of education, concentrating on the preparation of young people for paid and/or domestic labour (see Danylewycz 1991:127).

The early twentieth century saw some important experiments in practical education at the secondary level in Ontario. Jackson and Gaskell (1991:167-68) point out that vocational education was not completely new at the beginning of the twentieth century. Commercial programs had existed in the later nineteenth century, oriented primarily to preparing middle-class boys for office work. The vocationalism of the early twentieth century was a departure in so far as it was oriented towards working-class students, including both boys and girls in a gender-differentiated grid. New practical programs included home economics to prepare girls for domestic labour, shop to give boys a basic taste of manual training and various other vocational programs oriented primarily towards boys or girls depending on the sexual division of labour. Vocationalism, then, was a specifically and consciously gendered form of education (see Danylewycz 1991, Jackson and Gaskell 1991).

Vocationalism provided new ways of increasing school participation by differentiating education so that a wider variety of students could find their place. This paralleled an increase in the length of compulsory education. Seath argued for an increase in the school leaving age by extending the period of compulsory education from age 14 to age 16 or 17. However, he felt that such a move was impractical in 1911 and recommended instead sharper enforcement of truancy laws and a local option approach that would allow localities to increase the length of compulsory education (Ont DE 1911: 342-43).

Compulsory education was extended to the age of 16 in Ontario ten years later, in 1921 (Axelrod 1982:9-11; Royal Commission on Education 1950:19). The addition of two extra years of compulsory schooling was in some ways connected to changing work patterns that reduced the labour market opportunities for young people. Craig Heron (1995:224) argues that, in Hamilton, the demand for younger people in the labour market was reduced by the shift to heavy metal-working which called for a more mature workforce; the elimination of apprenticeships; the mechanization of certain forms of fetching and carrying that had formerly been done by younger workers; and the availability of newer immigrants as a source of cheaper unskilled labour.

The increase in formal education requirements was not driven narrowly by economic need for specific skills training, but also by the political project of forming young people into citizens. "Keeping adolescents in schools for two extra years, then, was a political project as much as a technocratic adjustment of the relationship between school and labour market" (Heron 1995:242). Indeed, it is arguable that the shift to vocational education was more about what to do with the young people who were being held longer in compulsory education but who had no aspirations for post-secondary education. This marked a clear shift to streaming in education to feed into the hierarchically structured labour market (Heron 1995:244). Streaming was in essence a strategy to resolve the contradiction between universal education for citizenship and the structured inequality of the labour market.

The proportion of 15–18 year olds in secondary school doubled in Ontario between 1921 and 1931, and one third of those were in vocational or technical schools (Jackson and Gaskell 1991:183). The proportion of Canadians aged 5–24 who were enrolled in the education system at any level increased from 44 percent in 1867 to 58.4 percent in 1921 and then dropped down to 55.4 percent in 1931 and 51.5 percent in 1941. Overall, the 1930s Depression and World War II interrupted the pattern of educational expansion which began again with the post-war welfare state (Statistics Canada 1978:15-17).

## The Broad Welfare State and Educational Expansion

The education system was substantially expanded and retooled to fit with the social policy of the broad welfare state. This was the apogee of liberal education associated with the most expansive period of social citizenship. The development of responsible and self-disciplined citizens who felt some degree of security was seen as the key to social peace and productivity during this period. A larger and more varied educational system was to be a crucial contribution to the formation of these citizens.

The themes of access and inclusion were reflected at all levels of the education system in Ontario during the broad welfare state period. The Hall-Dennis report (formally entitled the Report of the Provincial Committee on Aims and Objectives of Education in the Schools of Ontario [PCAOESO]), issued in 1968, was the apex of welfare stare educational policy. The commitment to access was central to the report: "The child's right to the best education available is now universally recognized" (PCAOESO 1969:9). It reflected a liberal-humanist ethos and focused centrally on the task of citizens for a democratic society. In the section on "training for democracy," for example, is the statement: "The heart of the problem of providing a general education in a democratic society is to ensure the continuance of the liberal and humane tradition" (PCAEOSO 1968:21). The report clearly opposed a narrow economist view of the fit between education and labour market. "The society whose educational system gives priority to the economic over the spiritual and emotional needs of man defines citizens in terms of economic units and in doing so debases them" (PCAEOSO 1968:27).

This report marked an important point in the trajectory of education reform and the ideology of the broad welfare state. It was the high point in the moment of inclusion, envisioning a form of citizenship that regulates the population through self-discipline. There were, of course, real limits to that inclusion and the period of the broad welfare state saw significant struggles around those limits. The civil rights movement in the United States fought bitter battles to attempt to break down the racialized boundaries of full citizenship and the women's movement fought against the gender inequality built into the citizenship system. The whole system of Canadian citizenship is founded on the destruction of aboriginal nations and cultures. Francophones outside Quebec struggled for access to French-language education while Quebecois fought for national self-determination. Many challenged the British Protestant version of national identity on offer in the Canadian state. Yet, for much of the welfare state period, there was broad political agreement that inclusionary citizenship strategies were essential to social well-being.

The Hall-Dennis report was not a sudden departure in a radical new direction. It was the culmination of a longer-term process of educational reform (Fiorino 1978:42; Fleming 1971b:10). This is stated quite clearly in the report, which notes that the 1937 reforms still sound contemporary thirty years later (PCAEOSO 1968:70). The Hall-Dennis report was considerably more secular in orientation than the 1937 reforms, which still included religious education (Fleming 1971b:10) and went beyond the 1937 reforms in advocating a shift away from traditional disciplines and strict conceptions of achievement levels (Gidney 1996:30).

In particular, the Hall-Dennis report was critical of the concept of failure at school. "A child who is learning cannot fail" (PCAEOSO 1968:62). After all, failure is not simply about a child not meeting a specific standard. If the aim of the school is to prepare the child for society, then it is a failure of the system if someone slips through the cracks. The welfare state at its broadest really did aim for a near-universal reach.

At the same time, a child's failure at school represents an indictment of the system for its inability to accommodate individuals. Joyce Carol Oates wrote movingly in the novel *Them* about a working-class woman whose entry into university marked a triumph in her dismal life. After all this, she failed. Later she wrote to the teacher: "I wanted to succeed in school and find a place, make my way along, get married, but my life was in a flurry and I was too nervous to do well.... You failed me. You flunked me out of school" (Oates 1969:314). Failure, then, cuts two ways: it can mean either the failure of the system to accommodate the individual or the failure of the individual to measure up to the requirements of the system. In the context of the broad welfare state, failure was regarded as a system problem, an educational challenge.

The Hall-Dennis report also weighed in against corporal punishment. "The use of physical punishment as a motivating factor in learning is highly questionable" (PCAEOSO 1968:57). It reaffirmed the need to address children's individual interests. "Learning by its very nature is a personal matter" (PCAEOSO 1968:48).

The direction of the report was to limit the extent of exclusion through the school system. The Hall-Dennis report represented the articulation of a series of pedagogical experiments designed to expand the inclusive reach of the school system, and thus the embrace of the state. It is no coincidence that this strategic direction received its sharpest statements in the late 1960s, at a high point of resistance within and outside of the school system. Students took action against the school system in many ways, ranging from organized actions against restrictive dress codes (for example, bans on blue jeans) to spontaneous challenges to the way teachers taught. The Hall-Dennis report notes that students reacted against being treated like children in schools. "Many young men and women protest against something in society which constricts them" (PCAEOSO 1968:41). Fleming argues that students in the late 1960s were rebelling against "irrational authority", insisting on their right to scrutinize rules and regulations "in terms of their own ideas of logic and common sense" (Fleming 1971b:78). The 1960s rebellion was met, in part, by reshaping the school system to allow it to accommodate elements of insurgency.

### Elementary Schools: Engaging the Individual

At the elementary level, the commitment to access was reflected more in qualitative than in quantitative terms. Participation rates were already high at the elementary school level and there was not much room for quantitative growth. In 1945–46, the vast majority of five- to fourteen-year-olds in Ontario (85 percent) were in school. This would increase to 95 percent over the next twenty years (Ont DE: 1963:S-5, 1966:S-5).

Clearly, there was not much room for increased participation at this level, which was fully compulsory.

The broad welfare state period did, however, see dramatic qualitative changes in elementary education. The impulse to inclusion was reflected in part in the commitment to "child-centred" learning. One of the great challenges of a universal system of education is to make places for children to find themselves within the school. Education must resonate with children's real experiences and needs if it is to operate as a relatively universal disciplinary form. Yet many children could not find a place for themselves within traditional educational approaches. Those who could not cope with the traditional approaches of drill-style learning and corporal punishment were driven into outsider status and resistance strategies. The challenge of child-centred approaches was to bring as many students as possible inside the system by allowing limited space for self-expression within a disciplinary environment. Children were to be allowed some space to develop a form of self-discipline appropriate to their background, their anticipated future and their personality structure.

The shift towards child-centred learning in Ontario was marked most sharply by the 1937 curriculum change[8] (Fleming 1971b:9-11, 122-28). Albert Fiorino (1978:41-42) stated in a background paper for the Commission on Declining Enrolment in Ontario that the 1937 curriculum change set the direction for Ontario education through to the 1970s. The committee of teachers responsible for the changes recommended dropping uniform standards, abolishing external exams and gearing program s of studies to the needs of the individual student (Fiorino 1978:43). McDiarmid argues that the aim of this new progressive educational direction was "to make schools less harsh, to modify rote learning practices and to make schools a little more meaningful to immigrant and working class children" (McDiarmid 1976:158).

This progressive direction was reinforced during World War II by a greater emphasis on citizenship and preparation for democracy. The 1941 edition of the Program of Studies explicitly raised the role of the schools in preparing the pupil to participate in a democratic society (Fiorino 1978:43). A similar emphasis on citizenship developed in British education during the war (CCCS 1981:53-54).

The issue of inclusion at the elementary level was not one of recruitment and retention. Enrolment was given under the system of compulsory attendance and the only reason for any major changes was a demographic shift. Rather, the aim was to engage the student more effectively to promote the internalization of a meaningful system of self-discipline and to engender appropriate relations with authority and the system of time-discipline. At the core of that self-discipline was an individualized ideology of personal growth that obscured social inequalities (Martell 1974:15-16).

## Secondary Schools: There's a Place for Us

The development of an inclusive secondary school system was a more complex task than it was at the elementary level. Here there were important issues of retention as compulsory attendance ended at age 16. In addition, the secondary school system had developed in a highly differentiated form reflecting fundamental class, gender and ethnic differences in student trajectories (the relation between background and life destination). Further, the question of citizenship becomes somewhat more complex when dealing with people who are burdened with certain adult responsibilities while having only the rights of children.

Secondary school enrolment increased dramatically during the years of the broad welfare state. The proportion of eighteen-year-olds who had graduated from secondary school increased from 30 percent in 1955–56 to 52 percent in 1965–66 and to 61 percent in 1975–76 (Ontario Ministry of Education and Training 1993:13). The question of retention of secondary students through to graduation was a major issue in Ontario secondary schools from 1950 onwards (McDiamid 1976:159).

The citizenship-formation strategies developed at the primary and secondary levels were very different. At the elementary level, the emphasis was on a renewed commitment to child-centred learning, which included the accentuation of individual attention and a softening of requirements for grade advancement. In contrast, the expansion of the secondary system was accomplished largely through a renewed emphasis on streaming, particularly the reorganization and enlargement of vocational streams. The core challenge was to include working-class students in a secondary system designed largely around the needs of what was still at that time a university-bound elite. The 1964 Grade 13 Study Committee described the challenge problem as: "how to provide in one institution a program of studies designed to prepare for admission to a university of learned profession the small number in the age group who at any given time are likely to benefit from such a programme and, as well, programmes of study which are designed to provide a solid general education, with some vocational elements, for the much larger number of students for whom a university-type course is inappropriate" (Ontario DE. Grade 13 Study Committee 1964:7-8).

The result was a renewed commitment to vocational education. The Roberts plan of 1962 increased access to high school completion through a massive expansion of the vocational streams (Fleming 1971b:145-49; Gidney 1996:26). This expansion of vocational education did not derive from a direct need for increased training for particular skills in the labour market (see Chapter 2). Instead it served to hold working-class students inside the system and to increase their chances of developing the discipline of citizenship.

One of the aims of the Roberts plan was to increase access to vocational education by destigmatizing streaming. The Ontario Legislative Assembly Select Committee on Manpower Training lauded this aspect of the Roberts plan. "One of the most impressive aspects of the plan is the intended objective of raising the status and prestige of the vocational streams to that of the traditional academic stream." (1963:25). Yet this was not the eventual outcome. Martell argues that the most dramatic expansion of the secondary system during this period was at the lower end of the vocational stream, "incorporating kids from the bottom levels of the class structure who would normally have dropped out of school by their early teens." (Martell 1974:8) With the exception of women trained for growing job markets in clerical and sales work, these students rarely ended up in the jobs for which they had been directly trained (8-10). The aim, rather, was "the development of a properly subordinate character structure suitable for the dead-end work that awaits these kids" (11). Curtis, Livingstone and Smaller (1992:88) describe vocational education in the 1960s and 1970s as the "dead end division" of the school system.

The expansion of vocational education aimed to extend the school experience of young people who would normally have left to enter the job market. This protracted school experience was important in the formation of particular attitudes, habits and expectations that were far more important than skills in themselves.

The period of the 1960s and 1970s also saw a shift towards a more student-centred approach in the academic streams of secondary schools. The number of required courses was reduced and the emphasis on traditional core subjects was relaxed. There was an increased emphasis on preparing students to be flexible in the face of rapid change (Fleming 1971b:33-34). The standardized matriculation exams at the end of the final year of high school (called Grade 13) were abolished in 1967. These exams "haunted" Grade 13 students and forced teachers to focus on test preparation (Ont DE Grade 13 Study Committee 1964:15) instead of teaching the curriculum thoroughly in a manner geared to the needs of a particular student body The abolition of the Grade 13 exams marked the final step in a longer-term process of eliminating standardized exams that posed obstacles to participation in the educational system. The high-school entrance exam had been previously eliminated in 1949 (Fleming 1971b:269-71).

In the late 1960s and early 1970s, a credit system was adopted to replace lockstep advancement in which a student needed to pass most or all subjects to pass on to the next grade. The credit system allowed students to advance in a course-by-course basis. These reforms were anticipated in pilot projects and generalized through the Hall-Dennis report (Gidney 1996:26-29). The same period also saw a dramatic shift towards a more user-friendly approach to teaching such courses as mathematics, social studies, science, English and French (Fleming 1971b:184-238).

The secondary school system grew through the expansion of the vocational stream and a more student-centred approach to the academic stream. Overall, the welfare state project of taking more students through more secondary schooling was a great success. Retention grew, despite the pull of a labour market in a period marked at times by a clear labour shortage. This was linked to changing conceptions of inclusion, an ideological commitment to educational access and the development of new forms of discipline that required contracted development.

## Post-Secondary Education: Increasing Access

The post-secondary system expanded rapidly during the period of the broad welfare state. And not only did it grow in size, it also changed character. The expansion was jump-started just after the war by programs to support education for veterans. The proto-welfare state for veterans represented a dress rehearsal for the development of the broad welfare state that soon followed. The broad welfare state saw the massive expansion of existing post-secondary institutions (primarily universities), the development of new universities and the introduction of new forms of technical education at the post-secondary level, particularly through community colleges. This is not a uniquely Canadian phenomenon, but it is one that took place in many of the "northern" welfare states. Gibbons et al. (1994:73) describe it as the development of mass higher education. They argue that this massification of higher education affected post-secondary education in many ways, including a diversification of functions (ranging, for example, from abstract research to practical training), a more diverse student profile (not just males from the professional and employing classes) and a more specific orientation towards preparing professional, white collar and technical workers (76-77).

## Access to Universities

The basic story of university enrolments in the welfare state period was a simple one. In general terms, Canadian university enrolments doubled every decade during the welfare state period. Expansion began at the end of World War II with the introduction of programs that offered tuition benefits and living allowances to veterans (Axelrod 1982:19). Enrolments doubled between the end of World War II and 1951, again by 1961, again by 1971 and then continued to grow throughout the 1970s (Statistics Canada 1978:15-17). The university system also grew and changed during this time.

During World War II, the emphasis in universities tilted towards professional and scientific courses, and away from arts and social sciences. The question of whether there was a future for the liberal arts was openly debated in Canadian universities during this period (Axelrod 1982:17-18). It was not only a debate about the needs of wartime society, but about the fit between the traditional liberal arts curriculum and a changing society with a heavy scientific-technological direction. McKillop argues that this period saw "a crisis of confidence within the academic community in the Western liberal tradition" (McKillop 1994:538).

The debates around the liberal arts during World War II raised many of the same issues that are being discussed today about the "relevance" of a liberal arts education in a society where the greatest economic need seems to be for higher-level scientific and technical skills. Yet the liberal arts curriculum was revived after the war. The form of liberal arts education changed through the period of the welfare state but its centrality in the university system remained.

The Massey Commission (officially the Royal Commission on National Development in the Arts, Letters and Sciences [RCNDALS 1951] contributed to the establishment of a direction for Canadian universities in the welfare state era. The Commission was created as a broad inquiry into national culture, and education was outside its terms of reference (due to the federal structure that made education a provincial responsibility). However, the Commissioners decided that an investigation of the future of the universities was crucial to their mission (RCNDALS 1951:6, 132).

The Massey Commission report makes an impassioned claim for the future of liberal arts education. It notes a trend towards scientific and technical education at the post-secondary level and describes a "tendency to adopt utilitarian and so-called scientific methods," noting these are "admirable in themselves but dangerous when misapplied" (RCNDALS 1951:138). This tendency reflects the demands of the economy. "The urge to 'speed up production' and to emphasize technology in the university's curriculum has led to a growing stress on purely utilitarian subjects in academic courses" (143).

The Commission argued that a liberal arts education makes an important practical contribution. It warns that employers pushing for a more practical curriculum may also ask, "Why can't my staff draft a lucid memorandum or an intelligible letter?" (RCNDALS 1951:137). But the report is not limited to an argument that the liberal arts help develop analytical and communicative skills. It also discusses the contributions of the liberal arts to the development of character, raising such considerations as the cultivation of "judgement and taste," as well as "intellectual curiosity and interest" (137-38). One of the contributions of the university must be "to enable persons to live more complete lives" (138).

The report also addresses itself to the "financial crisis" that universities faced in the post-war period, noting that average per student expenditures had dropped in the five years from 1943–44 to 1948–49 as funding levels had not kept up with a dramatic increase in enrolments (RCNDALS 1951:140-42). The Commission recommended an annual federal contribution to university costs and the development of a national scholarship system (352-60). Federal per capita support to universities was introduced quickly after the release of the report (McKillop 1994:565).

The theme of underfunding in the face of growing enrolments nonetheless remained a central one throughout the 1950s. A conference of representatives of Canadian universities in 1956 noted with concern the predictions that enrolment would double within ten years given that universities were already facing financial and other difficulties resulting from growth (Bissell 1956:244). The late 1950s and early 1960s saw the development of a rudimentary planning process and some level of organization of public funding (Axelrod 1982:77-95).

The shift towards technological education at the university level that worried the Massey Commission did not develop as the university system expanded through the 1950s and 1960s. On the contrary, curriculums in the 1960s changed much more in the direction of general liberal education with increased student choice over courses and sequences (Axelrod 1982:101-4). The proportion of undergraduate degrees in the arts and social sciences increased from 46.8 percent in 1960–61 to 60.6 percent in 1968–69 (Fleming 1971a:216). This in part reflected the need for a flexible white-collar workforce (which I will discuss below) but it also reflected a conception of citizenship and character-development in which jobs skills were not the only consideration. These themes resonate with remarkable consistency from the Massey Commission through to the Hall-Dennis report.

The shift of universities towards a more flexible liberal education resonated with conceptions of citizenship at the height of the broad welfare state. It was also a response to student activism. In the late 1960s and early 1970s, students mounted a serious challenge to authority in the universities. Administrations at various universities introduced parallel changes in response to student mobilization. At the level of curriculum, universities removed much of the rigidity of traditional program structures. Institutions such as Carleton, Queen's and the University of Toronto adopted new, more flexible, undergraduate programs that offered students more choice in the years 1969 to 1970. These institutions also attempted to improve teaching and adopt less punishing evaluation methods (Fleming 1971c:272-82). The innovations were in part a response to student pressure for a curriculum that was more socially and personally relevant (280-81). It is interesting to note how far the terms of debate have shifted in the ensuing thirty years, so that relevance is now constructed in occupational terms.

These broad shifts in curricular regime happened at the same time as the nature of disciplinary knowledge was being challenged by movement-based perspective, such as anti-racism, feminism, lesbian/gay liberation and Marxism. Multidimensional challenges, they combined the recovery of experience "hidden from history,"[9] disputes about fundamental ways of knowing built into disciplinary approaches and debates about content (where the disciplinary lens should be directed).

Universities also began to shift the terms of university governance and disciplinary procedure. Students won some degree of citizenship in these institutions. They gained the right to certain kinds of representation (for example, on university governing bodies). Universities withdrew from the pseudo-parental role they had been assigned historically (acting *in loco parentis*) and began to treat students as adults. New disciplinary procedures were also introduced, which recognized that students had certain rights (see Fleming 1971c:212-35, 374-402). Student citizenship in the university amounted to a pale reflection of the already weak model of citizenship in the capitalist state.

The university system grew and changed in important ways during the period of the broad welfare state – this was certainly related to changes in the occupational structure that included a massive expansion of the white-collar working class. At the same time, the growth of universities developed around the expansion of conceptions of citizenship and the augmentation of social rights through the period of the broad welfare state. Of course, access to university was far from universal, which is a reminder of the limited extent to which the "social rights" of the welfare state were actually rights in any strong sense. At the same time, university teaching was changed to resonate with the changing rhythms of citizenship so that at a time when government talked that language of "participatory democracy" the university was democratised in certain ways, allowing for greater student choice and participation. The broad welfare state captured social struggles, absorbing some of the impact of resistance and providing space to address (in some limited and displaced forms) the claims of people in motion.

The university played an important part in this process, providing a space for dissent while teaching forms of self-discipline that contributed to the enhancement of self-regulating citizenship. Universities offered students a tremendous degree of autonomy so that only those who acquired certain forms of self-discipline were able to fulfill requirements and obtain degrees. The university graduate had to develop the capacity to discipline herself or himself to meet externally established requirements. The university thus served as a site for the deep internalization of discipline in a situation of minimal supervision.

## A New Point of Access: Colleges and Polytechnics

The broad welfare state also saw the development of a whole new stream of post-secondary education in Ontario that focused on applied subjects aside from the traditional professions. The community college system in Ontario developed in the 1960s, through new forms of technical institutions that date back to the immediate post-World War II era. I will argue here that the college system provided the means to recruit a much broader segment of the population into the embrace of the state for longer periods of time. There was an important citizenship dimension to the development of this new post-secondary stream, which took the form of applied education.

As the community college system in Ontario developed, the universities were becoming notably less vocational in focus (Harvey 1974:57-58). The colleges had a distinctly vocational focus, although that does not mean that their growth was a direct response to a need for specific skills in the workplace. The development of the community college system must be understood in the light of the contradiction between increasing levels of formal education and deskilling, mentioned above and discussed in some detail in Chapter 2. The applied post-secondary stream provided a space for the more thorough formation of citizens. Colleges opened up the possibility of formal post-secondary education for a whole section of the population in a period where educational access was one of the key ideological markers of inclusive citizenship. At the same time, the applied post-secondary stream provided a place for the development of more refined modes of citizenship discipline that suited a more complex occupational hierarchy.[10]

The theme of access was central in the development of the applied post-secondary stream. Education Minister Bill Davis highlighted the theme of access when he described the mandate of the new college system to the Provincial Legislature. "Above all else, it goes far towards making a reality of the promise – indeed of the stated policy – of the Government to provide thorough education and training, not only an equality of opportunity to all sectors of our population, but the fullest possible development of each individual to the limit of his ability" (cited in Stokes 1989:1). Davis conceived the mandate of the colleges in expansive terms: "to meet the relevant needs of all adults within a community, at all socio-economic levels, of all kinds of interests and aptitudes, and all stages of educational achievements" (1).

Returning World War II veterans were pioneer beneficiaries of this new form of citizenship, which included access to post-secondary education. Those oriented towards a university education received tuition benefits and living allowances, as mentioned above. Other were offered new forms of training and assistance with re-establishment. The institution that is currently Ryerson Polytechnical University originated as the Ontario Training and Re-Establishment Institute to assist demobilized soldiers. Once the veterans were served, Ryerson reinvented itself as a specialist institution for technological education (Fleming 1971c:452-53).

A number of new post-secondary institutions focusing on technical education emerged during and after World War II. These included the Provincial Institute of Mining in Haileybury (1944), the Provincial Institute of Textiles in Hamilton (1946), Ryerson Institute of Technology in Toronto (1948), Lakehead Technical Institute in what is now Thunder Bay (1948) and new Technical Institutes in Ottawa and Windsor in the 1950s (Campbell 1971:14). These pioneering institutions (with the exception of Ryerson) were consolidated into the system of community colleges (formally called Colleges of Applied Arts and Technology) in 1965-66 (Fleming 1971c:520-21).

The colleges extended the educational preparation for entry into a variety of occupations, bringing into the public sector previously private apprenticeship and training systems and introducing upgraded requirements for many jobs.[11] One of the effects of the college system was to expose a broader layer of people to aspects of liberal education as part of a more vocational program. General education was supposed to constitute at least 30 percent of program content in the colleges, although in practice the programs often fell short of that goal (Vision 2000 1990:9). The creation of a second post-secondary stream laid the ground for an extended citizenship formation process with a much greater reach. The connection between citizenship formation and liberal education remains an important issue at colleges into the 1990s, as witnessed by the Vision 2000 report which emphasized a focus on general education and preparation for citizenship. "Helping people be good citizens, as well as productive workers with marketable skills, should be part of the educational experience at a College." (Vision 2000 1990:9)

### The End of Growth?

Educational growth, then, has been in large part a result of the centrality of schooling to processes of citizenship formation associated with the broad welfare state. The lean state represents an attempt to redefine citizenship both culturally and materially. At the same time, new obstacles to participation in education are being created, including user fees (particularly increased tuition fees), standardized testing procedures and new evaluation methods aimed at increasing the opportunity to fail. It might seem that we have reached the end of educational growth.

At this point, however, it seems quite possible that educational growth might continue into the lean state. It is much too early to know for sure what the implication of contemporary policy changes will be, but contemporary predictions do not seem to indicate an end to the increase in educational participation. The Council of Ontario Universities (2000:2) has predicted robust growth in the foreseeable future and the Harris government's plans emphasized increasing secondary completion and postsecondary participation (see Ontario 2001:11-12).

It is quite possible that rather than an end to growth, we are seeing a profound redefinition of education to align with new conceptions of citizenship associated with the lean state. Education reform is replacing the embrace of the state with a harsher market model of inclusion, marked by insecurity, user pay and increased opportunity to fail. The aim may be less to drive students out than to challenge them to survive in this new environment, hardening them for the lean world that awaits them after graduation.

## Notes

1. Katznelson, Gille and Weir (1982:39) argue that American educators at the end of the nineteenth century began to make their case for educational expansion on the basis of a claim for a monopoly on skill and knowledge and a position of neutrality as officials of the state.
2. The term hegemony is most importantly associated with Gramsci (see 1971:161). It describes a strategy for ruling in the face of struggle by securing some degree of consent from the ruled. Hegemony focuses largely on subordination through ideas, though it is built on a foundation of economic inequality.
3. I am drawing a parallel here to Mike Lebowitz's (1992) work on the relationship between capital and wage-labour. He argues that we can only understand class conflict if we are alert to the ways in which workers' agency is grounded in self-defined needs. Workers sell their capacity to work as a means to an end (sustenance) just as employers hire workers as a means to an end (surplus value, the basis for profit).
4. The state played a unique role in the development of social policy, even where philanthropic organizations initiated specific forms of intervention. The state alone could extend the reach of social programs to broad layers of the population, through the use of regulatory and funding powers as well as coercion. I disagree with Mariana Valverde's (1991) argument that taking seriously the contribution of philanthropic organizations means challenging a Marxist focus on the centrality of the state in social policy.
5. Giroux (1985:259) argues that one of the great defects of functionalist marxism can be the implication that school systems and other phenomena develop "behind the backs" of actors rather than through their activity. One of the central features of a marxist historical sociology must be to uncover the moments of intentional activity (for example in state formation) that gradually disappear into common sense (Gramsci's expression for taken-for granted world views).
6. Philip Corrigan (1977:ii-iii) argues that state intervention is seldom into a vacuum, but rather displaces the work of existing organizations. The establishment of social policy therefore involves a repression of alternatives. The recovery of these alternatives contributes to our ability to make sense of the way state institutions operate.
7. The role of inspection in the development of the state is discussed in Corrigan and Sayer (1985: 124-28) and Curtis (1992:195-97). State authority was not simply summoned up, but was negotiated through a process involving control over the circulation of information, the generalization of best (local) practices and a cautious enforcement of regulations.
8. Briefly, in terms of periodization, I would argue that the shift towards the broad welfare state was a longer-term process rather than an overnight development. The trajectory was particularly long in education, the pioneering universal program. It therefore does not seem to me to be problematic that a reform that set the tone for elementary education in the welfare state period occurred slightly before World War II. Indeed, many of the ideas central to the form of welfare state programs emerged from the struggles of the 1930s.
9. This expression draws on the titles to two books focused around acts of recovery: Rowbotham (1973) and Duberman, Vicinus and Chauncey (1989).
10. Bowles and Gintis (1976:132) argue that different levels of education prepared students for the disciplinary requirements that vary substantially across the occupational hierarchy.
11. The reorganization of apprenticeships by the state in Ontario is discussed in Fleming (1971c:479-80).

# Chapter 2

# Education for an Information Age?

The Harris government in Ontario presented education reform as a practical necessity. This was expressed in compressed form in the 1999 Budget Speech when Finance Minister Ernie Eves addressed education concerns in very practical terms. "Increased accountability, a stronger link between schools and the job market, and better career planning for students will continue to improve our education system" (Eves 1999:19). The shift to a post-liberal mode of education is portrayed as the sensible response to a rapidly changing occupational structure, driven particularly by the spread of information technology. In this chapter, I argue that education reform is not propelled by a dramatic shift in skills required in the labour market, although it is tied to the disciplinary requirements of systems of lean production.

## Skills for the Information Age?

The case for education reform is grounded in claims about the changing labour market. One of the stated aims of the educational system is to prepare people for the world of employment. The labour market is changing in important ways and so it must follow that the educational system should also change. The Ontario Ministry of Education makes the case that people will need more education to find a place in this changing labour market. "As the restructuring of Ontario's economy continues, it is expected that demand for both full-time and part-time study will increase, as people of all ages pursue learning to acquire knowledge and skills to remain competitive in the workplace"(OMET 1996b:51). Yet technological change in capitalist society has not usually been associated with a generalized increase in skill requirements. Indeed, Harry Braverman (1974) argued that there has been a tendency towards *deskilling* as labour processes have changed through the twentieth century. At the same time, formal educational requirements have increased.

This chapter will examine the contradictory relationship between skills and education.

There is an obvious basis for the widely held assumption that workers would need more education in the contemporary world. New information technologies seem to demand new levels of skill while new management strategies emphasize flexibility and "continuous improvement" methods that supposedly tap workers' creativity. Livingstone describes this assumption that increased skills should be required as the "prevailing myth of 'post-industrial' work" (Livingstone 996:79).

Claims about a skills shortage are based specifically on the immediate shortfall in the supply of trained workers for high technology jobs. Premier Harris made this point very strongly at an address to a conference on the future of Ontario Universities sponsored by the Council of Ontario Universities and the Bank of Nova Scotia. "Who in the university system will decide to reduce enrolments or close programs when there are few jobs available in a profession, like certain professional or PhD programs? For example, do we need ten PhD programs in geography, or six in sociology? Who is responsible for opening or expanding programs where there are significant shortages, like computer science and software engineering?" (Harris 1997:7)[1]

Industry-based organizations in the high-technology sector have certainly claimed that there is a skills shortage in the area. A Canadian Advanced Technology Association (CATA) member survey from 1997 estimated that there were 20,000 vacant information technology jobs in Canada at that point and the Software Human Resources Council estimated that there would be as many as 50,000 vacant information technology jobs by the year 2000 (OMET 1998a). Yet a paper by David Stager (1999) for the Applied Research Branch of Human Resources Development Canada argues: "The conclusion at this time in the debate about an IT [information technology] shortage, seems to be the Scottish verdict, 'Not proven'." He points out that there is no really solid basis for projecting labour supply and demand in the information technology field, but as far as it is possible to project "there should not be an emerging problem of shortage over the next five to seven years – which is a very long time in a sector where technology is changing quickly"(Stager 1999:47). Claims for a shortage of information technology specialists in the United States have been "clouded by a lack of unambiguous data" (47). These have been based largely on employer surveys that might reflect employers' wishes to see a greater supply of skilled labour in the sector to give them more control over the hiring process. "There is no doubt that employers prefer to have a large queue of applicants so that they have more scope to select those with specialized skills and even personalities to suit the firm's needs" (49).

The case for a labour shortage in information technology is open to debate. Even if there is a shortage in that sector, it seems excessive to retool the whole education system in response to a localized and temporary demand for just one category of workers. We need, then, to turn to the overall question of skill requirements in a changing labour market. Lean production is bringing into play new technologies and methods of work organization. The optimistic account of lean production presents it as a method for increasing worker autonomy and skill in the labour process. The classical statement of this is the comment by Womack, Jones and Roos that "by the end of the next century we expect that lean assembly plants will be populated almost entirely by highly skilled problem solvers" (Womack, Jones and Roos 1990:102).

## Skills and Lean Production

Studies on the changing world of work and lean production do not conclude that we are seeing a dramatic increase in autonomy and skill requirements. The optimistic story that lean production represents a sharp departure from the standardization and monitoring associated with Taylorist mass production methods does not hold up. Lean production builds on the central Taylorist techniques of breaking jobs down into elemental tasks, organizing work around a sequence of specified tasks to be carried out as management instructs and tight management control over the process as a whole (Parker and Slaughter 1994:75). It is in many ways a streamlined version of mass production that reduces buffers, increases stress and attempts to deploy workers' knowledge to intensify work (Moody 1997:85; Parker and Slaughter 1994:80-84).

Workers tend to develop their own knowledge of work processes, learning to do things better to gain some control over the pace of work or to gain break time. Lean production attempts to harvest this knowledge and use it to speed up the processes (Garrahan and Stewart 1992:76). Workers at the CAMI plant in Ingersoll, for example, realized over time that the suggestions they were submitting to management were actually being used to reduce staffing and speed up work intolerably (Rinehart, Huxley and Robertson 1997). Moody wrote that the outcome of lean production "is not worker empowerment or autonomy: it is highly standardized work timed down to the last breath" (Moody 1997:88).

There is a good argument, then, that the changes that we are seeing in the workplace are not in any simple sense about upping the level of skill. Lean production fits in with the general tendency, described in Braverman's influential work, *Labor and Monopoly Capital*, towards the degradation of work since the early twentieth century through the implementation of Taylorist scientific management methods. Braverman (1974:90-121) argues that Taylor's approach to scientific management was premised on detailed management control over the way work was executed. This was crucial if management were to control the labour process. The *conception* of the task should be separated as completely as possible from its *execution*. Workers would therefore be responsible for executing specified tasks with a minimum of discretion. Braverman traced the implementation of these principles through a variety of occupations, including clerical and service jobs as well as industrial work.

We are, therefore, not seeing a general trend towards increased skill and autonomy in Braverman's sense of combining conception and execution. Braverman himself disputed the claim that new levels of science and technology at work are associated with skills upgrading. Rather, there is often a polarization of skill, with a greater divergence between a small layer of highly trained specialists and the mass of workers (Braverman 1974:425-26).

## New Kinds of Problem-Solving?

Even if we are not seeing a trend towards upgrading, that does not necessarily mean that there is no change in the skill requirements for jobs. Tony Elger (1982:45) argues in his critique of Braverman that mass production throughout the twentieth century has not produced a homogenous deskilled labour force, but rather a complex and differentiated occupational structure requiring diverse skills and abilities. Different skills may be required as labour processes are transformed, even if this change does not mark an "upgrading" in Braverman's sense of the word.

John Holmes (1997) argues that skill requirements in the pulp industry have changed as part of the process of restructuring. There is a new emphasis on interpersonal skills (associated with teamwork) and on particular problem-solving skills (which he labels as "intellective" following Zuboff [1988]). "Workers need to make sense of data by using inferential reasoning and systemic thinking rather than by responding to physical cues (the sight, feel, smell or even taste of pulp finish or paper), which in the past made the worker a skilled papermaker" (Holmes 1997:10). The labour process has shifted so that the monitoring of the production process is mediated by machines rather than done in a direct hands-on fashion. This is a change in skills rather than "upgrading." Indeed, the occupational position of paper machine operators who had been crucial in older labour processes has been downgraded through technological change and work reorganization (21).

Zuboff (1988:75) argued that the spread of computer technologies has been associated with new requirements for "intellective skills"; that is, problem-solving capacities that draw on analytical skills, reasoning and a capacity for abstraction. It is difficult to ascertain just how universally true this is. Mishel and Teixiera (1991:22-24) state that there is very little basis for firm generalizations about these changes in skill requirements at a society-wide level but they do identify some general trends from scholarly literature, journalism and statements from business leaders. Overall, the requirement for a basic level of literacy and numeracy is widespread in the job market. Employers find it more difficult to deploy or retrain workers without these skills. This is an important consideration and there has been a curious lack of focus on mass literacy issues in debates about deskilling (Wood 1982:19).

Furthermore, there are new skill requirements among those innovative firms that are implementing "best practice" methods of work organization. "In these firms, jobs are being restructured so that workers are expected to independently solve technical problems that come up in the course of their work, to learn new tasks on a fairly regular basis, and to interact extensively with fellow workers, frequently as part of a 'team'" (Mishel and Teixiera 1991:23). The most important new requirements in these firms are "for the social and 'higher-order' skills upon which problem-solving, adaptability and team work are based" (52). These leading edge practices are not the norm, however. Competitive pressure might push more firms in this direction but there are many other restructuring options that do not rely on worker problem-solving or teamwork in these ways. Rather than being a model for widespread work restructuring, these "best practices" might be primarily responses to particular challenges relevant only to limited sections of the labour market. Longer-term studies seem to indicate that the rate of change in skill requirements has generally been declining rather than increasing since the 1960s (23-24, 17-18).

It is possible that restructuring has led to an increase in the need for intellective skills in the workplace, although it is difficult to know with certainty the extent of these requirements. Further, the need for intellective skills in the workplace does not explain the contemporary round of educational restructuring. Intellective skills, such as communications and problem-solving abilities, are already at the core of secondary and post-secondary curricula, particularly in the academic, liberal arts and general education streams and it is quite possible that the increased need for these skills contributed to the near doubling of post-secondary enrolments from 1971 to 1991.[2] This might also help explain the advantage that people with post-secondary currently have in the labour market. A Statistics Canada (1995:1) study showed that individuals with post-secondary education were less likely to be unemployed than those without. "In June 1992, the unemployment rate for less-educated young people (20- to 29-year-olds without a post-secondary degree, diploma or certificate) was nearly 17%. Among 1990 post-secondary graduates, only trade/vocational graduates experienced a higher rate (20%). All other categories of 1990 graduates had lower unemployment rates in June 1992. Graduates who fared better were those who earned career/technical (10%), bachelor's (11%), master's (8%) or doctorate (6%) degrees" (Statistics Canada 1995:1).

It is quite conceivable that one of the factors contributing to the increase in educational requirements for many jobs is the need for generic skills (broad conceptual abilities and communication skills without occupationally-specific content). These generic skills are already developed in humanities and social sciences programs (OECD 1993:25) and the Vision 2000 (1990:9) report on community colleges in Ontario argued that they should move more to the core of the college curriculum. At the secondary level, these skills would be most strongly associated with the academic stream.

The requirement for more generic skills might help explain a longer-term trend for increased educational requirements in the workforce dating back to before the education reforms were implemented. This is debatable, however, as it is quite possible that we are mainly seeing credential inflation in a tight labour market and an increasing stigmatization of people with a low level of formal education (Hoddinott and Overton 1996:210-14). In either case, the requirement for particular skills does not explain the direction of educational restructuring. Indeed, the restructuring has a heavy vocationalist emphasis that seems to emphasize more specific occupational preparation rather than generic skills. Mike Harris, for example, seemed to be arguing against an emphasis on generic skills when he said: "We seem to be graduating more people who are great thinkers, but they know nothing about math or science or engineering or the skill sets that are really needed (Mackie 2000: A7)."

## Standards Not Skills

Certainly, there is a claim that the current restructuring in Ontario is about developing generic skills in students. An Ontario government public discussion document argues that there is currently a problem with the skills students have upon graduation. "There are ... more young people who arrive at the next stage of their careers – university, college, or the search for a first job – without the skills and knowledge required for success.... Some high school graduates do not have high enough literacy and math skills to function effectively in the workplace" (OMET 1996a:3-4).

The solution to the challenge of skills development, according to the Ontario government, is quite simply to raise standards. "All students should have a high-quality curriculum with demanding standards" (OMET 1996a:6). The conception of "demanding standards" in OMET materials is twofold: increased compulsion and more measurement. The policy changes in Ontario suggest that education reformers strongly dispute the ways skills have been taught in the recent past. Education reformers believe students have been given too much choice and insufficient opportunity to fail. In general terms, the education reform agenda has focused on increasing the compulsion in the teaching of skills. At the most obvious level, this has meant increasing the number of required courses. In Ontario, the number of compulsory courses required for a secondary school degree will be increased from sixteen to eighteen out of thirty. This increase is attributed to a need for skills development, reflecting a "public desire for an increased emphasis on math, language and science, and preparation for responsible citizenship" (OMET 1998d:1).

More important than an overt increase in pedagogical compulsion is the emphasis on the construction of standards in terms of measurement. Standards are defined in a discussion document on the secondary school curriculum as "statements of required results whose meaning is made very clear by Performance Indicators" (OMET 1996c:5). This emphasis on standards is related specifically to generic skills. As the Ministry of Education business plan states, "The Ministry will finalize provincial standards, so that students will have a solid foundation in the areas of language and mathematics" (Ontario 1996:77).

The assertion here is that more detailed measurement combined with increased opportunity to fail, will increase the students' skill foundation. The curriculum is thus being reshaped around standardized testing. There are many problems with this kind of testing, which tends to focus classroom learning on test preparation and imposes limits on the curriculum. There is also a great deal of debate about whether the broad skills required in the workforce are those that will be measured in the tests. The problem is that breaking down skills into measurable units for province-wide tests severely limits what can be measured. Meaghan and Cassis argue that these tests measure the ability to "recall facts, define words, perform routine operations rather than higher learning skills such as analyzing, synthesizing, forming hypotheses and exploring alternative ways of solving problems" (Meaghan and Cassis 1995:46).

There is an even more fundamental issue about measurement here. Rather than ensuring that more people actually acquire these skills, the goal of educational restructuring seems to be to identify those who have learned them and those who have not. Programs that actually promote the "threshold level" literacy skills that might be required in the changing labour market are actually being cut in Ontario. The most important example of this is the slashing of adult education programs since the Harris government was elected. The government changed the funding model for adult education in 1996, reducing expenditure per student by over 50 percent (Battagello 1996:A3, Lewington 1998:A8). The new funding formula introduced the next year forced local boards to make even deeper cuts to adult education. In Toronto, angry protesters took over the meeting room as trustees voted to cut adult education programs serving 4,000 students (Sheppard 1998:A1). But this is not simply an Ontario phenomenon. Hoddinott and Overton (1996) illustrate the ways that the privatization of adult education, and the increased pathologization of people who are not literate, have eroded basic skills development through Newfoundland's literacy campaign which began in 1988 and peaked in the early 1990s.

Programs that teach literacy skills to adults are being cut while the measurement of these skills in the schools is being increased. The problem of teaching literacy is reduced to the question of "standards" in the Harris education reform agenda: if you test it, they will come. The challenge of teaching those students who have trouble meeting these standards is not really discussed – the emphasis is on measurement and classification.

New report cards in Ontario are part of this shift to measurement. The standardized report cards were introduced first at the elementary school level (Education Improvement Commission 1997:2). At the secondary school level, failure in the standardized Grade 10 literacy course is to be indicated on the transcript and will prevent graduation (OMET 1998d:3). Transcripts will also show all attempts at a course rather than just the successful one as had previously been the practice, ensuring that failure leaves its mark. "This reform will give students an incentive to excel the first time they take a course" (OMET 1996a:10).

## Streaming and Labour Market Polarization

The renewed emphasis on streaming is consistent with this focus on measurement and classification of students. Streaming is returning to Grade 9, although in such a way as to permit shifting between streams the following year. Overall, the secondary system will stream students towards universities, colleges or no post-secondary education[3] and a new teacher-advisor system will help direct students towards appropriate streaming choices beginning in Grade 7 (OMET 1998d:1-2). The more standardized testing and reporting procedures are sure to provide some of the basis for streaming.

It is difficult to see how this emphasis on measurement and streaming will equip more students with the generic skills (basic literacy, numeracy, reasoning and problem-solving) that might be required in the workforce. Rather, the aim seems to be to differentiate education on the basis of students' prior acquisition of these skills.[4] Those who have trouble with these skills will be streamed towards no post-secondary education and a very dismal future on the margins of the labour market.[5] Of course, more education in itself would not resolve the problem of labour market polarization that is built into the lean system.

This emphasis on the differentiation of students contradicts the universalistic pretensions of public education as a basis for citizenship. I argued above that the educational optimism of the broad welfare state was connected to an emphasis on the development of particular forms of subjectivity through schooling. The more "child-centred" approaches represented an attempt to keep more students in school by limiting the opportunities to fail out of the system. There was a confidence that simply keeping people in that space would contribute to the development of citizens with a basic cultural formation.

Educational restructuring marks an important shift away from that emphasis on citizenship associated with the liberal education model. Lean production requires a downward polarization of parts of the working class as part of the "management by stress" strategy that drives workers through insecurity[6]. The school system prepares students for that differentiation, trying to prevent the elevated humanistic expectations that might accompany citizenship.

Measuring and streaming students is associated with the new vocationalist approach to education. The new vocationalism centres on the acquisition of specific skills that are allegedly relevant in the job market, skills that are developed through the establishment of measurable performance goals in the training process (Jackson 1992:78). It also represents a behaviourist attack on traditional pedagogical approaches (Avis 1991:118-19). This vocationalism has very little to do with developing the kinds of generic literacy, numeracy or reasoning skills described above. It is concerned more with measurement than with teaching. This approach serves to shift the horizons of possibility for individual students by developing a measure of their performance so that their occupational expectations might fit the labour market they face. It is about new differentiated forms of subjectivity and discipline required for an increasingly polarized society. This means shattering any universalistic expectations that the welfare state educational system might have generated.

The Economic Council of Canada (1992) report, "A Lot to Learn," argued for a new attention to vocational education at the secondary level. It argues that too many students have shifted out of vocational programs that are not highly regarded (17-18) and identifies a problem of expectations. "Partly the problem is one of misplaced expectations: most parents, and the students themselves, aspire to the prestigious positions via university or college – often with little comprehension of what this actually entails" (17-18).

The report does not mention that in the real labour market it is not only "prestigious positions" that require post-secondary education. The job prospects for people with only secondary education are becoming increasingly limited. It is quite possible that the "academic bias" the report identifies (ECC 1992: 25, 53) is actually a rational response by students and parents to the changes in the labour market that increasingly marginalize those without post-secondary education in a situation of chronic youth unemployment. Many of the vocational programs in secondary schools are terminal streams that offer credentials for which there is little demand.

The overall problem facing young people entering the labour market seems to be a lack of employment prospects. Morisette, Myles and Picot cite evidence that there is an abundant supply of labour across Canada for the foreseeable future. In this view, young workers entering the labour force face a 'demand deficit' rather than a 'skills deficit': there is simply not enough demand for their labour irrespective of skills levels" (Morisette, Myles and Picot 1995:43).

This "demand deficit" has an impact on all young people, although it affects most sharply those without post-secondary education. In the present context a relatively educated workforce is in fact underemployed. Livingstone (1996:76-77) writes that this underemployment takes many forms. Some people are unemployed, while others who aspire to full-time work find themselves in part-time or temporary jobs. The skills and knowledge of those who are employed full-time are often under-used, their formal credentials might exceed requirements and many feel overqualified for their jobs. The response of business leaders and governments has been "to reform the educational system and encourage people to seek more and better training." (Livingstone 1996:77-78).

## The Ideology of Training

The emphasis on training was particularly prominent in the late 1980s and early 1990s. Dunk, McBride and Nelson (1996:3-4) discuss ways in which the training ideology read the structural problem of chronic unemployment as an issue of labour force preparation. The blame was thus divided between individuals, who were not taking responsibility for retooling themselves to meet the needs of a changing economy, and the educational system that was not keeping up. This focus provided a politically palatable argument for cutting social programs. "Indeed, the ideology of training may serve as the perfect rationale for stripping the income security programs and diverting funds towards retraining activities. The income security programs are viewed as 'passive' and dependency-inducing; retraining is 'active' and leads to independence" (Dunk, McBride and Nelson 1996:3). The training emphasis largely disappeared by the mid-1990s. The idea of a skills deficit is still useful in the educational field to support restructuring. "What's more, our world has changed, but our schools have not kept up. We have unemployed high school graduates and a shortage of technically skilled workers" (OMET 1996a:4).

Overall, however, there is far less focus on training ideology. This signals the exhaustion of what Jessop (1991:98) describes as the "neo-statist" social democratic response to capitalist restructuring, which emphasized the use of state resources to improve labour force preparation. This training orientation has a long history in social democratic policy. It was certainly prominent in British Labour Party policy in the 1960s (CCCS 1981:143-45). Education and training figured prominently in the political vocabularies of the both the Liberal and NDP Ontario governments that preceded the Harris Conservatives. This focus on training for high skills represented a strategy for a new form of social citizenship in the context of the emergence of lean production through capitalist restructuring. The high skills strategy was centrally nationalist, suggesting that the economic future of the nation lay in the skills of the population (Avis 1996b:74).

The shift away from training is not simply a result of the 1995 change of government in Ontario. Even before the NDP government was defeated the process of educational restructuring and attacks on public sector workers was already well underway (Martell 1995). The material and ideological lines of the lean state project sharpened dramatically throughout the 1990s and governments of every political stripe have largely accepted the new parameters. This has included a recognition that there is no national "high skills, high pay" route to prosperity in the contemporary context (see Avis 1996a:114). It is also associated with an ideological shift that has legitimized "welfare-bashing" and enabled governments to skip the training ideology and pass directly to welfare and education "reform."

David Livingstone (1996, 1999) argues that we need to reverse our perspective on the gap between education and jobs. We face a shortage of good jobs rather than a shortage of skills. An increasing number of employed people have more preparation than their jobs require, while many prepared people are unemployed or underemployed. This "education-jobs gap" has been disguised by credential inflation and employer concerns about skills shortages. The real problem we are seeing is the waste of the knowledge and abilities of workers who are underemployed or unemployed (Livingstone 1999:96).

It seems quite possible that the "education-jobs gap" is not a temporary conjunctural problem for young people, but the longer-term product of labour market restructuring. Morisette, Myles and Picot (1995:41-43) argue that young people might be pioneers in a new labour market. They are more likely to be employed in newer industries, workplaces where new technologies have been introduced, and in places where labour contracts have been substantially reworked. It is quite possible that the employment conditions of the young today will spread through the labour market as the position of older, more protected, workers is eroded through restructuring or attrition.

Educational restructuring aims to prepare young people for their place in this new labour market. This is not centrally a matter of augmenting skills but rather of diminishing expectations. The story about education during the broad welfare state period was that good jobs awaited those who made their way through the system. That no longer fits with experience and the next section examines the ways in which expectations are to be remade to fit with new realities.

**Lean Discipline**

The core of state education has been from the outset the development of particular forms of discipline. Citizenship has been the most important of those disciplinary forms since the public education system was developed in the nineteenth century. The focus on citizenship-formation has been so successful over time that it is now largely incorporated into the taken-for-granted world view of the population.

Educational restructuring involves a major reorientation of the system away from the discipline of welfare state citizenship. The process of capitalist restructuring has generated new disciplinary requirements for a lean world. The endless drive for intensification of work requires new forms of motivation to push people to try to meet ever-rising standards of productivity. A study comparing different ways of organizing work in the Canadian automobile parts sector found that workers in lean production plants were more likely than those in traditional "Fordist" workplaces to say that the workload was too heavy, that it was increasing, and that they would be unlikely to be able to maintain the pace until the age of sixty (Lewchuk and Robertson 1997:74-77). Domestic labour, unpaid work in the household such as cooking, cleaning and caring, has also intensified; the restructuring of health care and social programs increases the work required to care for household members, family or friends.

The welfare state educational system was not preparing students for this lean world of relentless intensification in all aspects of life. Citizenship generated too many expectations, whether ethical or material. The lean world requires the erosion of the expectations of citizenship to create an atmosphere of "management by stress" not only in the workplace, but in society as a whole (see Parker and Slaughter 1994). "Management by stress" in its educational form is one of the pillars of the new discipline.

Management by stress is necessary, but not sufficient, for the disciplinary reorientation associated with lean production. Garrahan and Stewart (1992:115-17, 138) argue that management by stress was combined with a new participatory ethos in the Nissan plant they studied in Britain. Teamwork played an important role in the development of that particpatory ethos, which they describe as "self-subordination." "Teamwork depends precisely upon self-subordination for it shifts the locus of control onto individuals who perceive themselves as guardians of quality and flexibility" (Garrahan and Stewart 1992:94).

Restructuring education involves a move from citizenship towards lean discipline combining increased stress with new forms of self-subordination. The stress level is upped by new performance standards, harsher consequences for failure to perform and an increasingly competitive atmosphere resulting from a harsh youth labour market combined with the focus on standards. At the same time, self-subordination is cultivated through the development of a hardened work ethos, new forms of individual responsibility, efforts to increase identification with corporate goals, the promotion of consumerism and consumer-empowerment strategies that include participatory elements.

## The Vocationalist Ethos

One of the central claims of educational restructuring has been that it will make education more "relevant." Students in Ontario, whatever their destination after high school, "must be focused on relevant learning" (OMET 1996c:3). The secondary school curriculum should be "rigorous, relevant and results-oriented" (Ontario 1996:77). Ontario schools began to focus excessively on citizenship to the detriment of work skills in the 1960s, "being more concerned with "civilizing" the young than with giving them the tools they need to become productive and independent" (OMET 1996a:4).

Relevance is defined particularly in terms of preparation for employment. The Economic Council of Canada argued that many "judge the quality of the educational system by its success in preparing students for the labour market" (1992:4). A central problem in the secondary schools is "a woeful lack of pragmatic technical and vocational programmes to prepare young people for the world of work" (47). The Canadian Chamber of Commerce Task Force on Education and Training (TEFT) echoes these concerns (1989:39), which also suggested that more practical preparation for the workforce was required.

This focus on "relevance" in terms of labour market preparation was central to the educational restructuring undertaken by Britain's Thatcher government. The "new vocationalism" was a central theme in Thatcherite education reform efforts by the middle of the 1980s (Johnson 1991:56). It combined specific concerns about the content of education with particular pedagogical approaches – the content was to become more job training-oriented, while the pedagogy was to shift in a behaviourist direction (Avis 1991:118-19).

The vocationalist focus is not centrally oriented on skills education, despite some of the rhetoric that surrounds it. Rather, it is about the development of new subjectivities more closely attuned to the requirements of the labour market (see Avis 1996a:108). This is about skill if we accept that the "skill" employers demand most is "a willingness to organize one's life according to the demands made by employers and to form an element in a mobile, flexible and malleable work force"(CCCS 1981:145).

In education the vocationalist direction places a great emphasis on work habits, measurement and identification with the goals of employers. The aim is to form students who fit into the labour market as it exists, rather than challenge its limits. At the core of this vocationalism is an assumption that students and capitalists share a common interest in the preparation of potential workers for whatever their place might be in the labour market, glossing over real conflicts (Avis 1996a:108). Students are taught to define their life goals in terms of the requirements of employers, rather than in terms of their own needs.

The business community quite strongly identifies a "skills" shortage at the level of labour discipline. This is clear in the survey of small businesses conducted by the Canadian Federation of Independent Business (CFIB) (1996) about employment issues. Respondents were asked to comment on the qualities they looked for in young employees. "The four most important are in fact character qualities, which have little to do with education levels. In their young workers, employers look for discipline, reliability, adaptability and the will to stay at the job. Basic education and good communication skills are other important factors. Technical or computer skills and a degree or diploma, while important in demonstrating raw skills, are not seen as the best indicators for measuring the quality of potential new young employees" (CFIB 1996:27).

More than 45 percent of those surveyed reported that they had trouble finding qualified people to hire (CFIB 1996:28). Most (68 percent) of those who reported this trouble identified a lack of potential employees with particular skills in their locality. The report discusses the sectors in which these shortages are most reported (manufacturing, transportation and communication sectors), but does not elaborate on which specific skills are in short supply.[7] A smaller number of employers (13 percent) identified specific problems with basic language and numbers skills (29). At the same time, almost half of those reporting difficulties finding qualified employees also identified problems with labour discipline. "A disturbingly high 45 per cent also said that worker indifference and poor work attitudes were at least partially responsible for the problem. These concerns are related to the fact that many small businesses have to compete with social assistance payments for workers. In other cases, business owners believe that workers' wage expectations are too high for the type of job performed" (CFIB1996:29).

This construction of the problem of labour discipline maps together indifference, bad work habits, overly high wage expectations and a "weakness" for social programs. The emphasis on labour discipline issues in the CFIB report corresponds with the findings of a survey of United States employers that reported that only 5 percent saw educational or skill requirements as increasing while 80 percent described their primary concern as the work habits and social comportment of potential employees (Commission on the Skills of the American Workforce 1990, cited in Mishel and Teixeira 1991:24).

The Canadian Chamber of Commerce Task Force on Education and Training (TFET 1989) discussed a number of employer concerns about the preparation of young people for the labour market: the lack of certain basic skills (reading, writing and analytical and interpersonal skills); underdeveloped work habits; a lack of knowledge of the labour market and employment opportunities; an undue emphasis on academic as opposed to vocational courses; obsolete approaches and equipment in vocational education; and an insufficient emphasis on overcoming the stereotypes that, for example, discourage women from pursuing math and the sciences.

The new vocationalism represents an attempt to reorient the educational system to address these and similar complaints from business. The professed aim is a closer integration of the school system with the labour market, to develop students who are better prepared for the world of work. Before examining the ways in which this is to be achieved, it is important to examine the claim about attuning education to the needs of the labour market.

**Skills Planning in a "Free" Market**
The very nature of the capitalist "free" labour makes specific job training on the basis of a detailed planning process both impossible and undesirable from the perspective of employers. The employment demand and occupational structure of capitalist societies changes constantly, albeit at a highly uneven and unpredictable pace. A paper on skills shortages published by the Applied Research Branch of Human Resources Canada puts this clearly. "Economic theory suggests that skills shortages and surpluses are expected to be a permanent feature of decentralized labour markets" (Roy, Henson and Lavoie 1996:58). Further, the emphasis on continuous improvement and constant change built into lean production methods makes skills planning particularly difficult at the present time (see Avis 1996b:75-76).

Even if it were possible to predict the occupational needs for a decade hence, it would not suit employers to have an exact match between supply and demand. While employers prefer to avoid labour shortages, they often benefit from situations of oversupply that weaken unions, drive down wages and allow for greater management control over the process of hiring and firing. There is therefore a long history of employer ambivalence about vocationalism in education. Employers have often seen vocational schooling that focuses too directly on narrow training as an intrusion into the free labour market and the workplace (Davies 1986:43-44). Capitalists do not necessarily want employees who know how to do the job "right" because that would interfere with management's prerogative to tell them precisely how to do it. Nor do they want graduates to feel entitled to a particular kind of job.

It is not necessarily obvious, then, that neo-liberal governments should be pushing for state intrusion into the job training realm at a time when a rapidly changing occupational structure makes the identification of future needs virtually impossible. The need for "flexibility" (to use a term that is popular with management) in conditions of rapid change would seem to constitute a strong argument for general rather than vocational education. "In light of considerable uncertainty about future requirements for specific skills and the increased importance of workplace-centered learning, there is growing consensus that the educational system should place greater emphasis on the transmission of fundamental skills" (Wolfe 1989:14). But the new vocationalism in education is not really about fine tuning the school system to particular occupational configurations and job-specific competencies. Instead, it represents a new approach to preparing students' subjectivities for the changing worlds of work, including both paid and domestic labour.

Liberal education employed a relatively indirect approach to preparing students for work, subordinating it to a larger process of moral formation. The goal of liberal education was to cultivate citizens, raising the cultural level of the presumably vulgar masses as a precondition to their full participation in society as citizens. This required a complex balance between the proscription of "indigenous" cultural forms among workers and oppressed peoples and the creation of new cultural spaces that provided for inclusion conditional on the internalization of particular habits and values. The complex balance has always been a terrain of class struggle.

The cultural apparatus of citizenship prepared people for the world of work in various ways. At the core of the liberal educational system is the acceptance of authority, although in complex ways that combine punishment, deference to "expertise" and self-regulation. Time-discipline is deeply internalized to the point of naturalization. The individual who emerges at the end of the process of liberal education is self-active and self-regulating, accepting in "normal times" the horizons of possibility imposed by existing social relations. Of course, this acceptance is often partial and contradictory.

### Undermining the Culture of Citizenship

The problem is that capital is seeking to shift those horizons of possibility in the effort to form a lean world. This means undermining the culture of citizenship. Lloyd and Thomas (1998) argue that one of the central aspects of the cultivation of citizenship was the creation of a pedagogical space that combined the formal equality of students with authority relations based on the act of attending to the teacher.[8] The teacher role combines surveillance and punishment with exposition based on presumed expertise and disinterest. Education thus plays a key role in creating the space for the formation of an "imagined community" oriented around the capitalist state.⁹ "What is practically required to effect this ideal is the moral formation of the citizen by an increasingly specialized cultural, not technical, pedagogy that occupies a separate space in its own right – a space that is steadily delineated by the state for society" (Lloyd and Thomas 1998:146).

The looser connection between liberal education and the world of work is actually central to the formation of citizens. The creation of a more abstract realm in the classroom allows for the creation of a supposedly neutral space in which the real inequalities, conflicts and interests of everyday life can be (formally) put aside. "In effect, education is the process which draws the subject from immediacy and particularism, from a class perspective, to a general perspective through which he can be united, not only with middle class reformers, but with the nation as a whole, as citizens" (Lloyd and Thomas 1998:132).

The construction of a supposedly neutral space of culture is conceived as the place of true humanity, in which the person who is fragmented by the complex divisions of labour in contemporary society is put back together again (Hunter 1990:163-67; Lloyd and Thomas 1998:117). All of this is founded on the constitution of economics, politics and culture as separate spheres of existence in capitalist society (Lloyd and Thomas 1998:80). The space of culture is thus neutralized by leaving aside politics and economics; rising above them into the moral domain of true humanity.

In short, liberal education relies heavily on the appearance of neutrality in the preparation of individuals for their place in capitalist society. It does not demean students by treating them as mere economic units (see the Hall-Dennis report cited earlier, PCAEOSO 1968:27). Nor does it insult them by preaching a specific political creed. Rather, it elevates people, turning vulgar children into worthy citizens. Of course, this process is not nearly so innocent of politics and economics as it pretends. Through liberal education, students are taught (objectively) that the limits of capitalist society are the natural and eternal boundaries of human possibility. Thus their personal horizons of possibility are caught up within the existing world of the labour market, the family form and organized or commercialized leisure.

The new vocationalism represents a willingness on the part of education reformers to dispense with this appearance of neutrality. The lean world has less room for the aesthetic realm of culture and its pretensions of disinterest. Politics and culture are to be bluntly subordinated to economics as social life is reoriented sharply towards the market. Education must prepare students for their place in the market: as sellers of their capacity to work and as consumers of goods and services that include commodified culture. Note that the state is not written out of this account, despite any neo-liberal protestations about free markets. The state must actively pursue the project of placing people in the market, proscribing alternatives and prescribing appropriate codes of behaviour.

There are serious risks in this strategy. The high ground of "disinterest" is being abandoned. This shift has already contributed to an important wave of resistance by teachers, students, trustees and parents (discussed in Chapter 7). It is quite conceivable that a more "interested" form of education will give rise to new forms of contestation. But capitalists and state policy-makers are clearly willing to take risks to reshape society in ways they see as more advantageous.

## Developing a Market Orientation

The new vocationalism serves to orient education to the market. There is a constituency for this market-defined conception of relevance. Students facing a dismal labour market are likely to be somewhat sympathetic to the idea that education should provide them with competitive advantages. Parents may have some sympathy for the direction of these reforms as they seek out opportunities for their children to succeed. Corrigan put it quite starkly: "Put in its extreme form, a further commodification of education will only work because, for a significant section of parents their children represent commodities through which they realize themselves" (Corrigan 1988:30). Further, the intensive commodification of everyday life in capitalist society and the entry of large portions of the working class into consumer society have paved the way for an ideology of the market that emphasizes diversity, choice and self-realization rather than cruelty, dislocation and the chronic inability to match resources to needs. The meaning of the market is different in a society where shopping is a major leisure activity.

Vocationalism is a central means by which education is being reoriented towards the market. The goal of lean schooling is to teach students how to realize themselves through the market, both by marketing themselves and meeting their needs through the market. In the language of OMET (1996d:6), students are to "develop enterprising skills and attitudes such as self-reliance, network-building, informed risk taking and flexibility." This means that school life must be redefined in terms of an increased emphasis on work rather than socialization of the "whole person"; a raised level of competition to meet standards and not fail; an individualization of responsibility; and a remodelling of pedagogical relationships to cast students as developing entrepreneurs and consumers rather than budding citizens.

The new vocationalism, then, is part of the orientation towards the market. It represents an attempt to retool schools to fit in with "post-Fordist economic culture" (Arnold 1996:234). This moves what has been described in the British context as "enterprise culture" to the heart of the educational system (see Deem 1994:30). Students are to commodify themselves, to develop the competencies and habits that will suit the needs of the ultimate consumer, their employer (see Jackson 1987:355). This involves a sharp turn towards a utilitarian education in which work discipline and required skills become the supreme achievement. The "neutral" orientation of education towards meeting the needs of employers thinly veils an ideological alignment of schooling with pro-business politics (see Tasker and Packham 1994:154).

The shift towards a new vocationalism can be found at all levels in the Ontario educational system. One of the important ways that it is being accomplished at the Grade 1–9 levels is through a focus on "outcomes-based" curriculum, which was reflected in the 1995 Common Curriculum and has been intensified by the subsequent Harris reforms.[10] The focus is on the measurement of observable results so that the "content, learning activities, and learning resources are means for achieving outcomes, not ends in themselves" (Wideman 1995:4). Nancy Jackson (1987:356-58) argues that outcomes-based learning has its roots in Taylorist scientific management and focuses on the development of those competencies that employers define as desirable. Outcomes-based learning is the pedagogical foundation for the utilitarian education represented by the new vocationalism.

The new vocationalism imposes elements of a work orientation onto schooling from a very early age. Beginning in Grade 1 students are to compile a portfolio that reflects their "progress in the areas of learner, interpersonal and career development" (OMET 1996d:12). This portfolio is to include evidence of their achievements, documentation of extracurricular activities and personal reflections. By Grade 7 it is to include an annual education plan with identified goals; by Grade 9 or 10 it is to include "the student's tentative post-secondary destination"

(OMET 1996d:12). The portfolio is both an "objective" source of information for career planning and the beginnings of an orientation towards self-marketing.

This portfolio is an important part of the policy to "teach career awareness early and throughout the students' education." (OMET 1996d:2). Even in the Grade 1–6 curriculum students are expected to "make connections with the world of work" (OMET 1996d:5). In Grades 7–9 students will begin "to consider choices among real alternatives that will affect their lives and careers"; by Grades 10–12 they are to "target career options" (OMET 1996d:6). Of course, this is a lean world where the best laid plans may go awry and so students should learn to "make choices without losing the flexibility to respond to changing circumstances" (OMET 1996d:6).

A similar emphasis on career planning was a feature of educational restructuring in Thatcher's Britain. Phil Hodkinson (1996) argued that the career planning strategies that were promoted there had little to do with the ways young people actually navigate through the job market. The assumption underlying "career planning" is that young people should use technically rational decision-making in their "choice" of a career. The career planning model assumes the young person should dispassionately assess her or his own capacities, throughly examine the actual possibilities available in the job market (now and in the future) and then make a rational choice. "Such a technical view of decision-making assumes that the process is fundamentally unproblematic, beyond the engineering difficulty of improving information and guidance" (Hodkinson 1996:124).

Hodkinson (1996:125-27) found that this technically rational approach to career planning did not fit with the actual experiences of young people finding their way into paid employment. They used a more complex process that brought together their actual contacts in the work world; their own aspirations and tastes; the aspirations others (for example, parents) had for them; and their work-related experiences, which could reinforce or erode their desire for a particular direction.

Career planning is difficult at any time in a capitalist economy, let alone in a period of rapid restructuring. The problem of "transition from school to work" has much more to do with chronic youth unemployment than with the job search skills of young people. It is difficult to imagine that a career planning approach that does not engage with the real world that students inhabit is going to have a huge impact on their actual job market experiences.

However, the orientation of education around a rationalized conception of career planning does have important ideological implications. It places the responsibility for success or failure in the job market on the shoulders of individual students. It hides the real obstacles to procuring 'satisfactory employment' (a contradictory term at the best of times). The "career planning" model ignores the very real constraints and opportunities that young people face as a result of their location in relations of structured inequality (Hodkinson 1996:121).

Career planning places a labour market orientation at the centre of the educational experience so that students are prepared to sell themselves. Education is then oriented to the needs of employers, who are the ultimate consumers of students' capacity to work (see Dickson 1991:110). It then opens to the door to new "partners" from the business community who can help orient students to the "real world" of what employers want in a workforce (see OMET 1996d:7).

The career planning orientation also imparts a "lean ethos" to students, teaching them that education (and other aspects of life) should be approached instrumentally as a means to the only end that counts: the world of work. The forty hours of forced "volunteer" work in the community similarly contributes to imparting the "lean ethos." Being a productive citizen means working for free as well as being paid as we all pitch in together to fill the void left by cuts to social programs. The compulsory community service is to be paired with an increased emphasis on co-operative education and work placements to offer students "real-life experience" (OMET 1998). "Real life" in a lean world means work, generally under supervision.

At the post-secondary level, it is arguable that this lean ethos underlies much of the shift away from the liberal arts currently in place in universities. It seems highly unlikely that it is actually a question of skills. Above, I argued that insofar as there is a real shift in skill requirements, it is actually about an increased need for "intellective" skills. It would seem that a liberal arts education would fit the bill. Yet the liberal arts seem to be going out of fashion as educational restructuring continues. The problem with the liberal arts seems to be that they are not "practical" enough (see OECD 1993:28-30) but there is every reason to believe that a liberal education contributes to the development of "intellective" skills. The concern seems to be less practicality as such (that is, the applicability of learned skills to the world of work) than it is instrumentality (the idea that every aspect of schooling should be assessed only in terms of its apparent utility in the world of work). This instrumentality is concerned with the assertion of utility in the workplace rather than the development of the skills actually required. It is rather like a competitive swimmer who refuses to lift weights and only wants to prepare for a race by doing something useful: swimming.

We are seeing an important shift towards a more instrumental ethos in education. The University of Phoenix, with its business-oriented curriculum, part-time teaching faculty and heavy use of information technologies, is in many ways the model for a lean post-secondary institution (or enterprise) that has dispensed with many of the practices of older liberal arts institutions. This university is now being recognized in Canada (British Columbia and Ontario) as part of the new opening towards privatized post-secondary education. An article in *New Yorker* magazine described discussion in classes at the University of Phoenix. "[i]n this class and the others I attended the students were engaged and the discussion was spirited. What was a little hard to get used to, though, was the lack of intellectual, as opposed to professional, curiosity. Ideas had value only insofar as they could be put to use – if they could *do* something for you" (Traub 1997:121).

This lack of "intellectual curiosity" may actually be a deficit when it comes to learning generic skills. I would argue that the instrumental approach to education has little to do with skills and a great deal to do with attitudes. The lean ethos does not fit comfortably with the rather open-ended and contemplative tradition of the liberal arts. As I will show in the next chapter, education reform is much more about promoting a particular kind of culture shift than it is about teaching specific skills.

## Notes

1. There are two versions of this speech issued from Premier Harris' office, one of which omits the specific reference to sociology and geography.
2. The near doubling of enrolments is discussed in Goodall (1994:41). See also Canadian Educational Statistics Council (1996:115) discussing the dramatic increase in university participation rates from 1977–78 until 1992–93. The proportion of 18–24 year olds attending university jumped from 11 percent in 1985 to 19.5 percent in 1993.
3. For an excellent critique of the class bias in streaming, see Curtis, Livingstone and Smaller (1992).
4. The idea that measurement was in large part aimed at identifying abilities rather than teaching them drew on an early discussion of Thatcherite education reforms which suggested that the "back to basics" approach was aimed at "revealing natural differences in ability" and achieving "competitive differentiation"(CCCS 1981:251).
5. This is not to argue that generic skills cannot be learned in more vocationally grounded ways. Indeed, in many ways the aim of education should be to bring together our physical and intellectual work on the world and to move between concrete practices and more abstract generalizations. The separation of academic and vocational training limits these possibilities.
6. Parker and Slaughter (1994) discuss management by stress at the level of the firm. I would argue that the same conception cen be applied more broadly at the level of society as a whole.
7. The report also notes that, "businesses in the services sector are less likely than those in the goods producing sectors to report shortages, even though service sector employment tends to be faster growing." (CFIB 1996:28)
8. Hunter (1988:59-61) discussed this space in terms of the formation of a disciplinary regime through a process of sympathetic surveillance by the teacher in the classroom and the playground.
9. The term "imagined community" derives from Anderson (1983:16).
10. The Common Curriculum began as a project of the Liberal Peterson government and was completed towards the end of the Rae NDP government (Wideman 1995:2-3). It is an important reminder that educational restructuring was well underway before the Harris Tories were elected.

# Chapter 3

# Education for the Nation

Schooling played a central role in the project of forming citizens during the broad welfare state period. One of the core aspects of citizenship-formation was the creation of national identity. This meant the construction of "invented traditions"' for "imagined communities," the development of a national culture supposedly grounded in a shared history.[1] Nigel Harris described this process: "Every major state endeavoured to instil social homogeneity in its people, to force their unruly shape into a predetermined corset of national identity – as witnessed in the social marginalization of languages and accents not recognized as socially acceptable" (Harris 1995:5)

The project of constructing a national culture in the Canadian state had a particular character given the context of aboriginal struggles for self-determination, official bi-nationalism (anglophone and francophone), large-scale immigration, and the proximity of the United States. Pevere and Dymond state, "there may no other country which has managed to turn the process of self-definition into such an industrious national pastime.... Canadians seem to enjoy nothing more than sitting around and fretting about who they are" (Pevere and Dymond 1996:viii-ix).

This chapter begins with an examination of the cultural project of the broad welfare state, which was based in an educational optimism that assumed people were relatively plastic and susceptible to moulding. The project aimed to enlighten the population by teaching the elevated ways of knowing associated with a cultural education grounded in the "great books" and a solid foundation in the scientific method. This cultural education was to be grounded in a liberal arts tradition that drew heavily on the discipline of history to locate students in time and place. Liberal education would contribute to the enlightenment of the people by teaching culture and science to form the ethical basis of social citizenship.

This cultural project has been abandoned with the shift to the lean state and post-liberal education. It does not mean, however, that the lean state has no cultural agenda. Rather, the aim is to create a more entrepreneurial "innovation culture" that draws on the commercialized culture of television, movies and amusement parks rather than the "great books" or the lessons of history. As part of this innovation culture, science is cast as the replacement for history as a vehicle for locating students in time and place. The Harris government's education reform agenda aimed to shift schooling towards this innovation culture.

## Educational Optimism and the Broad Welfare State

The development of a national culture was one of the great educational and cultural goals of the Canadian state in the era of the broad welfare state. The welfare state is often understood as a set of specific social programs providing particular benefits, including unemployment insurance, social assistance, pensions, mothers' allowances and state-funded health care. This definition in terms of programs is important, but it can sometimes eclipse the educational dimension of the welfare state project. The provision of material benefits and the enlightenment of the population were integrally connected in the project of the welfare state.

The broad welfare state was founded on a tremendous educational optimism. The population was seen as pliant formed through effective state action into a productive and harmonious citizenry. In contrast, early twentieth-century social policy centred around conceptions of degeneration that focused on a residual layer of the population that was either biologically damaged (in eugenic versions) or demoralized beyond repair (in environmentalist versions). This residuum was not susceptible to improvement through education or changed conditions. Any assistance to the residual layer would either perpetuate or deepen their damaged state. Social policy, then, had the twofold task of sorting out and removing the residuum while cautiously improving the culture and conditions of the "respectable" poor (widows, those unemployed through no "fault" of their own, people temporarily disabled by illness) in ways that would not drive them into permanent dependence (Bacchi 1978; Clarke 1980; Stedman Jones 1971).

The development of the broad welfare state was associated with a new optimism about shaping the population. Tomlinson argues that a major shift in the conception of poverty took place in Britain by about the 1920s. "The whole intellectual context of what might loosely be called Social Darwinism and eugenics was removed from the discussion of unemployment, as poverty was no longer linked to the degeneration of the race, and no longer therefore had the same significance as a symptom of a general threat to society" (Tomlinson 1981:67). This shift occurred slightly later in Canada and marks an important reconception of the character of the population and the nature of social problems. Poverty was no longer conceived as an individual moral failing that would be reinforced by state policies alleged to create a culture of dependence, but rather as a social problem requiring the intervention of social policy (Corrigan and Sayer 1985:171). Bowles and Gintis argued that the great periods of education reform in the United States, including that of the 1960s at the height of the welfare state, "were characterized by a lack of concern with genetically inherited characteristics and a profound optimism concerning the malleability, even the perfectability of youth" (Bowles and Gintis 1976:115). This optimism is evident in social democratic approaches to youth in Britain in the 1960s, which stressed the possibility of remoralizing even the most difficult children through a fine-tuned and multifaceted state apparatus that combined material assistance with more guidance (Clarke 1980:74).

This educational optimism was not limited to the realm of formal schooling. Indeed, much of the state apparatus shifted towards rehabilitation and reform, including a rehabilitative emphasis in the prison system, new methods of community psychiatry and the so-called "normalization" of people with developmental handicaps. This emphasis at the level of state policy was also reflected in civil society as the culture of child-rearing was recast. Benjamin Spock's best-selling *Baby and Child Care* was an important example of educational optimism, reflecting a commitment to shaping children through positive educative interactions.[2] (Current shifts in the culture of childhood will be discussed in Chapter 6.)

Educational optimism placed a heavy burden on the education system. Alan Thomas (1976:104-5) states that it was fashionable in the 1960s to argue that "a much larger segment of social need could be interpreted as learning needs and, with only a brief pause at this step, could be translated into educational needs and efforts at recruitment." The education system was central to a project of dealing with social problems by engineering citizens, particularly in their younger years – before problematic orientations hardened into character defects. Donzelot (1979) captured some of the disciplinary character of this educational optimism, pointing out that it involved intervention on the basis of perceived potential for problems.

Educational optimism lay at the heart of a broad project of social elevation through better schooling and the promotion of a liberal humanist national culture.[3] The aim was one of inclusion, bringing the population into the nation by producing citizens. Material needs were to be addressed in a limited way, to create a situation in which people were educable[4] without undermining self-reliance (meaning dependence on wage-labour). Citizenship in a capitalist society is a rich form of discipline that leans heavily towards consent (as opposed to coercion). It moves to the rhythm of time-discipline,[5] speaks the language of democracy and participation, and enforces a particular configuration of public and private. It rests on a conception of balancing rights and obligations, with the state cast as the embodiment of collectivity and requires a solid basis of minima and standards as the basic marks of inclusion and security.

The Danish author Peter Høeg (1994) captures the place of educational optimism in this project of forming citizens in his novel *Borderliners*. A few "problem" children are taken into a prestigious school as part of an educational experiment in mainstreaming. The central figure in the school is the headmaster Biehl, who aspires to a kind of enlightenment through the internalization of self-regulatory norms. The themes of time-discipline (Høeg 1994:67), order (214-15) and enlightenment (227) resonate through the book. The visionary project of those who run the school is described as follows: "[t]hey were working with something that would spread and inspire first the entire public school system and then the rest of the country.... They might not have said it straight out, they might not have thought it straight out either. But somewhere inside and among themselves they have been absolutely certain that they were right.... That it would be possible, sometime in the not too distant future, to have everyone respect their ideal of diligence and precision. And on that day, all living things in the universe would live at peace with one another (215-16).

The idea that citizenship as a disciplinary form revolves around "precision and diligence" seems just about right. The odd combination of liberal humanism and authoritarianism that drives the headmaster Biehl neatly summarizes the broad welfare state project. Biehl is relentlessly optimistic that everyone can be elevated if they can only be made to internalize the right methods of self-regulation. This optimistic conception of people as plastic and subject to moulding lay at the core of the welfare state project, particularly in education.

The project of forming citizens required the provision of a minimal level of benefits and services to create a population open to enlightenment. This was impelled largely from below, through the mass unionization that provided a means for many working-class households to win substantial improvements in their standard of living and the right to enter consumer society and, consequently, the self-defined "middle class".[6] It was reflected in the defining myth of the broad welfare state education system, that of "equality of opportunity" and education for a "more classless society" (see Bowles and Gintis 1976:123-24; CCCS 1981:65-71). Improved access to education was necessary to perpetuate that myth.

## Seeing Like a State[7]

Schooling contributes to the project of nation-building by teaching specific ways of seeing that are associated with the "universal" standpoint of the state. The state, which supposedly rises above specific conflicts of interest to represent the interests of society as a whole, is associated with specific supposedly universal ways of knowing that claim to transcend particular perspectives. These ways of knowing are taught in school, providing students with new capacities to see that are founded on particular (partial but claiming to be universal) perspectives. Students therefore learn *what* to think rather than *how* to think.

The project of teaching students how to think is founded on a hierarchical view of knowledge. This works in two main ways. Certain ways of knowing are privileged over others and are presumed to be richer and more powerful. At the same time, the distribution of knowledge amongst individuals is presumed to be hierarchical in such a way that individuals can be ranked in terms of their mental abilities. As a result, specific ways of knowing and particular individuals are recognized while others are marginalized. Indigenous ways of knowing, for example, have been displaced by a specific perspective that claims superiority based on universality (see Dei, Hall and Rosenberg 2000).

Hierarchies of knowledge lie at the core of the construction of the "hegemonic curriculum" (Connell 1993:34). Indeed, contemporary conceptions of professionalism across a range of specific occupations share a foundation in a conception of hierarchies of knowledge. "Professionalism and related therapeutic, technocratic and meritocractic postures are grounded in a common outlook that acknowledges the social and ethical propriety of a hierarchy of knowledge and expertise" (Reed 1997:18).

Of course, it goes without saying that vast amounts of learning take place outside of the formal educational system. Livingstone (1999:13) contrasts the icebergs of informal learning with the pyramids of formal education. People learn about the world through their co-operative practical activity in it, engaging in various forms of work and play. A great deal of rich and intricate knowledge is acquired through cooking, playing a sport or doing a paid alongside others. This learning is situated and social, it involves co-operation around specific experiences of practical activity (Castellena 1997:191). For example, in the workplace people tend to learn a great deal from fellow workers. "Workers do much more than accommodate each other, for they typically participate in interpersonal networks that generate, retain and transmit crucial work-related knowledge" (Darrah 1997:265).

This informal learning is denigrated and underestimated in contemporary discussions of illiteracy (Livingstone 1999:42). Oral and non-linguistic communications are regarded as inferior to written forms. The focus on literacy is not neutral, but is bound up with class inequality and other forms of oppression. Access to literacy varies with class, gender, migration patterns and other factors aligned with existing systems of structured inequality. The emphasis on literacy over other ways of knowing thus reinforces the position of the most privileged (who are most likely to be literate) and undercuts the disadvantaged (who are least likely to be literate). Stuckey argues that "literacy is a system of oppression that works against entire societies as well as against certain groups within given populations and against certain individual people" (Stuckey 1991:64).

Formal education plays a crucial role in the elevation of literacy over other forms of interchange. Literacy is a crucial foundation of educational classification, the organization of the student population around specific measures and assessments. It tends to be valued as a credential, an externally imposed measure of the individual that conditions educational and life trajectories, rather than as a tool for the literate person to make sense of the world (see Stuckey 1991:108, 118-19).

With the privileging of literacy goes the devaluation of other ways of knowing acquired outside of school. In contrast to the social and situated character of informal learning, classroom education is largely individualized through the competitive grading system and abstracted through the emphasis on learning that is severed from activity in the world. The individualization of the learning process includes the systematic disruption of the interpersonal exchanges that accompany informal learning, particularly when it counts (for example, during a test). As Michael Holzman wrote "Only in schools are people who fail to decode a text not helped by those around them ('This is a test.')" (Holzman 1986:30). The competitive assessment system treats learning as an individual acquisition, reflected in personal scores that locate the person within some sort of rank order (Connell 1993:75). This rank ordering gains legitimacy from the identification of individual capacities with one specific measure of intelligence (the I.Q. test) that maps ability in the form of a bell curve or "normal" distribution (Livingstone 1995:335).

The education system emphasizes competitive grading to earn credentials rather than the subjective value of learning for the individual. This emphasis is currently growing and it complements the increasing emphasis on formal academic credentials in the workplace (Connell 1993:26; Livingstone 1999:72-78). The identification of schooling as the unique source of learning helps drive the trend to require higher levels of formal education to fill jobs. At the same time, credentialism reinforces the conception that school learning is of utmost importance.

Formal education also severs theory from practice, abstracting classroom learning from the real experience of acting in the world. Students check their everyday problem-solving experiences at the classroom door to enter the world of formalized and abstracted exercises (with the partial exception of the technical education stream). The pedagogical form of classroom instruction suggests that the knowledge that counts is that which is learned in formal educational settings. This is central to the establishment of a hegemonic curriculum that marginalizes other ways of knowing and acquires common sense status as the model of real learning (Connell 1993:38). Schooling, then, runs against C.L.R. James's conception of a genuine democracy in which theory and practice unite to create the conditions in which "the workers as such and the thinker as such will disappear" (James 1993:276).

The exclusion of situated and social learning plays an important role in the production and reproduction of social inequality through the education system. It is one of the factors in the educational discrimination against children from working-class families who tend to fare less well at school than children from the managerial and entrepreneurial classes (Curtis, Livingstone and Smaller 1992:7; see also Connell 1993:36). Children whose parents have received more formal instruction will have easier access to resources to help them make sense of abstracted classroom learning. The organization of schooling severs mental from manual labour and valorizes abstracted intellectual skills (as opposed to grounded intellectual skills that might be associated with concrete problem-solving in physical work). Practical problem-solving generally involves some combination of mental and manual work. In school, mental labour is generally detached from practical work on the world. Manual work is thus devalued both through the abstracted character of formal learning and the organization of students into academic (mental) and technical (manual) streams (see Curtis, Livingstone and Smaller 1992:104-6).

Bernstein's (1971:77-80,175-77) work on linguistic codes offers another way of understanding the way that individualized and abstracted learning tends to count against working-class students. Children from working-class backgrounds are more likely to arrive at school oriented towards *restricted* speech codes, in which speech tends to be concrete, descriptive and narrative in form. Formal education, however, is generally organized around *elaborated* speech codes, in which speech is more analytical and abstract. Elaborated speech codes are also associated with the self-conscious manipulation of language, the ability to find the "right" way to say something and to justify that choice. Working-class children often have to change their speech codes to succeed in school and this has an impact on their relationship to their family and community. In short, the mode of expression rewarded in the classroom is more likely to be outside of the experience of working-class students than of those from middle- or employing-class families.

At the same time, the exclusion of social and situated forms of knowledge from the school setting works against women and people from cultures other than the dominant one. There is an important literature that argues that women's ways of knowing the world are more likely to be situated and social than those of men, given the gendered character of life-experience (see Smith 1990:18). People from non-dominant cultures will find themselves at odds with the language and culture of the classroom. This effect will be exaggerated by the presumed universality and inclusiveness of the culture created from the front of the classroom. The "universal" standpoint of the classroom actually casts doubt on the authenticity of students' experiences of estrangement. (These gender and cultural dimensions will be discussed in detail in Chapters 4 and 5.)

The pedagogical form of schooling, then, contributes to the construction of hierarchies of knowledge. This hierarchical organization of knowledge has been reinforced historically by the development of monopolistic forms of state education and the displacement of other forms of learning. The nineteenth and early twentieth centuries saw the development of robust forms of working-class self-education through formal organizations and informal networks (see Hahn 1976; Radforth and Sangster 1981). J.T. Murphy (1972:94-95), a revolutionary British shop steward writing in the 1930s, described the rise of the Labour College Movement around 1907 as a struggle for "independent working-class education." Other institutions engaged in working-class education were imbued with conservative, collaborationist ideologies. The Labour College Movement, in contrast, had a frankly radical agenda: "What the present position of the workers as a class is. How and why it came to be so. How the workers can alter it" (Horrabins cited in Murphy 1972:95).

These forms of education have waned with the spread of state schooling (see Lloyd and Thomas 1998: 98-106 and Connell 1993:36). The forms of working-class self-education that remain are largely confined to specialized forms of trade union training. Jeffrey Taylor (2001:239) examined the history of labour education in Canada. He points out that trade union organizations took over labour education just after World War II, marginalizing the Workers' Education Association (WEA) with its emphasis on "non-sectarian, militant, autonomous and critical" working-class education. The new union-run education programs focused primarily on stewards training and industrial relations preparation. By the 1990s, however, he found that a more activist approach, in response to the sustained employers offensive, had spread across much of the union education movement. I would add that, despite these hopeful signs, union-run working-class education is still fragmented (between unions), limited only to union members (and their families on occasion), shaped around the power structure of bureaucratized unions and not positioned to challenge the state's monopolistic claim to "education."

The decline of working-class self-education needs to be understood in terms of the broad trajectory of class formation (see Introduction). I am not claiming that working-class self-education offered a full-fledged alternative to state schooling. I am simply making the point that the hegemony of state schooling has been accomplished in part by the elimination of alternatives so that the educational system is seen as the only point of access to many forms of valued knowledge. In the absence of any alternatives, working-class demands tend to focus on more access to the existing educational system rather than the development of new and potentially more appropriate forms of learning.

The hegemony of the official school curriculum does not depend only on the elimination of alternatives and the exclusion of the learning gained through everyday practical experience. It relies on the crucial idea that certain ways of knowing are better than others. The hegemonic curriculum is founded on the twin pillars of science and liberal-humanist culture. These ways of knowing share common claims to a uniquely elevated vantage point, from which the most penetrating and far-ranging insights in the history of humankind have been possible. Schooling thus founds the "universal" standpoint of the state on the elevated epistemological claims of science and liberal-humanist culture.

## Making National Culture

The development of national cultures has been an important component of capitalist state formation, providing a basis for the development of imaginary communities out of heterogenous and divided populations (see Anderson 1983). Culture is constructed as a common space of disinterest, rooted in the supposedly universal perspective of the state, that seems to rise above the give and take of daily conflicts to represent a shared asset of considerable worth. The state thus assumes an ethical form on the basis of its identification with culture, claiming to represent the best in humanity and attempting to raise the population up to that level (Lloyd and Thomas 1998:47).

Cultural education can be seen as enlightenment rather than social control, offering people access to beauty, insight and the wisdom of the ages. With this approach, teaching invites students into the space of culture, offering them a hand up towards the community of the enlightened. Stuckey points out that this conception of teaching rests on "the view of the safe, benevolent inside, the place where we are and a place others might be persuaded to inhabit" (Stuckey 1991:114). "Inside" is a unique and beautiful space of open-mindedness and disinterest but the teacher must shed specific interests to create this space. This conception of teaching and scholarship is exemplified in a statement characterizing the humanist that was made by Desmond Pacey in 1967 when he was head of the Association of Universities and Colleges of Canada. "It is not that he advocates any specific aesthetic or ethical doctrine – he may do so as a man but not as a scholar – but that he seeks to make his students aware of the range of alternatives, of the complexity of choice, of the need for the finest possible intelligent discrimination" (cited in Fleming 1971c:269).[8]

National cultures require conscious development. The period of the broad welfare state in Canada saw a great deal of attention focused on the question of national culture. The cultivation of a national culture figured prominently in both the Massey Commission and the Hall-Dennis report. There is a great deal of similarity in the way the two reports construct the challenge of establishing Canadian identity, although there are also important differences reflecting in part the challenges of the 1960s movements that are reflected in the Hall-Dennis report.

The Massey Commission referred to culture as a feature of national security in a Cold War context. "Our military defences must be made secure; but our cultural defences equally demand national attention; the two cannot be separated" (RCNDALS 1951:275). But culture was not just a line of defence, it was also a means of elevating the population, a spiritual leavening. "The work with which we have been entrusted is concerned with nothing less than the spiritual foundations of our national life. Canadian achievement in every field depends on the quality of the Canadian mind and spirit" (RCNDALS 1951:271). The report also discussed the importance of national culture to the maintenance of national unity (271). Educational systems were crucial to that cultural development. The report described the universities (in the words of a submission from the universities themselves) as the "nurseries of a truly Canadian civilization and culture" (143). In the face of this important mission, the universities faced serious problems. The influence of the United States loomed large in English-speaking universities, through the presence of American faculty or American-educated Canadians, and a general cultural dependence that included the use of American textbooks (13-16). The universities did not have adequate funding sources and faced chronic underfunding (140-42). This report stressed the cultural project of post-secondary education rather than the economic tasks of skills development.

The Hall-Dennis report, issued seventeen years later with quite a different mandate (provincial not federal, educational rather than broadly cultural, elementary and secondary rather than post-secondary), touched on many of the same themes. Its core commitment was to prepare for democracy: "freedom to think, to dissent and to bring about change in a lawful manner in the interest to all" (PCAEOSO 1968:21). Training for democracy meant exposing the whole population to the great ideas of the liberal humanist tradition. "All aspects of learning must be supported for the great ideas are not the exclusive property of an intellectual elite" (PCAEOSO 1968:21). Schooling should not be simply about work preparation it should also be about education for the constructive use of leisure time (13).

This training was to be rooted in a particular from of national identity to counter external influences. "If a national – as opposed to nationalistic – ideology is not firm, the mass culture and economic resources imported from abroad will tend to make an economic and cultural colony of Canada" (PCAEOSO 1968:30). There was an almost poetic search for the mythical roots of this "national but not nationalistic" identity. "It is in the soul of the people that the Canadian identity can be found; and despite frequent self-evaluation, sometimes positive though muted and frequently negative and banal, Canadians sense an identity that is not rooted in Britain, France or America, but in themselves and their own land" (23).

The Hall-Dennis report offers a conception of citizenship under threat, contested by external forces (especially American influences) and by internal fractures along lines of language, culture and generation. It reflected the development of multiculturalism, a more sensitive vehicle for incorporation developed in part as a response to the challenge to racist and ethnocentric education (discussed in Chapter 4). The report called for a citizenship education that reflected cultural diversity (see PCAEOSO 1968:30). The education system played a huge role in the linguistic and cultural assimilation of young people from diverse backgrounds. It created complex dynamics in families as children became more competent than their parents in dealing with certain areas of daily life. The multicultural strategy registered awareness of this complexity resulting in a more nuanced process of incorporation.

There was particular attention to the politics of youth in the 1960s, including discussions of the generation gap, young people's rejection of traditional values, an awareness of world problems and the chafing of teenagers who continue to be treated as children (PCAEOSO 1968:34-35, 42). Yet here we see the contradictions in this conception of education for democracy at their starkest. Despite all the rhetoric about democracy, students were not to become citizens of the school and had none of the participatory rights of citizenship in this context. The Hall-Dennis report did not call for this kind of enfranchisement, even as it argued, "Our children need to be treated as human beings – exquisite, complex, and elegant in their diversity" (48). The non-citizenship of children in schools, wrapped in ideological commitments to democracy, is perhaps the appropriate preparation for the limited form of citizenship that comes with the attainment of full adulthood in capitalist society. National identity in this liberal-humanist form is perhaps the most supple and sophisticated disciplinary approach that has been developed in capitalist society. It is, however, based on the construction of an extra-economic space of "culture" that is increasingly seen as an obstacle to a leaner state rooted in more coercive disciplinary approaches and market-based consumerism.

## Science and National Culture

Thus far, this chapter has examined the link between cultural education and the nationalization project. Lloyd and Thomas (1998), who make a powerful case for the importance of cultural education to capitalist state formation, inspired this approach. They do not discuss the complementary role that science has played in the construction of national cultures and state-centred ways of knowing. Education systems have employed both scientific and cultural methods to form citizens in relation to the state. Scientific and cultural education have shared claims to universality, disinterest and locations at the pinnacle of the hierarchy of knowledge.

During the twentieth century, science has come to play an important place in liberal education. The period of the broad welfare state saw a new emphasis on science education, driven by military (the Cold War) and economic competition (see Fleming 1971b:35). Cultural education retained a central place in conceptions of citizenship formation. At the same time, the natural and social sciences acquired a new prominence.

Science education covers many areas of study, ranging from very concrete aspects of technological education to the grand abstractions of theoretical physics. This range of study becomes even greater if we include the social sciences. These diverse courses tend to share very little except for a formal commitment to the power of the scientific method in penetrating the mysteries of the natural universe and (although this is more contentious) the social world. These claims for the power of the scientific method provide a crucial grounding for the development of particular ways of knowing through a hegemonic approach to formal education.

The positivist account of the scientific method attributed its powers to the combination of particular research methods (for example, the accuracy claimed for quantification and statistical measures) with a specific theoretical legacy (resting particularly on the contributions of particular great men, such as Einstein, Darwin, Newton and Pasteur). This combination of theory and empirical research was seen as the foundation for a unique objectivity, a powerful universality (as demonstrated by the development of general laws) and a dynamic capacity to incorporate new developments. There have been important debates about this traditional account of the scientific method since the 1960s, occasioned by Kuhn's (1970) new social history of science and politicized challenges to the "neutrality" of science associated with rising social movements (see Harding 1998). At the same time, the positivist conception of science has remained influential.

Cultural and scientific education are sometimes seen as inherently in conflict with one another, representing different world views and pedagogical approaches. Yet scientific education can also complement the cultural orientation of liberal education. The objectivity associated with science provides an important ground for the position of the disinterested educator. Scientific knowledge can lay claim to particular forms of universality, which transcend the specifics of students' own experiences or interests. Indeed, science, on the basis of its ability to answer difficult questions, ranging from the most practical to the most abstract, claims an almost mystical place atop hierarchies of knowledge.

The specific place claimed by European science in these hierarchies of knowledge reinforces the ethnocentric conception that the peoples enter history only when they come into contact with Europeans. The non-European "peoples without a history" have also been portrayed as not having science (or indeed any serious knowledge of their environment) (see Wolf 1982). Science is presented as a marker of European superiority rather than a product of unique historical circumstances (such as the massive accumulation of wealth through plunder, the mobilization of knowledge to serve imperialism, the appropriation of indigenous knowledge and the destruction of alternative ways of knowing based in suppressed economic and social institutions) (see Harding 1998:39-54).

There are three other features of science that have contributed to its place in the formation of citizens. First, the development of scientific methods (particularly those of the social sciences) has been bound up in the process of state formation. The emergence of British sociology, for example, was interwoven with the development of state administration (see Abrams 1968). Sociological inquiry helped to enumerate the population and frame social problems. At the same time, the state's point of view was incorporated into sociological inquiry as a hidden presupposition. Statistical methods, for example, developed largely as a means for the state to know its population. A great deal of social science thus came to share a technocratic viewpoint with the state, developing an allegedly disinterested approach to social problems that claimed to leave politics aside (see Shaw and Miles 1979). Science education can help to locate people inside administration, taking for granted the power and perspective of state regulation.

Second, science as a way of knowing may at times seem uniquely well-suited to the revolutionary character of capitalism as a social and economic system. Marx spent a considerable amount of time in the *Communist Manifesto* discussing the dynamism of capitalism. "All fixed, fast-frozen relations ... are swept away, all new-formed ones become antiquated before they can ossify. All that is solid melts into air." (Marx 1969:111). The positivist account has presented the scientific method as an endlessly flexible way of knowing that is always capable of assimilating new data (by confirming, revising or rejecting theories) and keeping pace with a changing universe. Cultural education, in contrast, has often relied on canonical approaches that might seem inherently conservative. Science education might therefore be seen as particularly useful preparation for a society in which order must be constantly reconciled with change.

Finally, the traditions of science education have often incorporated forms of practical experience (such as labs) that tend to be less common in the liberal arts. Science seems, in certain ways, to be able to overcome the division between head and hand that is so central to the development of liberal education. However, we should not go too far with this. The experiential component of science education occurs in a highly formalized setting that is almost by definition (that is, the rules of experimental procedure) hermetically sealed off from daily experience (that might contaminate results). Nonetheless, the combination of a practice component in lab work and the possibility of an applied technological orientation, might seem to make science more credibly "practical" at times than cultural education when applied education is valued (for example, during World War II and in the current round of restructuring). Interestingly, it also means that science tends to suffer at times when instrumental education is less popular (for example, during the 1960s radicalization).

## Culture in a Lean State

The expansion of the educational system through the period of the broad welfare state saw more people exposed to greater amounts of cultural education. At the same time, the sciences came to occupy an increasingly central place in the educational system. Culture and science contributed in different and often complementary ways to the project of state formation and the making of citizens.

The education reform agenda associated with the shift towards the lean state has tended to counterpose scientific and cultural education. Across the breadth of the educational system we are seeing a tilt towards the sciences and away from the liberal arts. I will argue here that this tilt is associated with a narrowing in the conception of citizenship and an increasing emphasis on instrumental approaches to education. I will also discuss the degree of distortion involved in the association of science with practical education and the liberal arts with impractical aestheticism.

The 1990s in Ontario saw an important shift towards the prioritization of scientific and professional education and the diminution of the liberal arts. The dimensions of this shift should not be overstated; there is no immediate program to eliminate liberal arts education. There is, however, a consistent orientation towards scientific and professional education in government documents and policy decisions. This orientation is strongly connected to the new vocationalism, discussed previously in Chapter 2. The argument is premised on the assumption that education has lost its balance, tilting away from its first role (skills-building) and towards its second role (forming good citizens). "Many argue that changes to Ontario high schools that began in the 1960s have focussed excessively on the second role – being more concerned with 'civilizing' the young than with giving them the skills they need to become productive and independent. But education can succeed only if the two roles are balanced" (OMET 1996a:4).

The shift towards science and professional education is cast as a practical response to changes in the real world, both in the labour market specifically and in society more generally. The 1999 Science Curriculum for students in Grades 9–10 argues that science education is more relevant than ever. "During the twentieth century, science has come to play an increasingly important role in the lives of all Canadians. It underpins many of the technologies that we now take for granted, from life-saving pharmaceuticals to computers and other information technologies. There is every reason to expect that science and its impact on our lives will continue to grow as we enter the twenty-first century" (OMET 1999a).

The OMET is taking steps to reorient the curriculum towards the sciences. A March 1999 press release announced that the new high school curriculum will increase the emphasis on math, science and English (OMET 1999b). The presence of English in the list is a significant reminder that this reorientation does not represent a complete shift away from liberal education, a point I will return to below. However, it is clear, in overall terms, that math and science requirements for Ontario elementary and secondary students are being increased (see OMET 1996d:23, 1998c, 1999b). *The Globe and Mail* wrote in its coverage of the release of the new elementary-school curriculum: "Education Minister Dave Johnson said Ontario children have been poorly served by the school system in science and technology and have lagged behind students in other jurisdictions" (Galt 1998b:A1).

The Ontario government is also intervening to shift post-secondary curricula in the direction of the sciences. One step in this direction was the Access to Opportunities program, developed to double enrolment in certain computer-oriented university programs while increasing by 50 percent enrolment in college computer technology programs (OMET 1998a). New incentives for students to study in these areas were developed in the form of a special graduate scholarship program (OMET 1998b). But this should not be seen as a unique one-time effort. The Ontario Jobs and Investment Board (1999:20), headed by David Lindsay (a close associate of Premier Harris), argued that the province should make more use of this kind of targeted initiative to reorient post-secondary programs.

This positive shift towards the sciences was accompanied by a denigration of the liberal arts. In Chapter 2, I quoted Mike Harris' controversial statement about sociology and geography. Paul Axelrod argues that liberal education in Canadian universities is under threat due to "government polices that privilege certain academic endeavours over others, namely applied science, high technology, business, selected professions, and mission-oriented research, all at the expense of the social sciences and humanities, the fine arts, and basic scholarly inquiry" (Axelrod 2002:86). This policy away from the liberal arts has been matched by severe funding cuts in the cultural realm. The Harris government significantly cut funding to cultural agencies, most dramatically through a 40 percent reduction in the budget of the Ontario Arts Council, a body that serves as a funding and support service to many Ontario cultural organizations (see Scott 2000:A17).

The emphasis on English in the high school curriculum might seem encouraging for advocates of the liberal arts and cultural education. There are important signs in the new English curriculum, however, that the focus is to be instrumental. "Students need literacy skills to enable them to receive and comprehend ideas and information, to inquire further into areas of interest and study, to express themselves clearly, and to demonstrate their learning. Literacy skills are important for higher education and for eventual entry into the workplace. Students who are preparing for postsecondary education must develop these skills in order to succeed in the challenging academic work of college and university programs. Students who are preparing for careers in business and industry also need these skills in order to adapt to a workplace that is constantly changing" (OMET 1999c).

The new English curriculum does also include some discussion of the more traditionally cultural aspects of language education. Cultural education is not being eliminated, but rather downgraded. This cannot be explained strictly in terms of institutional inertia. There is some advocacy of the liberal arts among policy-makers and business representatives. In April 2000, chief executives at thirty Canadian high-technology firms released a statement calling for a "balanced" approach to educational system that included the liberal arts (Luke 2000).

I would speculate at this point that there is some tendency in the current educational regime to stratify cultural education, so that an elite has access to a more traditional liberal education while the mass of students are offered a more instrumental competency-oriented curriculum. This seems to be the direction in the United States, for example, where many elite schools continue to offer a very strong liberal arts education as mass education becomes increasingly instrumental. We might be headed towards a new level of streaming at the university level, where the liberal arts are seen to be good training for a layer of managers and professionals who work in a problem-solving mode with wide discretion and a heavy emphasis on social networking, while those destined to work in jobs that are not managerial or elite professional are offered a more vocationalist education.

There are also important signs that emphasis in the secondary school English curriculum is shifting away from a traditionally cultural liberal-humanist orientation. The new standardized testing tilts the educational system towards a more instrumental orientation. Students will need to pass a Grade 10 literacy test to graduate from high school (see OMET 1999d). Student performances on a Grade 3 language competence test are now posted and used as an accountability measure for schools (and possibly for teachers). A new system of annual standardized tests will account for 20 percent of the final grades for all students from Grades 3–11 (Marowits 2001). The standardized testing regime sends out a clear message to students about the importance of skills-development as opposed to more broadly conceived cultural education, which is far more difficult to measure. Standardized testing is bound to inflect all English studies courses with an instrumental focus on skills and competencies.

An increasingly instrumental approach is evident even in traditionally cultural subject areas. The Ontario Jobs and Investment Board (1999:28) argues that fine arts education can contribute to the development of an entrpreneurial ethos through, for example, the introduction of courses in business management and intellectual property. This is quite a shift from the idea that aesthetic culture as such has specific leavening qualities that commend it to the project of making citizens.

Across the educational system in Ontario, then, a shift towards science, technology and professional education is underway. This is closely linked to the new vocationalism. Yet this does not mean that education will no longer have a cultural dimension. Rather, it represents a shift in the method of cultural education, away from a focus on the liberal arts towards an emphasis on skills development (with a particular emphasis on science and technology) that has its own "culture." Schools are in the business of cultural formation, whichever approach they take. I will argue later that the shift towards science, technology and skills development is connected to the focus on an "innovation culture." But first, it is important to examine the context for the denigration of traditional cultural education approaches.

## The Culture Industries After National Culture

The erosion of the role of cultural education is linked to a shift away from government participation in the realm of arts and culture. Federal, provincial and municipal governments in Canada are seriously downgrading their commitments to fostering cultural activities. This is part of a broader reorganization of citizenship, as discussed above. Here, I want to briefly trace the specific cultural context for the recasting of citizenship in a lean state.

National culture in the context of the broad welfare state provided the basis for new forms of identification with the nation-state that offered sections of the working class a sense of belonging in capitalist society. At the same time, workers fought their way into the market as consumers,[9] gaining new access to the commercialized culture industries that flourished on the basis of a massively expanded potential audience. These commercialized culture industries have made official national culture far less important.[10] Indeed, in the context of restructuring national culture has come to be seen as an obstacle.

The twentieth century has seen a burgeoning of commercialized leisure, driven in part by the increased consumption capacities of many working-class households. This has significantly altered patterns of working-class leisure and the character of cultural production. Clarke and Critcher (1985:60-74) argue that the commercialization of leisure activities began in the 1880s in Britain and then intensified in the 1920s and 1930s with the increased popularity of the cinema and spectator sports. The 1950s and 1960s saw these trends accelerate with the spread of television and other forms of family-centred leisure (see Clarke and Critcher 1985:79-80; and Spigel 1992). The period from the 1970s to the 1990s saw yet another dramatic increase in the penetration of commercialized leisure with the introduction of the VCR, personal stereos and computer games. It is arguable that we are moving from family-centred leisure to more individualized forms.

The culture industries have flourished in the age of commercialized leisure. This has been a contradictory phenomenon, opening up new possibilities for expression while at the same time frankly subordinating the cultural realm to market relations. For example, the rise of militant industrial unions such as the United Auto Workers and the United Steel Workers in the 1930s and 1940s was linked to a great expansion of commercial culture, which gave rise to new forms of popular culture grounded in certain aspects of working-class experience and radicalism (see Denning 1996 and Lipsitz 1994). African-American popular culture gained new prominence with the spread of the culture industries, offering new forms of voice on the condition of relentless commercialization.[11] We thus arrive at the contemporary situation in which cultural diversity is expressed as market differentiation.

The popularization of commercial culture either absorbed, or at the least marginalized, semi-autonomous forms of folk culture expressing common experiences of class, community, ethnicity, gender or sexuality.[12] This immediately opened up a broader audience for "local" folk cultures and shut down non-commodified spaces for self-expression. A variety of cultural forms withered (ranging from the fair to the tavern, from the sing-along to the radical press) as leisure was commercialized. The commercialization of culture paralleled an erosion of community. This process did not stem simply from the spread of the culture industries, but was part of a process of social reconfiguration connected with the spread of mass production and consumption (or Fordism). Social reconfiguration included the concentration of industry, revolutions in transportation and communication, the reshaping of cities (metropolitanization, suburbanization) and the dramatic growth of the service sector along with the spread of the culture industries (see Harvey 1989a).

The commercialization of culture opened up new possibilities for expression and caught them in the web of market relations. This had important consequences. The profit-making aspects of the culture industries have become an important part of the allure of the commodities they produce (see Horkheimer and Adorno1972:121; and Jameson 1991:351). Films are ranked by the amount of money they make and the incomes of stars are widely publicized. The fascination with popular culture is inflected with the veneration of money. The legitimation of capitalist relations becomes internal to the culture industries which, in their very form, celebrate the quest for profit. Indeed, the form of cultural industries is more important than their content in establishing an association with the dominant capitalist order (Horkeimer and Adorno 1972:136-7, 139,152).

However, Horkheimer and Adorno's depiction of the culture industries goes too far in suggesting a closure of the system that eliminates contradictions (see Eagleton 1991:46-47). I think it is possible to draw on this powerful conception without losing the sense that the culture industries have opened up contradictory spaces. Robin D.G. Kelley (1996) captures the character of these contradictions powerfully in his account of rap music, which at once captures elements of the experiences, aspirations and radical dissent of some African-American youth and frankly celebrates its own commercialization. The expansion of the culture industries has opened up new contradictions even as it has woven aesthetic expression and leisure activities deeper into the fabric of capitalist social relations (see Williams 1981:204-5, 232-33).

The culture industries spread with the expansion of mass production and consumption in conjunction with new forms of working-class self-organization, particularly the spread of unions to the industrial and public sectors during and after World War II. The deep penetration of commercialized culture into every aspect of everyday life has been both a condition of possibility and a result of the social changes associated with the rise of lean production. It has certainly been an important factor in the restructuring of social policy and the rise of the lean state. Quite simply, commercialized culture has effectively become the location of identifications that a national culture once aspired to develop. The need for the state to play a cultural role may be reduced in circumstances where the culture industries provide a potent ground for developing identification with actual, existing capitalism (see Jameson 1991:315, 351-52). Further, the project of national culture may be less viable given the context in which national identities are being undercut by processes of globalization (see Esland 1996:22).

Indeed, the culture industries may do a better job of providing a ground for the development of identifications than national culture ever could. National culture, with its leavening mission, could not escape the hierarchical distinction between "high" or elite culture (for example, opera, symphony, art galleries) and 'low' or popular culture (for example, television, pop music, Hollywood movies). Cultural education was cast as a medium for moral elevation on the basis of the aesthetic powers of high culture (see Lloyd and Thomas 1998:42). Elite tastes were thus established as the national standards and reproduced in an exclusionary manner that stigmatized the broad masses with their uncultivated palettes (see Bourdieu 1984). The project of national culture was, in many ways, to generalize elite culture as the basis for new forms of identification (see Clarke and Critcher 1985:130), but elite culture could not escape the symbolic moats and fortifications built around it in order to keep out the masses.

It is not surprising, then, that we should see cultural education downgraded in the shift to the lean state. New market identities may have reduced the need for politically mediated national cultures. Television, for example, is arguably a potent source of "imagined community," grounded in conceptions of privacy and property rights (see Spigel 1992:100). The borders of this imagined community do not correspond to the boundaries of the nation-state, but tends to be at once broader (the globalization of American commercial culture) and narrower (through processes of market differentiation and exclusion).

Indeed, national culture has in some ways become a fetter on capitalist intensification in the cultural realm, creating a certain space of decommodification in which principles (however imperfectly realized) of access, national particularity, diversity of representation and aesthetic merit are supposed to rate over market viability. We are seeing a deliberate shift away from this particular form of state activity in many areas including the educational system. The arts are being privatized and made increasingly reliant on philanthropy, user pay or full commercialization.

Yet we must not mistake the withering of certain forms of national culture for the disappearance of the state itself or of politically mediated cultural formation. We are seeing instead an important change in the form of state activity. The state in Ontario, for example, is not simply getting out of the business of culture. Rather, the Harris government seems to be replacing the broad welfare state project of national culture with a new orientation to "innovation culture," which I will discuss below.

## Science After History?

The study of history has been an important feature of cultural education. National histories provide foundations for national cultures. The core of cultural education has been the presumption of a common culture that is constructed as the logical outcome of a sequence of historical events. This requires work on the past, a retrospective organization of events into a logical sequence that naturalizes the constitutional and cultural forms of a specific nation-state. Jack Granatstein made a case for this kind of history as part of an unfinished project of nation-building in Canada. "If Canada is to be worthy of its envied standing in the world, if it is to offer something to its own people and to humanity, it will have to forge a national spirit that can unite its increasingly diverse peoples. We cannot achieve this unanimity unless we teach our national history, celebrate our founders, establish new symbols and strengthen the terms of our citizenship" (Granatstein 1998:148-49).

Hobsbawm (1983) powerfully describes this work on the past as the "invention of tradition." He argued that the invention of traditions began as a specific response to the threat that working-class mobilization posed to the social order at the end of the nineteenth and beginning of the twentieth centuries. These traditions were invented to secure the loyalty of working-class citizens by incorporating them into political society.

Historical study thus occupied a prestigious location within the hierarchies of knowledge. This has an important ethnocentric dimension as non-European peoples exist outside of history until the moment of conquest or contact that brings them into history. European conquest has been constructed as the moment of cultural elevation in which isolated and static peoples were brought onto the stage of "history" (Wolf 1982).

The shift away from state-organized national cultures has occasioned a reduction in the centrality of history education. There seems to be some connection between the "end of history," the demise of cultural education and the increased prominence of science in contemporary schooling. Jameson (1991) argues that there is a fit between postmodern conditions and a withering of historical consciousness. The cultural logic of late capitalism includes a sense of historical closure, in part a reflection of the deep penetration of capitalist social relations into every pore of society. This produces a very presentist orientation in which the past has little to teach us and the future is simply an extension of the present (see Jameson 1991:360). The only possibility for a different future seems to be a catastrophic breakdown, as envisioned in popular culture through a whole series of post-apocalypse movies like the Mad Max series (Jameson 1991:286). The longing for some connection to the past is expressed in a nostalgic craving for "ye olde" images of a reality that never existed or in hobbies like genealogy (Jameson 1991:46, 361).

In short, we are in a period in which there appears to be a radical discontinuity between past and present. The accelerated rate of change (for example, in technologies) seems on its own to be a convincing argument that the gap between the present and the past is widening rapidly. Segregating the present from the past shuts down the vision of other possible futures that animate radical social movements, as it hides the story of how things got to be this way and how they might be changed. But this should not be seen as a permanent and irreversible change.

I subscribe to the radical version of this analysis of historical closure that casts it as a product of particular circumstances that are subject to change. Contemporary capitalism continues to be founded on violent inequalities that provide the basis for mobilizations. Through such mobilizations, the exploited and oppressed will develop a new historical consciousness as they begin to make history (see Callinicos 1995:160-65, 209-11 and Jameson 1991:406). Social movements create a hunger for history as people seek to interrogate the past to understand the forces that shaped the development of the present and the possibilities for the future. Radical workers' movements, for example, have created a new hunger for historical knowledge; a hunger satisfied, for example, in Britain's labour colleges that emphasized the study of history (see Murphy 1972:94-95). The social movements of the 1960s inspired important works of historical recovery, exploring the "hidden" histories of (and these are not mutually exclusive categories): aboriginal peoples, lesbians and gays, anti-Stalinist socialisms, people of colour, women and workers.[13] The contemporary experience of historical closure is the result of the character of contemporary capitalism in conjunction with the relatively low ebb of struggles at this specific moment. A new hunger for history should be awakened as the next major wave of social struggles confronts activists with important questions of how the world came to be this way and how it might be changed. This view is emphatically pro-historical, arguing in the end that the reduced emphasis on the awareness of history amounts to depriving an entire generation of its political memory (Davis 1995). This must be accompanied by the caution that school history teaching can, in its own way, suppress political memory and radical vision.

There are, for example, proponents of history education who seek a return to the formerly dominant approaches to historical and cultural education. They present an internal critique that argues that the discipline of history lost its way with the impact of the 1960s social movements, with their politicized and pluralistic historical accounts. Jack Granatstein argues, for example, that the redress of historic grievances has crowded out the teaching of genuine Canadian history. "The history taught is that of the grievers among us, the present-day crusaders against public policy or discrimination. The history omitted is that of the Canadian nation and people" (Granatstein 1999:xi). From this point of view, it is defects in the development of the discipline of history that are to blame for the marginalization of historical education. History has been captured by the margins and there is no place left for the old centre, political history (see Granatstein 1999:63-66). Further, historians have lost the knack of telling a good story and have lost touch with a broader public (see Granatstein 1999:48-49, 67-71). The defence of the narrative is a centrepiece in the right-wing counterattack against the increased prominence of social history.

It is true that university-based intellectuals often do not communicate well with a broader audience but it is disingenuous to blame this on one particular school of thought. Rather, we should understand the decline of the "public intellectual," the thinker oriented to communicating with a broader public, in the context of the growth of the universities (creating the conditions for the professionalization of academics) on the one hand and the impact of deepened commercialization on the culture industries (shutting down avenues of communication that once existed) (see Jacoby 1987). I would argue further that the withering of the left (in the broadest sense) has led to the demise of a broad cultural and political infrastructure that once provided a place for public intellectuals (including those with little formal education as well as those with a great deal) to engage with a broader audience around a wide range of political and cultural questions.[14]

It is clever, but inaccurate, to locate the defence of the narrative form in history as a populist critique of academic obscurity. The problem is not that history has abandoned good old-fashioned storytelling, but rather that the number of public spaces available for the discussion and debate of ideas has diminished significantly. There are different ways to tell a good story; modernist techniques of montage can also be compelling. The narrative form can certainly be criticized for the way it can be used as a vehicle for presenting a particular interpretation as *the* history of the nation, dissolving the analytic perspective into the sequence of facts.[15] Yet Jameson defends the critical power of the narrative in revealing historical necessity, identifying "why what happened (at first received as 'empirical' fact) had to happen the way it did" (Jameson 1981:101)

In the end, it is not the narrative form as such that is really the issue here, but rather the claim to naive and disinterested storytelling. Traditional political history tells the national story from the perspective of the state. Just as the state has been presented as a neutral body representing the whole of society, political history has presented itself as the (only) story of the nation, even though it is told from the perspective of the powerful. There are very good reasons to defend the narrative form against the attacks of poststructuralists who argue that historical processes are essentially unknowable and have been apprehended only through the distorted lens of grand narrative schemes (see Callinicos 1995). At the same time, however, it is important to dispute the claims of the right-wing historians who long for a return to the "good old days" when partial stories could be passed off as the whole truth.

The ultimate success of the right-wing historians in waging a civil war against radical social historians within the discipline of history is not clear at this point. They are, in any case, unlikely to accomplish a broader revival of national histories in present circumstances. Such a revival would run up against notions of historical closure, which at the moment seem to fit with contemporary common sense. The right-wing version of historical closure equates the "end of history" with triumphant capitalism (see Fukuyama 1992). In this version, contemporary capitalism is the last stage of history, marked by the elimination of meaningful contradictions through, for example, the collapse of the "other" side in the Cold War. As Fukuyama argues, "At the end of history, there are no serious competitors left to liberal democracy" (Fukuyama 1992:211).

The study of history thus loses much of its cogency. I would argue that "end of history" thinking is an important factor underlying the increasing marginalization of the study of history within the education system.[16] This does not mean that policy-makers have been influenced by Fukuyama as such, but he does provide the scholarly articulation of an analysis shared by the many proponents of contemporary restructuring processes. As discussed above, "end of history" thinking fits with what Jameson (1991) describes as the "cultural logic" of the current period. It is largely taken for granted by contemporary reformers, yet it guides thinking in important ways as we will see below in the discussion of innovation culture.

The idea of historical closure, then, can help us understand the current realignment of the educational system along an axis in which traditional historical and cultural studies are downgraded while science, math and vocational studies receive more attention. The downgrading of the liberal arts relative to the sciences is not simply about sharpening the vocational orientation of contemporary education. This realignment of educational priorities fits with the conception that science has, in effect, superseded history. Fukuyama (1992:72) argues that the emergence of modern science in the sixteenth and seventeenth centuries provided the direction for subsequent historical developments. His argument hinges on the claim that science alone among human undertakings is "unequivocally cumulative and directional." "The scientific understanding of nature is neither cyclical nor random; mankind does not return periodically to the same state of ignorance, nor are the results of modern natural science subject to human caprice" (72).

Science impelled modernization processes, producing important kinds of convergence in societies with very different starting points, largely by providing a basis for technological progress (Fukuyama 1992:77). It drove historical processes to the end of history, to the point where the world of liberal capitalism was near-universal and essentially irreversible (89-97). Science will continue to drive progress even if history, in the sense of epochal change, is at an end.

This argument draws on the positivist account of science discussed earlier. The positivist view tends to place science outside of history, offering up a decontextualized understanding of scientific advances. In this view, the logic of science itself accounts for advances in knowledge. Science is understood in terms of commitments to rationality, objectivity and empirical precision that free it from the fetters of tradition and interest, eliminating the friction that might otherwise inhibit the development of better knowledge (see Harding 1998:2-3). This traditional view was, however, rejected by Kuhn (1962 [1970]), who played a key role in opening up a new approach that placed science back inside history. The various social historical approaches to science that have flourished since Kuhn's time reject the claim that scientific advances result from an internal regime of objectivity, rationality and precision. Science is no more disinterested or detached than any other form of human knowledge (see Harding 1998).

Fukuyama (1992:352-53, n.2) rejects the Kuhnian approach to science in a lengthy footnote that favours the positivist view. The view that scientific perspectives are uniquely progressive and disinterested lies at the core of many contemporary policy approaches. This positivist view is particularly compatible with the technocratic orientation implicit in contemporary social policy restructuring (including education reform) that casts political issues as technical problems to be solved by sound management in the interest of all (see Apple 1995:140; and Avis 1996a:111). The positivist view also presents science as a repository of absolutes as opposed to the ever-increasing relativism of the humanities and social sciences.

Science, as opposed to history, is being constructed as the reference point for contemporary culture. This expresses itself, for example, in the technological determinism that features prominently in some discussions of the "information age" (see Dyer-Witherford 1999:22-26) where the computer is placed at the centre of a new set of social relations to which we must adapt. The computer is cast not only as a teaching and learning tool in the school setting, but as the symbol of a new social order to which children must be acculturated.[17] Indeed, contemporary right-wing analysis often deploys a vulgar materialism in the form of economic and technological determinism; one that far exceeds the excesses the oft-criticized mechanistic readings of Marx (see Jameson 1991:265).

Science is presented as a uniquely dynamic approach to knowledge which, once freed from the ballast of history, is capable of moving quickly enough to capture the contemporary world with its ever more rapid pace of change. The humanities, in contrast, have been anchored to histories of various sorts and now seem to be moving from the core of the world of knowledge to the periphery. "In some sense, the humanities stand a little aside, as quizzical commentators who offer doom-laden prophecies or playful critiques, and as performers who offer pastiche entertainment or heritage culture as a diversion from threatening complexity or volatility" (Gibbons et al. 1994:110).

The periphery, however, is not the same as oblivion. While there is a significant tilt away from the humanities in contemporary education reform, it does not yet seem that we are headed towards their elimination. The latest high school curriculum in Ontario maintains a certain commitment to the place of humanities in education, even if it is dramatically diminished relative to the high point of liberal education. It is difficult to believe that the humanities are headed to extinction, given that the highly influential culture industries have assimilated elements of the humanist ethos (Gibbons et al. 1994:110). It also seems that there will be a place for the liberal arts in elite education as the stratification of the post-secondary system increases. As discussed above, it is possible to imagine that the liberal arts will be retained at the elite end of the spectrum (that is, institutions emphasizing research as well as graduate and professional education) while they suffer erosion at the mass end (that is, at institutions emphasizing undergraduate or technical education).

**Innovation Culture**

I am arguing, then, that one of the important assumptions of contemporary education reform is that the school system must be restructured to prepare students properly for a world after "the end of history." Education reform is founded on the assumption that the old tools of aesthetic culture and history, rooted in the way things were, will not adequately equip students to navigate their way through our rapidly changing world. Aesthetic culture and history also bear the marks of the old political mediations, winning loyalty to the existing social order through identification with the nation-state. These mediations are no longer required in this world after history. As should be clear by now, I also believe this diagnosis is completely wrong. I believe, however, that it is worth examining in detail as it helps us understand the logic of contemporary education reform.

The Harris government in Ontario, along with many other governments in Canada and around the world, set itself the daunting task of remaking society economically and culturally to try to consolidate an emerging order, which could be seen as a new stage of capitalism. The commitment to this task was made clear in an important document released near the end of Harris's first term in office. Early in 1998, Premier Harris commissioned the Ontario Jobs and Investment Board (OJIB) to develop a broad economic vision for the province's future (Ontario Jobs and Investment Board 1999:4). The OJIB was headed by David Lindsay, one of Harris's close advisors (Ibbitson 1999:A15).[18] The broad-ranging OJIB report argues that important social and cultural changes would be required to enhance Ontario's economic prosperity in the next two decades. It is a highly developed articulation of the Harris government's cultural agenda, including education reform.

One of the five strategic goals set out in the OJIB report is the establishment of an innovation culture.[19] The report argues that the economic context of a knowledge-based economy compels us to do things differently and to do new things. After all, we inhabit a world "in which rapid change is a constant" (OJIB 1999:25). An innovation culture appreciates new approaches and looks with suspicion on continuity. An OJIB background paper on innovation culture stresses that carrying on in the same old way is not an option. "[b]y following our current path, Ontario will – at best – maintain its position. In order to improve, it will take change to innovate – to break stride" (OJIB 1998a:5).

A better future, then, requires that we break with the past. Implicit in this argument is the idea that we are at a moment when history has little to offer us. The break with the past will not be accomplished simply on the economic front. "It could be argued that our ability to innovate depends largely on two factors: The people, organizations and institutions in our society; and our system of values and incentives and the way they guide our behaviour, collectively and individually. It is, therefore, an *issue of culture*" (OJIB 1998a:5, emphasis added).

We need to develop a culture that promotes innovation. That means destroying elements of the old. "Innovations not only create new products, processes and institutions, but also destroy the status quo" (OJIB 1998a:9). The only path to a better future is a break with the past and a thoroughgoing commitment to innovation. "As a society, Ontario needs to embrace innovation. We need to support and move innovation within and across the full 'innovation spectrum' from leading edge research to process improvements in our manufacturing facilities, from our management and marketing expertise to our cultural and artistic expression" (25). It is not a stretch, then, to argue that innovation culture takes the lean production principle of continuous improvement ("process improvements in our manufacturing facilities") and applies it more broadly across the "innovation spectrum."

The creation of an innovation culture in Ontario will require the coordinated effort of many actors.[20] At the level of the individual, it is necessary to "develop a culture ... that fosters and encourages initiative, creativity and risk-taking...." (OJIB 1999:25). Governments must "undertake bold and unique actions to remove impediments to innovation and review the incentive structures so that risk-taking and success is not penalized"(26). The educational system needs to "strive for excellence and relevance and adapt to change and respond to market opportunities" (26).

The innovation culture pictured in the OJIB report is built on the twin foundations of science and entrepreneurship. It is here, rather than in the traditional liberal arts, that the values for a prosperous future must be sought. I emphasize values here because the discussion of an innovation culture in this report draws on the *ideological* importance of science and entrepreneurship along with their practical impact. In other words, the import of science and entrepreneurship is not only practical but also cultural.

## Science As Innovation Culture

Science (at times linked specifically to technology and engineering) is the only realm of knowledge singled out for particular attention in the OJIB report. The emphasis in the report is not generally on science as a crucial feature in skills development. Neither is there any particular emphasis on science in either the discussion paper on "Preparing People for Tomorrow's Jobs" (OJIB 1998b) or the chapter of the final report on "knowledge and skills for prosperity" (OJIB 1999:16-24). Instead, science is discussed in the context of promoting an innovation culture. "As a key component of this innovation culture, Ontario needs to build awareness of and strengthen our 'scientific literacy' (understanding and skill in biology, mathematics, chemistry, physics, biology, astronomy, etc.) throughout the education system, our institutions and society as a whole" (32).

Notice that there is discussion of "scientific literacy" in this report but virtually no mention of literacy in its traditional sense of reading and writing. There is a brief statement suggesting that current approaches to literacy education do not excel by global standards as "adult literacy in Ontario is only in the middle of the pack internationally" (OJIB 1999:17). However, no solution is proposed in the context of this report. Indeed, the discussion of Ontario school reform mentions an increased emphasis on mathematics, science, technology and career counselling but does not discuss the new literacy testing program, in contrast to an Education Ministry press release heralding the new high school curriculum (OJIB 1999:18 in contrast with OMET 1999b). The omission of literacy is telling here. Indeed, references to the liberal or fine arts in this report are confined largely to the opportunities these areas offer for entrepreneurship, as discussed below.

Science education is not simply about teaching skills. Its impact is also cultural. An innovation culture must have some basis in scientific values. "Understanding and embracing science and technology should be part of Ontario's 'culture' – to enable the province to take full advantage of new opportunities in a rapidly changing world" (OJIB 1999:63. This means raising the level of public awareness about science and society. "Informed public debate should take place on the social and regulatory impact of scientific discovery and technological change and strengthen our literacy in science and technology" (OJIB 1999:33).

Science is strongly identified with technology in this document. The report makes connections between science, technology and the commercialization of ideas (see, for example, OJIB 1999:31-33). The stress on technology is at once economic and cultural. There is considerable discussion of the importance of technological research and development. It also goes beyond that to discuss what could be considered the cultural implications of technological change. The report and working papers are inflected with a certain technological determinism. "Today change comes from the rapid introduction of new technology [and] increased competition as a result of globalization. These changes are irreversible. We cannot turn back the clock" (OJIB 1998b:5; see also OJIB 1999:16).

New technologies are creating the world which we are to inhabit. We need to organize ourselves to fit into this world technologies are making. "Digital technology will be the basis of much of the innovation that will take place in new products, new services and new ways of doing business. Information and communications technology and new marketing arrangements will create the pressure and opportunities for innovations in all kinds of non-technological areas, from arts to auto parts" (OJIB 1999:25).

## The Culture of Entrepreneurship

The other central foundation of an innovation culture is a commitment to entrepreneurship. There is discussion of entrepreneurship as a practical skill in the report and working papers (see OJIB 1998b:5; and OJIB 1999:16). Yet beyond this, innovation culture is founded on entrepreneurial values and practices. Entrepreneurship is not simply a practical skill set, it is also a desirable cultural value, linked to creativity and initiative (OJIB 1999:63). The teaching of entrepreneurship at many places within the education system is accorded high priority in this report. The report calls for action to: "Promote entrepreneurship and innovation learning at an early age and continue through the education system [by] teaching courses in entrepreneurship and business in secondary school ... [and] following through to post-secondary education...."(OJIB 1999:28, see also 63). Education reforms in Thatcher's Britain similarly emphasized the promotion of an entrpreneurial culture (see Deem 1994:30, Tasker and Packham 1994:151-54). It is important to note that this entrepreneurial culture is to be highly conformist. Dissident forms of entrepreneurship, such as the use of squeegees to clean windshields, are denounced, policed and crushed.

The arts enter into this report not as a cultural good in themselves but as a place for important entrepreneurial opportunities. Suggested sites for entrepreneurship education at the post-secondary level include "courses in business management and intellectual property in disciplines like engineering and fine arts" (OJIB 1999:28). Globalization creates a new need to market the arts. The report calls on businesses and governments to: "Aggressively market Ontario's cultural industries – film and television production, musicians, authors, designers, etc. – internationally highlighting their high quality, professionalism and expression of the unique Canadian experience" (OJIB 1999:43). "This, then, is the pale shadow of the once-mighty national culture project. The cultural representation of the "unique Canadian experience" is contingent on its transformation into exportable commodities. The successful example of Roots Canada, a producer of clothing and leather products often bearing prominent labels, is noted in one of the discussion documents. "While Roots is about selling high quality clothing and leather products, it is also about selling a culture and marketing concept around the world" (OJIB 1998a:8).

Indeed, the report is quite clear that the old pairing of citizenship with national cultures needs to go, calling on individuals to "embrace a 'citizens of the world' attitude" (OJIB 1999:35). Of course, immigration controls demonstrate that the actual commitment of the Canadian state to genuine internationalism is far more tenuous than this kind of statement might imply (see Basok 1996). This statement marks an important change in the ideology of citizenship, but not in the practice of dividing workers along national lines and claiming them for particular states.

A culture of entrepreneurship, then, will corrode certain established relationships (such as that between the citizen and the state) and permit innovation. This shift is therefore likely to encounter opposition (see OJIB 1998a:9). The best ways to break down such opposition is through the creation of competitive environments. People and institutions will learn entrepreneurship as they are forced to use it to keep themselves afloat. "The more demanding the environment in certain respects, the more likely the organization or individual is to respond innovatively.... Competition creates a demanding environment.... Each competitive environment tends to foster its own type of innovation culture" (OJIB 1998a:17).

If the educational system is to "break stride," it will clearly need its entrepreneurial spirits heated up with a more competitive environment and new partnerships with business. The OJIB report discusses ways to make the funding environment for post-secondary institutions more competitive. It argues that funding to post-secondary and training institutions should be targeted on the basis of the success of their graduates in obtaining employment (OJIB 1999:20). It also calls for consideration of a voucher system for Ontario's post-secondary education system, "a more student-driven funding system, to replace some or all of the province's grants to colleges and universities" (OJIB 1999:20). A voucher system would mean that the government would fund students and not institutions. Direct, stable funding to institutions would be eliminated or dramatically reduced. This would increase the competition between institutions and possibly also between programs for students and the funding they bring with them.[21] Indeed, competition between institutions and between programs within institutions is already increasing dramatically in Ontario as enrolments are being used as a primary measure of viability.

It is not only a question of increasing the competition between and within Ontario educational institutions, but also of pushing these institutions into a global competitive environment. This means creating a more stratified educational system in which a few institutions are promoted to the "world-class" level. The report returns a number of times to the theme of attracting and holding on to the "best and the brightest" (OJIB 1999:30, 36, 61). One of the ways to do this is by "focusing government support and encouraging private-sector participation, towards the creation of world-class institutions"(30). We can presume that very few post-secondary institutions will meet this "world-class" standard and that others are likely to suffer from this focusing of support.

Another strategy for increasing the entrepreneurial orientation of educational institutions is to push them into partnerships with business (OJIB 1999:17, 29, 53). The research work carried out in educational institutions will need a new balance "between the need to engage in basic research, applied research and the transfer and commercialization of new ideas" (OJIB 1999:26). Of course, these entrepreneurial values are inseparable from pro-business ideologies. One of the boldest commitments in this direction is the call for a new "business impact" test to assess the effect of new regulatory measures (OJIB 1999:59, 65). Just as environmental impact tests aim to ensure that new developments will do no harm to the physical and social environment, this test would presumably assess the impact of new regulatory measures on the business environment. This is a world turned upside down, where measures that might improve the health and welfare of citizens will be first assessed on their effect on businesses.

## Conclusion

I have discussed "innovation culture" here at some length as it constitutes an important articulation of the character of the "cultural revolution" that employers and allied policy-makers are trying to foment. This conception of "innovation culture" is not simply the fantasy of a clique of Ontario right-wingers, rather it draws out the cultural aspects of the contemporary round of capitalist restructuring. It is worth understanding these links in some depth as it reminds us that we are not simply struggling against a mistake, a historical misstep that will easily be reversed when a different government is elected. There is logic to these changes; they have a powerful base in a series of related social and economic changes.

Yet none of this means any of these changes are "irreversible." And here we move to the realm of political fantasy. This is not the end of history. Capitalism has penetrated deeper into the pores of human societies, creating important changes in the conditions for reproduction and resistance. Yet capitalism itself is contradictory, although this is disavowed by its advocates. Capitalism necessarily reproduces conditions of struggle and agents with the power to challenge the system. As workers, women, people of colour, lesbians, gays, bisexuals and transgendered people organize and fight back, they make history, forcing open questions that Fukuyama and others consider to be closed for good. This chapter has tried to map out some of the conditions that such struggles will have to face in the realm of education.

# Notes

1. This statement draws together Hobsbawm's (1983) discussion of the "invention of traditions" (the retrospective ordering of the past to naturalize the nation-state) and Anderson's (1983) conception of the "imagined community" (discussed above). This synthesis draws on Palmer's (1999) discussion of the role of the discipline of history in the formation of a national history.
2. Hardyment (1983:225-26) argues that the combination of pleasure and learning in Dr. Spock's book was representative of post-World War II child-rearing guides in contrast to those that came before the War. I would argue that this approach to child-rearing fits well with the ethos of the broad welfare state and the form of liberal education associated with it (exemplified in Ontario by the Hall-Dennis report).
3. The liberal humanist ethos is an important part of the character of the broad welfare state. John Clarke (1980:80, 88) discusses the specific need for a humanization of the state apparatus to match the humanist ethos of the post-war welfare state in Britain.
4. I am using "educable" in the broad sense here, referring not only to formal education through the school system but to a broader system of moral regulation, following the work of Corrigan and Sayer (1985).
5. Time-discipline is the naturalization of clock-time as a central regulator of our behaviour. E.P. Thompson (1993b [1967]) traces the specific struggles required to establish this form of regulation in the face of resistance by producers who had other ideas about where they should be at a given time, driven by a different rhythm
6. The popular definition for the minimal criterion of membership in the "middle class" is the capacity to purchase more than bare subsistence requirements, which equates with membership in consumer society. Lizabeth Cohen (1990) traces out this trajectory among Chicago workers.
7. This phrase comes from Scott 1998. Note, though, that the project of Scott's book is rather different from this book.
8. This echoes Max Weber's (1958:145) distinction between the scientist and the citizen, in which disinterested scientists strictly excludes personal commitments and beliefs from the classroom, confining them to the separate sphere of citizenship outside of the educational system.
9. The study of changing patterns of working-class consumption is an important addition to the literature on gendered class formation. Significant contributions on this theme include: Cohen (1990), Cross (1993), de Grazia (1996), Glickman (1997) and Parr (1999).
10. I am arguing that the significance of national culture in the project of state formation is declining. This is not the same thing as arguing that the significance of nationalism as a political force is declining, which is emphatically not true.
11. This contradiction is explored in Stuart Hall's (1996) discussion of the contradictory character of "black" popular culture in the context of deep commodification.
12. This meant the erosion of semi-autonomous forms of bourgeois culture as well as those of the working class (see Anderson 1998:86 on bourgeois culture and Palmer 1992 on working-class culture).
13. The recovery of "hidden histories" is reflected in titles of works by Duberman, Rowbotham (1973) and Vicinus and Chauncey (1989).
14. Denning (1996) offers an impressive overview of the broad political and cultural spaces that opened up with the rise of the C.I.O. unions in the United States. An impressive range of artists, critics and other thinkers oriented themselves around these political and cultural spaces in the 1930s and 1940s. Wald (1987) traces the particular trajectory of the anti-Stalinist cultural left. While I do not know of a similar comprehensive survey of Canadian left culture in the same period, this kind of infrastructure did also develop in Canada. One can catch glimpses of it in the memoirs of participants, including: radical writer Earle Birney (1975), who wrote fictionalized reminiscences in *Down the Long Table*; left-wing poet Dorothy Livesay's memoirs (1977) or Toby Gordon Ryan's (1981) memoirs of the left-wing theatre milieu.

15. There can also be a tendency to closure in the narrative form, constructing the present as the only possible outcome and indeed the completion of the past. This can have the effect of naturalizing the status of the citizen within a framework of laws that come to represent order (vs. chaos) as opposed to the defence of one particular order (see White 1987:87-88). These are interesting insights about uses of the narrative, but at the same time it is wrong to argue (as White does) that this tendency to closure is inherent in the narrative form as such (see Callinicos 1995:49-53, 210-11 for a critique of White).
16. Davis (1995) documents the declining emphasis on historical education in high schools.
17. This argument is implicit in the discussions of information technology in the (pre-Harris) Royal Commission on Learning (1994), particularly in Chapter 13, Volume 4. See the critique of this aspect of the Royal Commission report in Livingstone (1995a).
18. Ibbitson's (1999:A15) article was a revealing critique of the OJIB report, arguing that it marked the transition from the "autonomous liberal-arts university" to the "provincially-controlled, market sensitive, advanced polytechnic that will replace it."
19. The five strategic goals are: "1. Knowledge and skills for prosperity, 2. Innovation culture, 3. Strong global orientation, 4. Building on our industry and regional strengths, 5. Favourable investment climate" (OJIB 1999:4).
20. The report proposes action ideas for seven key players under each of its strategic goals. These players include individuals, businesses, educational institutions and various levels of government (OJIB 1999:14). Education reform is cast in an important role in the development of an innovation culture in Ontario
21. The 2001 Ontario Budget moved university funding in this direction.

# Chapter 4

# Education, Citizenship and Inequality

## Introduction: Education for Equity?

The education system has long been promoted as a haven of equity, and movements to improve the situation of disadvantaged people have often focused prominently on winning access to schooling and transforming it. Yet the actual practices of the educational system are far from emancipatory. Schooling suppresses real diversity in the name of a relatively standardized curriculum and a homogenized national culture. At the same time, it prepares students for a world of inequality by categorizing them differentially by, for example, grading and streaming.

The discussion of universality and inequality in education is particularly important given the prominence that the fight for educational equity often holds in freedom struggles. The struggle to integrate schools was central to the earlier battles of the African-American civil rights movement in the 1950s and 1960s. It has since been followed by struggles for educational inclusion and new forms of African and/or multicultural studies. Women's movements have waged twin struggles for access to education and the reorientation of curriculum and pedagogy to address women's particular needs and experiences.

These struggles for educational inclusion have been associated with quite different political objectives. Some have fought to open up access to the elite for small numbers of individuals from disadvantaged groups, while leaving the basic structure of exploitation and oppression untouched. Others have treated educational transformation as a crucial site in broader struggles to change the world. Indeed, education is almost by definition a crucial issue in counter-hegemonic struggles as individuals and groups seek a new sense of themselves, their possibilities and the way the world works as part of a fight for change. Much of this counter-hegemonic education takes place outside of formal educational institutions through various individual and group activities ranging from personal reading through feminist consciousness-raising to movement-based discussion and debate, anti-racist education and socialist organizing.[1] Indeed, this chapter will raise questions about the degree to which the formal education system can actually be transformed to play an emancipatory role.

In this chapter I use race and ethnicity as a case study in educational equity. I begin with a discussion of debates around the contribution of W.E.B. Du Bois, a theorist and activist who argued that education had a central place in the freedom struggle. I then relate the struggle for educational equity to the contradictory character of capitalist citizenship, which both promotes uniformity and reinforces differentiation. This sets the ground for an investigation of the ways in which racialization is built into the framework of liberal education, which is oriented around capitalist citizenship. Finally, I look at the ways that the shift to post-liberal education with its emphasis on "standards," threatens the limited forms of multiculturalism that have developed in liberal education.

## W.E.B Du Bois on Education for Freedom

I will begin this discussion of education and liberation with a brief review of certain debates within the African-American freedom movement over the past hundred years. An important starting point for this discussion is the work of the African-American theorist and activist W.E.B. Du Bois who argued that education would play a key role in the liberation of African-Americans. In 1903, he wrote an influential article entitled "The Talented Tenth" that promoted higher education for the 10 percent of the black population who would constitute its natural leadership in a process of uplift. "The Negro race, like all races, is going to be saved by its exceptional men. The problem of education, then, among Negroes must first of all deal with the Talented Tenth; it is the problem of developing the Best of this race that they may guide the Mass away from the contamination and death of the Worst, in their own and other races" (Du Bois 1986a:842).

For Du Bois, the formation of an African-American elite was crucial to the project of improving conditions and combatting racism. "The Talented Tenth rises and pulls all that are worth the saving up to their vantage ground" (Du Bois 1986a:847). Education, and specifically cultural education would play a central role in this project of elite formation. The Talented Tenth would then become the teachers of the rest of the African-American population, both in the very specific sense of classroom education and in the more general sense of establishing community and family standards (852-55). Reed (1997:62) summarizes the idea of the Talented Tenth, arguing that in Du Bois's view, "[the] cultivation of a stratum of broadly-trained, eminently civilized blacks who exercised full citizenship rights was a logical precondition for the commonly accepted task of racial uplift."

Du Bois's conception of the Talented Tenth developed from sharp debate with Booker T. Washington, who advocated industrial education for African-American youth (Reed 1997:60-64). Du Bois (1986b:393) characterized Washington's program as "industrial education, conciliation of the South and submission as to civil and political rights." Industrial education, then, was part of a broader program of preparing American blacks to accept their place in a racist society by becoming good workers. "The tendency is here, born of slavery and quickened to renewed life by the crazy imperialism of the day, to regard human beings as among the material resources of the land to be trained with an eye single to future dividends. Race-prejudices, which keep brown and black men in their 'places,' we are coming to regard as useful allies with such a theory, no matter how much they may dull the ambition and sicken the hearts of struggling human beings" (428).

Du Bois advocated instead a liberal-humanist education that opened up cultural development. This meant challenging those who would restrict the access of African-Americans to higher education. "[W]e daily hear that an education that encourages aspiration, that sets the loftiest of ideals and seeks as an end culture and character rather than bread-winning, is the privilege of white men and the danger and delusion of black" (Du Bois 1986b:398). Washington, in Du Bois's opinion (400), was among those opponents of cultural education for African-Americans.

Du Bois emphasized liberal humanist education for the Talented Tenth as there was an important cultural dimension to their work. He focused on "cultural revitalization," a project that involved "combatting the stigma attached to race and building racial pride by taking note of black accomplishment" (Reed 1997:62). A great deal of cultural work was required to repair the damage of racist silencing. In his 1940 autobiographical reflections, Du Bois referred to his own experience of education in which the glaring absence of any investigation of African culture or history was combined with biologistic claims of racial inferiority. "I began to see that the cultural equipment attributed to any people depended largely on who estimated it; and conviction came later in a rush as I realized what in my education had been suppressed concerning Asiatic and African culture" (Du Bois 1986d:626-27.)

Thus, Du Bois's strategy of the Talented Tenth emphasized the importance of a liberal education to the development of a leadership layer among African-Americans who could stimulate a broader process of cultural change. This strategy has served as an important reference point in contemporary debates about the place of the black intellectual. These debates take place against a backdrop of increasing social polarization in American society which has included widening income and lifestyle gaps among African-Americans (see Kelley 1997:6-8). The same process of economic restructuring has produced the immiseration of many blacks and the expanded wealth of a growing professional class.[2] The civil rights and black power movements of the 1960s and 1970s were crucial in opening up the possibility for African-Americans to move in larger numbers into positions as employers, managers, academics and self-employed professional or entrepreneurs (Joseph 1996:52). These movements have gone into decline at the same time as restructuring processes have increased social and economic polarization, including that among African-Americans (Marable 1995:36).

This broad polarization process has had particular implications for intellectuals. The mobilizations of the 1960s and 1970s created new access to elite educational institutions for a small number of African-Americans, as both students and faculty members. At the same time, subsequent developments in the 1980s and 1990s, ranging from anti-affirmative action measures to cuts in social programs, have reduced access for others. "On the one hand we have an educated elite and elite educators with access to academe (and its resources) and the students privileged to enter. On the other hand we have the non-elites who, since the 1970s, have faced growing barriers to their access to the university as a traditional training site for the Talented Tenth, and a source of economic as well as social mobility" (James 1997:156).

This has widened the gap between university-based intellectuals (particularly those in elite institutions) and the majority of the population. Some of these university-based intellectuals, such as Henry Louis Gates Jr. and Cornel West describe themselves as the inheritors of Du Bois's Talented Tenth (James 1997:29; Reed 1997:160). Yet this "Talented Tenth" seems to be increasingly detached from the task of contributing to improving the lot of the majority of African-Americans. "Before this post-civil rights era of integration (disproportionately benefiting elites), black intellectuals debated not whether they were obligated to serve in the advancement of a besieged people, but how best to fulfill these obligations" (James 1997:8). One important indicator of this detachment has been the way that some African-American intellectuals have taken up the right-wing conception of the "culture of poverty," blaming the poor for their own immiseration as a result of their attachment to particular beliefs and ways of life (Joseph 1997:53; Reed 1997:158-59).[3]

The struggles of the 1960s and 1970s, then, opened up limited access to membership of the cultural elite for members of various subordinated groups, including African-Americans. This in itself is an accomplishment but people of colour, women and lesbians or gays who achieve elite membership continue to face discrimination, but the accomplishment of elite status for a few has other implications. It can create a false sense that racism (or sexism or heterosexism) has actually been overcome. "The publicity surrounding black 'public intellectuals,' most of whom are black men and women at ivy league (sic) or prestigious public universities, popularizes the fiction that race and gender equity within a virulently racist sexist academy have finally been attained" (Joseph 1997:53). This is particularly important given that these individuals come to be taken as representative experts and spokespeople for their group (53).

This debate tells us a great deal about the place of formal (state) education in processes of emancipation. Demands on the educational system have been an incredibly important focus for mobilization and have yielded crucial gains. Yet there are serious limits to what can be obtained through the reform of existing educational institutions. The education system reproduces a degree of uniformity in culture[4] and differentiation in terms of social stratification.

Du Bois recognized some of these contradictions. He developed and changed his conception of the Talented Tenth over his long career as an activist and theorist (see James (1997:16-27). His emphasis shifted from the development of a cultured elite to the role of radical working-class leadership. This shift was a response to the pattern of development of the black middle class and his ongoing political conflicts with the moderate leadership of the black movement, particularly the NAACP. The emerging black middle class often lost its identification with the struggle of the majority of African-Americans. "The very loosening of outer racial discriminatory pressures has not, as I had once believed, left Negroes free to become a group cemented into a new cultural unity.... But rather, partial emancipation is freeing some of them to ape the worst of American and Anglo-Saxon chauvinism, luxury, showing-off and 'social climbing'.... I have discovered that a large and powerful portion of the educated and well-to-do Negroes are refusing to forge forward in social leadership of anyone, even their own people" (Du Bois 1986e:1108).

Du Bois noted that his defence, when he was charged with being a Soviet agent during the McCarthy era, came from the workers' movement and radicals. "I am free from jail today, not only by the efforts of that smaller part of the Negro intelligentsia which has shared my vision, but also by the steadily increasing help of Negro masses and of whites who have risen above race prejudice not by philanthropy but by brotherly and sympathetic sharing of the Negro's burden" (Du Bois 1986e:1109). Adolph Reed (1997:70) argues that even this radically revised conception of black leadership was oriented to the development of a "mass, working-class-based – but intellectual-led -- movement." This orientation is consistent with Du Bois's essentially Fabian[5] politics, which remained relatively consistent throughout his life (Reed 1997:88). The idea that emancipation is delivered from above remained a consistent theme in his work, even if his emphasis shifted from the specific agency of a culturally-educated elite to that of an intellectually-led workers' movement.

Du Bois's Fabian orientation towards liberal education as an agency of emancipation is one of the most important statements of a theoretical position that has been broadly influential in a variety of labour and social movements. That Du Bois himself moved some steps away from that position is a testament to his life-long activism that included a commitment to creativity and a willingness to learn from experience. Liberal education offers up a contradictory ground for oppositional activity. On the one hand, oppositional movements must demand access to liberal education, which potentially offers a real space for the development of cultural skills that can contribute to independent thinking. On the other hand, liberal education is integrally tied to the reproduction of an unequal social system and a stratified population

## Education and the Contradictions of Citizenship

Education, then, is a contradictory place for freedom struggles. It can be an important place for mobilizing and there is room for real gains. Yet those victories tend to get caught up in the limits of an unequal society, so that they tend to disproportionately benefit a small elite and offer little substantive change for most of those who are exploited and oppressed. These contradictions are not based in the education system alone but are rooted in the broader relations of liberal-democratic citizenship in a capitalist society.

Liberal-democratic citizenship consists of a complex set of relations of universality and difference. Citizenship promises a certain kind of universality – but only to those granted official membership in the nation. This means that the "universality" of citizenship contains within it a great exclusion – that of non-citizens. Even among citizens, access to the full rights of citizenship has been far from universal. Indeed, many of the great struggles of the nineteenth and twentieth centuries have involved the mobilization of workers, women, people of colour, lesbians and gays to fight for access to full citizenship rights. But full citizenship in itself has offered only the thinnest version of universal rights, formal equality in a society based on substantive inequality. Access to even these limited rights is conditional upon acquiescence to certain forms of regulation and the suppression of diversity.

These complex relations of universality and difference are played out in very important ways in the educational system. The making of citizens involves certain forms of universality intertwined with processes of differentiation. Schools are on the front line of assimilation for aboriginal peoples, immigrants and other culturally subordinated groups. They suppress diversity in important ways even as they sort students into highly differentiated categories and streams. At the same time, demands for increased access to schooling and changes to education systems have figured prominently in the various struggles of these subordinated groups.

Iris Marion Young (1995) investigated the ways in which citizenship both promotes uniformity and reinforces differentiation. Universal citizenship offers the promise of inclusion and participation, yet at the same time suppresses diversity and imposes standards in ways that deny the specific needs and experiences of many disadvantaged and excluded people (Young 1995:176). The construction of a shared space of "general interest" to bind together a community of citizens has been accomplished through the imposition of standards of uniformity. "The ideal of the public realm of citizenship as expressing a general will, a point of view and an interest that all citizens have in common and that transcends their differences, has operated in fact as a demand for homogeneity among citizens" (178). People who are different have either been overtly excluded from citizenship or forced into practices that have little to do with their needs or experiences. For example, citizenship has developed along with a conception of the public realm built on masculinized standards of disinterest and dispassion that exclude many women's experiences of care-giving in the private realm (178-84).

Rather than providing a basis for increased equality, the uniform standards that the capitalist state imposes on its citizens promote hierarchical differentiation. The commitment to equal treatment might offer the promise of guaranteed minima that provide resources to people who are disadvantaged but in the face of structural differentiation on the basis of systemic inequalities, equal treatment can reinforce and perpetuate disadvantage (Young 1995:198). All too often, equal treatment can mean the denial of different needs as a result of experience and social location. We will see in the case of schooling, for example, that universal standards (in testing, to name but one) profoundly reinforce social inequities.

The broad welfare state provides an important reference point for this discussion. The welfare state was oriented around reinforcing the dependence on wage labour – it was designed not to be a real alternative to paid employment. For women, this often reinforced the constraints of the domestic situation, offering benefits in a form that increased dependency on the (primarily) male wage-earner. Mimi Abramowitz (1992:30) argued that social programs in the United States, "rewarded the two-parent, one-earner, heterosexual family unit and punished those families that did not follow this idealized version of the family unit." Welfare state benefits for women linked to domestic labour were generally at a lesser level and more highly stigmatized than those directed primarily to men on the basis of paid employment. The broad welfare state was organized around the family wage ideal to promote a particular household structure (Gordon 1990:182-83). The broad welfare state did not actually offer security to women who were not employed, except through the mediation of a male wage. A system of "universal" benefits, then, offered security in a highly gender-differentiated way.

The contradictory relationship between universality and inequality in liberal citizenship is deeply inscribed in the character of capitalist social relations. The market system creates individuals who are autonomous and legally equivalent agents in contract and exchange. In principle, the class, gender, race or sexuality of the buyer or seller should not matter in market exchange. Yet these formally equal individuals inhabit a world of fundamental inequality. The supposed universality of market exchange under capitalism is integrally linked to social processes that naturalize certain differences. The failure to prosper in the market is attributed to individual or group incapacities, which supposedly prevent full actualization through the market. Thus racism and sexism in capitalist societies naturalize substantive inequality in the face of formal equality (see Wood 1988).

The separation of the economic from the political in capitalist society narrows citizenship to the extent that even full enfranchisement offers little real control over defining aspects of social life (Young 1995:176). Ellen Wood argues that this allows for the formal political equality of democratic citizenship without threatening the economic domination of the capitalists: "The state – which stands apart from the economy even though it *intervenes* in it – can ostensibly (notably by means of universal suffrage) belong to everyone, producer and appropriator, without usurping the exploitive power of the appropriator" (Wood 1995:40)

We can then return to the education system specifically. I am arguing here that educational inequality needs to be understood as a specific case of the contradictions of liberal citizenship. Students face the formal equality and substantive inequality of capitalist citizenship. All students are formally equal, yet they inhabit an educational system rooted in fundamental inequalities. The failure of individuals or groups to achieve in this setting is attributed to supposedly inherent differences that prevent them from actualizing themselves in the system. In school, students become habituated to the naturalization of differences that make sense of the inequalities that emerge in a supposedly fair and equal system. In education, as in citizenship relations more broadly, supposedly universalistic standards can in fact suppress, naturalize and reinforce difference and disadvantage.

## Equity and Education Reform

One of the central features of liberal education has been the naturalization of inequity. "Education systems persistently promote the belief that people who are advantaged in the distribution of social assets deserve their advantages"(Connell 1993:27). The reproduction of inequality is not a contingent feature of liberal education, but rather is central to its perspectives and methods. At the same time, the struggles of anti-racist and feminist movements have opened up some small spaces within liberal education (associated, for example, with official multiculturalism and equity programs) to contest aspects of the eurocentric and masculinist 'common sense' at the core of the curriculum.[6] Contemporary education reforms threaten to shut down these limited spaces, shoring up the closures that are already built into liberal education. This leaves us with the very contradictory task of defending elements of liberal education (or at least some of the gains made within that regime) against the right-wing reforms in such a way as to critique and point beyond it.

There are five central themes in liberal education that will recur in the discussion of various dimensions of inequity below.

1) Liberal education lays unique claims to a universal (and therefore neutral) standpoint while producing profound differentiation.
2) The inclusive grasp of liberal education has expanded through its history, yet has always been limited and conditional.
3) Liberal education severs mind from body, casting aside the knowledge that comes from active (physical and mental) exploration of the world, reducing the physical to specific instrumental functions and prioritizing passive mental learning.
4) Competitive individualism is at the core of liberal education, yet that individuality is constructed in relation to a collectivization of a particular mediated type that exists only through the activity of the teacher (and/or the system she personifies).
5) Liberal education is founded on a cultural project of citizen-formation, though this has always been combined with elements of skills training.

The shift to post-liberal educational forms in the lean state can be understood in terms of these same themes.

1) The universal standpoint is central to new educational forms that emphasize standards and intensify differentiation.
2) The drive to inclusion is being set against an emphatic orientation to disentitlement.
3) Pedagogies oriented around information technology are being used to intensify the separation of mind and body, with an obsessive focus on the virtual.
4) Individuation is being prioritized over collectivization, as the task of creating a 'public' citizenry erodes in the face of atomized market relations. The state remains the embodiment of the collective primarily in its role as dispenser of authoritarian discipline.

5) As commercialized (popular) culture takes over from national culture, education is free to reorient around a rhetoric of training. The focus is on the development of self-commodifying students who will market themselves and seek satisfaction as consumers.

Education reform, then, threatens to shut down the limited spaces of equity that had opened up in liberal education. While liberal education was firmly rooted in relations of inequality, its orientation around social citizenship made it susceptible to certain demands for inclusion. In contrast, post-liberal education makes no promises of inclusion as it is founded on market exchange and a rigid conception of standards.

## Education and Racialization

There is very little discussion of race and ethnicity in the Harris government's education reform agenda but this should not persuade us that education reform is therefore neutral in areas of race and ethnicity. Contemporary education reforms will have a profound impact on processes of racialization and ethnicity formation in Ontario. We do not have to scratch very deep beneath the surface of official rhetoric about "educational standards" to unearth a very narrow and exclusionary cultural agenda.

This section will discuss the endemic character of racism within liberal education. The racism of liberal education does not flow simply from a set of content errors that can be revised away, although such corrections are certainly crucial. Rather, racism is deeply incorporated into the core educational dynamics of the liberal system. At the same time, the struggles of oppressed peoples have opened up spaces within liberal education for limited challenges to racism, even if those spaces are small and finite. Post-liberal education threatens to shut down these small spaces and return schooling to a frankly monocultural agenda.

This discussion of the racial and ethnic dimensions of education reform will require an orienting discussion to develop key concepts. Racism in the Canadian state is so deeply taken for granted that many of its dimensions are not immediately obvious, except to those who experience marginalization and violence in their everyday lives. This is in part a result of the official "colour-blind" multiculturalism that has informed liberal education since the late 1960s. Official multiculturalism claimed to render racism (if its existence in Canada were even acknowledged) a thing of the past. This attitude was founded on the myth of Canada as a less-racist society, a myth that has been reproduced by the state, the educational system and popular culture. It is necessary first to challenge this myth as a way to open up a discussion of racialization and education reform.

Liberal education is founded on the claim of a universal perspective, represented in the classroom by the practices of the teacher (see Chapter 1). The teacher in a classroom plays the role of the disinterested representative of the general interest associated with the state. The capacity to represent the general interest derives from the possession of (supposedly) universal knowledge that transcends particular interests, experiences and perspectives. These claims about universality of knowledge and generality of interest are founded on the assumption that specific forms of cultural and (more recently) scientific education pass along the highest intellectual accomplishments of humanity (see Lloyd and Thomas 1998). These allegedly universalistic ways of knowing have become the common stock of a particular form of collectivity that is developed in the classroom, through the activity of the teacher who becomes the actual embodiment of the common good and therefore the personification of the state.

The supposedly universalistic ways of knowing that form the core of liberal education are, in fact, historically and culturally specific. This is not to argue that science (or indeed "high culture") itself is necessarily so irredeemably Eurocentric and male-biased as to be without any value beyond its specific cultural base. The problem is rather that actual existing scientific and cultural methods disavow their own partiality, staking universalistic claims for bits of knowledge that are specifically located in time and place as products of real people living in particular circumstances. Lewis R. Gordon expressed this elegantly in his description of Frantz Fanon's approach to science. "Fanon did believe that science itself can avoid being European. Ultimately, he believed so because European science has been so much like the history of television. Its producers continue to believe that they are bringing us the world because they have defined the world so narrowly" (Gordon 1995:3).

Liberal education is founded on partial perspectives with universalistic pretensions. Most importantly, liberal education incorporates the world view of "European man" who mistakes himself for all of humankind (see Gordon 1995). Liberal education attempts to teach students to aspire to the position of bourgeois, heterosexual, European man in culture and science. This is presented as the unique viewpoint for universal knowledge. Students who are not "European men" have been (at various moments in the development of liberal education) either excluded from this circle of knowledge (through practices of overt segregation) or invited to aspire to this standpoint by casting themselves aside. Liberal education thus reproduces the dynamics of a racist social order that confronts blacks with the dilemma that Fanon (1967:100) describes: "turn white or disappear."

In other words, everyday racism is built into a liberal education system that casts particular ways of knowing the world as universal and inclusive even though they are actually partial and exclusive. This can be seen both in the heartland of empire (Europe, North America, Australia and New Zealand) and in the (former) colonies. The everyday racism at the core of liberal education is evident in the colonial education systems developed by the imperialist powers. Liberal education was directly exported to the colonies. The core curriculum was simply transplanted, so that students were taught from an explicitly European perspective, without regard to their own geographical locations or cultural experiences.

Colonial education taught students to aspire to become someone else. Dionne Brand reflected on her schooling in Trinidad around the time of independence from Britain. "We went to school to become people we were not, we went to school to become people we would not be ashamed of, we went to school to uplift the new Black nation, we went to school to become people who could be acceptable to the country we were seeking independence from. We went to school not to become ourselves but to get rid of ourselves" (Brand 1998:176). It bluntly reflected the perspectives and experiences of European man and rigorously excluded the viewpoint of colonized. George J.S. Dei reflected on what he was not taught in school in Ghana. "My frustrations were not so much with what the colonial curriculum taught me, but even to this day I am angry about what was not taught. I have wondered in my later years why learning about Niagara Falls in Canada was more important that being taught about the local rivers in my village. After all, these were the rivers in which I swam, bathed, caught fish and fetched water" (Dei 1996:14).

The colonial curriculum clearly centred on European geography and history. Fanon (1967:147-48) argued that colonial education taught people of colour to think of themselves as white, at least until they confronted the walls of racist exclusion and condescension. "The black schoolboy in the Antilles, who in his lessons is forever talking about 'our ancestors, the Gauls,' identifies himself with the explorer, the bringer of civilization, the white man who carries truth to savages – an all-white truth" (147). The claims for the portability of a European curriculum were grounded in claims of universality. Himani Bannerji was educated in English language and culture when she grew up in Pakistan and India. "Great literature or culture were universal, we learnt" (Bannerji 1995:56)

This same liberal education was racist both in the colonies and in the centres of the empires, though the racism is perhaps less visible and more taken for granted in white-majority settings. People of colour are rendered invisible by this taken-for-granted white perspective on the world that casts Europeans alone as the makers of history (see Gordon 1995:29; Wolf 1982). Assimilation into this supposedly universal regime of knowledge means shedding one's own particular culture, experience and history in the name of a supposedly inclusive Europeanized world view. The indigenous knowledges rooted in the immediate experience of subordinated peoples are devalued and marginalized (see Dei, Hall and Rosenberg 2000).

Autobiographical accounts provide us with examples of people who actually felt themselves slipping away. Bannerji (1995:56) notes that during her studies in England she had to "put up a struggle to keep something of myself from vanishing and to maintain a little sense of significance." Dionne Brand ended her graduate studies when she "felt as if the completion of this PhD would mean the complete takeover of my 'self' by all that I had been resisting even while absorbing" (Brand 1998:172)

bell hooks argues that this assimilationist direction in education reflects "the white-supremacist assumption that blackness must be eradicated so that a new self, in this case a 'white' self, can come into being" (hooks 1989:67). Liberal education compels people of colour to aspire to become white to be visible. Fanon described this pressure. "Then I will quite simply try to make myself white: that is, I will compel the white man to acknowledge that I am human" (Fanon 1967:98). Thus, inclusion in the system of liberal education has the effect of erasing the experience of people who are not of European ancestry. W.E.B. Du Bois engaged in a lifelong campaign to improve educational access for African-Americans, yet at the same time recognized the dangers in this assimilationist direction. "I am not fighting to settle the question of racial equality in America by getting rid of the Negro race; getting rid of black folk, not producing black children, forgetting the slave trade and slavery, and the struggle for emancipation; of forgetting abolition and especially of ignoring the whole cultural history of Africans in the world" (Du Bois 1973:150).

Liberal education, then, teaches certain forms of knowledge and silences others. It attempts quite deliberately to induce a kind of cultural amnesia in students from subordinated groups, radically disconnecting them from their own people, place and time. This strategy of dislocation was certainly abundantly clear in the residential schools developed for aboriginal people in Canada by church and state. I will draw on the vivid characterization of these schools in Thomson Highway's (1998) novel *Kiss of the Fur Queen*. The school experience begins when children are transported by airplane from their Northern community to the remote South (Highway 1998:47). This dramatic dislocation is reinforced at the school where heads are shaved, uniforms dispensed, names are changed and children are forbidden to speak their own language (52-55, 70). When he returns home for the summer after his first year of school, Champion-Jeremiah faces a real challenge when it comes to playing with his younger brother. He can no longer speak Cree and his brother does not speak English. "Fortunately, before the week was out, Champion-Jeremiah experienced an epiphany. At their fish camp on Mamaskatch Island one stormy evening, inside the tent, he tripped ... causing him to burst out in a torrent of Cree expletives that shocked his mother. From that moment, he chattered with such blinding speed that people could barely understand him. The family breathed a collective sigh of relief. (67).

This is clearly an education that rips out tongues, suppressing the capacity to speak except in the language of the dominant group. This deliberate act was based on the assumption "that European thought and feeling were superior, and that these superiorities were embodied in languages" (Chamberlin 1993:69). Lillian Allen described the feeling of cultural loss associated with learning "proper" English at school. "Growing up in Spanish Town, Jamaica, in a British-style school system, I was conscious of the tension between how you expressed yourself in a natural, joyous and feisty way outside the school context and how you were supposed to express yourself at school" (Allen 1993:11).

Assimilationist education, then, attempts to create a new self, radically separated from her or his own culture and deprived of self-expression that is "natural, joyous and feisty." This loss is all in the name of an assimilation that cannot really be accomplished. The "promise" of inclusion on the basis of assimilation is never fully kept "since we who are black can never be white" (hooks 1989:67). Pervasive racism means that people of colour are always visible as such. Even those who adopt the "universal" (European) standpoint will be reminded every day that they are not white. The perspective of European man is thoroughly racialized so that he always sees skin colour. Fanon wrote that his skin colour was a constant issue whenever he entered a room with white people in France. "I am the slave not of the 'idea' that others have of me but of my own appearance.... I am dissected under white eyes, the only real eyes. I am *fixed*.... I feel, I see in those white faces that it is not a new man who has come in, but a new kind of man, a new genus. Why, it's a Negro!" (Fanon 1967:116).

The universalistic pretensions of European culture are thus falsified by the everyday racism of white folks. Aboriginal, Asian or black people who have taken the inclusive claims this culture seriously may feel a second dislocation when they are granted permanent outsider status. "My alienation from this 'universal culture' began in England. That 'our' Dickens might have looked at me in the streets of London, as others did, with a thinly veiled hostility – and not seen our common ground in the "universality of a refined literary sensibility" – became apparent to me many years ago in Porto Bello (sic) Road" (Bannerji 1995:56).

Students and teachers of colour, then, face a simultaneous invisibility and visibility in the face of liberal education (see Chamberlin 1993:21). European man does not see their history or culture, yet he always sees their "colour." Liberal education creates a community in which only those located inside European ways of knowing can be seen or heard. Yet people of colour who make themselves invisible by assimilating into this community are always visible as outsiders in the racialized perspective of European man.

As discussed above, the classroom is the locus for the development of a very specific form of community mediated by the activity of the teacher, anticipating the "imagined community" centred around the capitalist state. The educational system folds individuals into this community through a process that differentiates, marginalizes and excludes. Himani Bannerji powerfully discusses the marginalization she experienced in university literature classes in Canada. "Deprived of a general sense of social belonging, of being a comfortable user of the local cultural grammar, divided by my gender, race and marxism, I was an 'outsider' in and to my discipline and the classrooms that I inhabited. Often I was the only non-white student in these classes.... They carried on discussions as though I was not there, or if I made a comment ... the flow would be interrupted. Then they would look at each other and teachers would wait in the distance for me to finish" (Bannerji 1995:57)

Classroom discussion "flows" within the limits of an accepted common sense. The illusory community of the classroom operates through the construction of a specific terrain of inquiry (official culture) and a manner of engagement (reason) that reproduces common-sense understandings of the world. Brand (1998:168) argues that her most important learning took place outside of formal university classrooms, "since those classrooms, their social structures, their curriculum, all of their arrangements, ergonomic, administrative, as well as pedagogical, were commonsensically and institutionally embedded with racism and sexism." This racism is potently visible to students (and teachers) of colour, though it is deeply embedded in the taken-for-granted assumptions of "white" students (and teachers) who might therefore not see it. Students whose experience is not reflected in the teaching from the front of the room (or the "common culture" among students) are estranged from the educational system. George Dei et al. (1997) argue that black/African students are "pushed out" of Ontario's schools by a Eurocentric curriculum that does not meet their needs or reflect their experiences.

This is not simply a matter of overt racist content in the curriculum, although that is certainly important. The bedrock of common-sense racism in the educational system is the formation of an imagined community around the viewpoint of "European man" who thinks he represents the pinnacle of human achievement. The reproduction of cultured "European man" is at the core of the project of liberal education, which is explicitly founded on the supposedly unique leavening qualities of a specific set of intellectual traditions and cultural products.

The partiality of liberal education can be very difficult to see from within, as it is easy to get caught up in its inclusive and universalistic claims that are so closely tied to everyday racism. Critical assessments of colonial education provide an important reference point for this discussion as they highlight the non-portability of ways of knowing that claim to be universal.[7] Neil Lazarus (1999a:40-41) argues that the dislocation and alienation associated with colonial education served as an important reference point in the experiences of a wide variety of colonial and postcolonial Marxist (or Marxist-influenced) intellectuals, including Cabral, Césaire, Fanon, James, Sivanandan and many others. These theorists and activists tended to share a contradictory relationship with the Westernized education they received, simultaneously drawing on and rejecting European thought. They were keenly aware of the limits of European thought and its universalistic claims, yet at the same time they retained aspirations towards totalistic analysis as a tool in struggles for liberation. To put it simply, they could put important elements of European thought to use because their own experiences helped them to recognize the partiality of its false universalistic claims and, therefore, to seek more solid foundations for more genuinely global approaches.

Colonial education outlasted direct rule by the imperialist powers. Even after long struggles for independence, curricula often retained crucial European inflections. "The white man finally had left us, the states were ours, but inscriptions and fossils of colonialism lay everywhere, though often unrecognizable as such because they were so effectively internalized" (Bannerji 1995:55). Independence in some cases brought education reforms that remedied the extreme geographical dislocation and overt racism of a directly imported European curriculum in former colonies. Yet even cleaned-up versions of this curriculum often maintained the implicit assumption that really important knowledge (scientific or cultural) derived from specific European intellectual traditions that could be traced back to the Enlightenment and indeed to the "classics."

Autobiographical reflections on experiences of colonial education provide a crucial point of reference in powerful writings about racism in Canadian schools and universities, including Bannerji (1995), Brand (1998) Dei (1996) and Highway (1998)[8]. These reflections provide penetrating insights into the common-sense racism at the core of Canadian educational systems. Once one comes to the conclusion that a given educational approach is racist in India, Trinidad, Ghana or an aboriginal First Nation, it should follow that it is also racist in (other) Canadian schools. However, students and teachers who are deeply implicated in the relations of whiteness in Canada are much less likely to see the Eurocentrism of a liberal education than are students and teachers of colour, whether studying in Canada or elsewhere.

Colonial education, then, should not be thought of as a special case but as an important example of the deployment of liberal education in a specific context. Of course, liberal education has not been static and unchanging. In fact, liberal education has proven to be remarkably dynamic and it has changed substantially through the course of the twentieth century. In Canada, a bluntly racist and Anglocentric curriculum was supplanted by a more nuanced official multiculturalism. It is important at this point to establish the extent to which official multiculturalism marked both a departure from and a continuity with eurocentric liberal education in Canada.

## Official Multiculturalism: The Highest Stage of Liberalism

Official multiculturalism has been an important feature of the national policy of the Canadian state since the early 1970s.[9] The educational system was one of the areas of state policy in which official multiculturalism had its greatest impact. I will argue in this section that its impact was highly contradictory. On the one hand, in conjunction with the struggles of aboriginal peoples and people of colour, multiculturalist policies opened up real spaces to challenge aspects of racism in education systems. Some of the overt racism was removed from school and university curricula and new programs such as heritage language and culture classes created room for the recognition of aboriginal, African, Asian, Caribbean, Central or South American and non-anglophone European cultures. On the other hand, official multiculturalism created a more tenable form for the maintenance of Eurocentrism and hegemonic whiteness. It was associated with "state efforts to manage race and ethnic relations as ongoing problems without providing assurances of full equality for all groups" (Wotherspoon 1998:173).

Official multiculturalism emerged as state policy in the context of three major challenges: a resurgent aboriginal movement, new forms of anti-racist organizing and militant francophone nationalism (Ng 1995:37-38). The policy direction actually began in the 1960s as an emphasis on official bilingualism and biculturalism designed to accommodate francophone national demands and weaken the powerful Quebec independence movement. It was criticized by aboriginal people, anti-racist activists and European cultural communities whose mother tongue was neither English nor French, all of whom who were left out of national policy. The exclusion of aboriginal people from this "bi-national" conception of Canada was particularly striking given that it coincided with federal government initiatives to eliminate aboriginal status all together in a move to intensify assimilation (see Purich 1986). The policy was redefined as multiculturalism in the early 1970s.

Official multiculturalism thus emerged as an attempt to recast citizenship in somewhat more inclusive terms in order to manage dissent. At the same time, official multiculturalism did fit in with the broad welfare state cultural project of developing an autonomous English-Canadian identity.

At the beginning of the twentieth century, the reference point for English-Canadian identity was primarily the British Empire. Over the century, Canadian national policy shifted from a primarily imperial focus towards the development of an autonomous English-Canadian identity. The development of the broad welfare state in the post-World War II period marked an important moment in this shift. One of the central goals of cultural policy in the welfare state period was to consolidate a distinctly "Canadian" identity, as discussed above with reference to the Massey Commission and the Hall Dennis Report. The precise place of francophones within this new "Canadian" identity was hotly contested.

This new Canadian identity was founded on changing ideas of whiteness in the Canadian context. At the beginning of the twentieth century, Europeans were not regarded as uniformly "white," but rather were organized into a racialized hierarchy (for example, making racial distinctions between Anglo-Saxons, Irish people, Jews, Southern Europeans and Eastern Europeans). While there was some dispute about the precise location of particular peoples within this hierarchy, the racialization of Europeans was a consistent theme. It marked a differentiation within one segment of a broader racialized hierarchy that Day (2000:145) refers to this as the "Canadian Great Chain of Race." The lowest "white" ranks received considerable privileges in relation to aboriginal people and people of colour who were, in various ways, excluded from Canadian society.

The racial hierarchy among Europeans gave way to a more inclusive whiteness as the twentieth century progressed. The specific history of the development of this more inclusive whiteness in Canada has yet to be written and it cannot be accomplished here.[10] The most important point for our purposes is that emerging forms of English-Canadian identity were grounded in more inclusive forms of whiteness that encompassed Europeans from a wider variety of backgrounds. "Canadian" identity thus became broader through the twentieth century, though it was firmly anchored in a taken-for-granted whiteness (see Day 2000). The policies of official multiculturalism in many ways marked a formal recognition of the place of Europeans from outside Britain and France to full membership in Canadian society. These policies were not, however, a challenge to the racist conception of Canada as a European settler nation.

One of the places where the national policy of official multiculturalism had the greatest impact was in the educational system. This development was in part a response to an increasing mobilization in the 1960s and 1970s against racist education, including important movements within black communities (Calliste 1996:92-99). As stated earlier, liberal pedagogy tilted towards inclusion in the era of the broad welfare state. Official multiculturalism broadened the embrace of the state to capture a more diverse population. Of course, there were firm limits to this inclusion as membership (in the illusory community of the classroom or the state) is based on conditions that exclude others.

Overt racism is a barrier to the broadened embrace of the state in the classroom. Liberal education is based on the role of the disinterested teacher who is equally distant from all students. A teacher who openly discriminates on racial/ethnic grounds violates her or his own claims to legitimately evaluate students from a supposedly neutral standpoint (see McCaskell 1995:264). Official multiculturalism provides the grounds for such claims of neutrality while simultaneously preserving the traditional (that is, European) cultural core of liberal education.

Before the development of official multiculturalism, Ontario's educational system was bluntly monocultural, premised on a single dominant culture. Theo Goldberg's (1994:3-6) account of the shift from monoculturalism to integrationism in the United States provides a useful framework for considering developments in Canada. He argues that monoculturalism emerged as an official ideology only in the late nineteenth century, linked to the emergence of new regimes of immigration control and social policies oriented around "melting-pot assimilationism." This monoculturalism was grounded in the claim for an uniquely American tradition. American monoculturalism was fully consolidated by about the 1950s and was soon after supplanted by a new integrationist ethos that accepted a certain amount of diversity, developed in response to demographic shifts and social movement demands.

The passage from monoculturalism to official multiculturalism in Canada roughly parallels this move from monoculturalism to integrationism in the United States. The consolidation of monoculturalism in Canada, however, took a somewhat different form. The British Empire remained an important reference point in English-Canadian monoculturalism, providing a barrier to assimilationism as only British peoples were deemed fully assimilable. The "Canadianness" of non-British European immigrants was only fully established in the 1950s and 1960s (see Day 2000:175). At the same time, English-Canadian monoculturalism developed in relation to an official policy of bi-nationalism (English and French). This was not a bi-nationalism of full partnership and consent. Instead, it was a way of managing the militant refusal of francophones (primarily in Quebec) to surrender their language and culture in the face of the original British conquest and ongoing Anglo-chauvinism.

Despite these differences, there are important parallels with the American case in the establishment of monoculturalism. In the period from around 1880 to 1950 Canada developed regimes of immigration control and social policy focused on assimilationism. Black and Asian immigrants were deemed unassimilable and were essentially barred from migrating or given "guest worker" status (see Avery 1995; Baeker 2000; Li 1998, Troper 1972). The assimilability of immigrants from Southern and Eastern Europe was assessed largely on a case-by case basis. Those who were admitted became the objects of assimilationist social agencies who sought to teach them "Canadian" standards (see Avery 1995; Sears 1990; Valverde 1991).

The educational system was clearly on the front-line of this new assimilationism. One sign of the shift towards official monoculturalism was the attempted suppression of French-language education in Ontario. The period 1912-27 saw pitched struggles between a provincial government intent on eliminating French as a primary language of instruction and the francophone population who mobilized to defend their right to an education in their mother tongue (Godbout 1979:55-61). At the same time, there was increased concern about the role of the urban school in the assimilation of new immigrants.

Racism had certainly been present in Ontario schools before monoculturalism was consolidated around the turn of the twentieth century. There was an official policy of segregation in south-western Ontario with separate schools for black students that ended with the closure of the last segregated school in 1891 (Royal Commission on Education in Ontario 1950:535-36). In British Columbia, students of Chinese origin were placed in separate classrooms and schools in Victoria until parents of Chinese origin organized a year-long school boycott against segregation in 1922-23 (Ashworth 1979:70-77).

The most important example of segregated education in Canada was the residential school system developed for aboriginal people. This school system was assimilationist only in the sense that it attempted to destroy any vestiges of aboriginal culture in its students. It was not assimilationist in the other sense of entry into full citizenship through inclusion in a common culture – this was not an option for aboriginal people. Nor did the policy reflect separateness in the sense of self-determination. The aboriginal education system, modelled in some ways on the industrial school system for blacks in the United States South, was preparation for second-class status and economic marginality (see Johnston 1988; Milloy 1999).

It is arguable that the monoculturalist project was never fully consolidated in English-speaking Canada. The bi-national character of the Canadian state was reflected in certain constitutional provisions, including the right to separate Catholic schools which was initially to protect French language rights (francophones in Canada were primarily Catholic while anglophones were mostly Protestant). Thus, Ontario's monoculturalist education system was divided between Separate (Catholic) and Public systems. The Public system included compulsory Protestant religious education from 1944 to the 1960s. This was an obstacle to assimilation, so Jewish students, for example, were to some extent marked off as unassimilable. The government-appointed Committee on Religious Education in the Public Schools of the Province of Ontario (CREPSPO) (1969:23-5) argued that formal Protestant religious education in the public school system was incompatible with the development of Ontario from an Anglo-Saxon to a pluralistic culture. Organizations such as the Ethical Education Association waged a long battle to eliminate religious instruction from the Public Schools (CREPSPO 1969:13).

Monoculturalism was thus an obstacle to the development of a more inclusive and autonomous English-Canadian identity for "white" Canadians who were not from British backgrounds. This became clearly unsustainable by the 1960s. The later 1960s and early 1970s saw an important increase in the immigration of people of colour to Canada as certain overtly racist exclusionary policies were relaxed. At the same time, antiracist movements developed a more militant and activist orientation, in part due to the inspiration of African-American struggles and of national liberation movements in Africa, Asia and the Carribean.

Official multiculturalism was enshrined as official education policy throughout the later 1960s and early 1970s. Heritage language programs were introduced, allowing non-anglophone and non-francophone students access to instruction (outside of school hours) in their parents' mother tongues (Gidney 1999:150-51). School boards adopted anti-discrimination policies in the mid-1970s and the Toronto Board of Education went beyond that to adopt a more systematic race relations policy in 1979 (Gidney 1999:150; McCaskell 1995:258-61). Although heritage language programs were in themselves often not relevant to African-Canadians, in some cases there was an opportunity to develop specific African heritage classes (James and Braithwaite 1996:23). Schools began to symbolically recognize events such as Black History month and acknowledge some variety of cultural or religious holidays. Although limited, these gains do open up real spaces. "A child that grows up hating or being ashamed of her own looks, body, language and people can be traumatized and self-destructive.... In this light, for reasons of personal empowerment, cultural projects with a political nuance – such as Black History month, for example, or heritage language training – are precious to us" (Bannerji 1995:37).

While acknowledging these precious spaces, we need to recognize the limits of official multiculturalism. At the most general level, official multiculturalism is the foundation for the official story of Canada as a "less racist" nation (particularly when compared to the United States). Bannerji (1995:9) describes Canada as a country that has not owned up to its place in the racist order, "has not paid its blood debt yet" and, therefore, "its halls and corridors of power and wealth still echo with the sound of shackles and indenture ships 'landing'." Official multiculturalism provides some of the cover that helps Canada to avoid facing its "blood debt." It can thus become a "buzzword" masking inaction in challenging racism and cultural exclusion (Allen 1992:6).

Official multiculturalism is grounded in a model of cultural pluralism in which difference is tolerated. Sivanandan (1985) argues that this model was used by the state in Britain to depoliticize anti-racist struggle, shifting the focus of intervention towards individualistic training to promote the tolerance of difference. "Racism was not a matter of racial oppression and exploitation, of race and class, but of cultural differences and their acceptability" (Sivanandan 1985:3).

One of the key problems is that official multiculturalism is not really very pluralistic. It allows for a profusion of difference in the margins while preserving in the centre a liberal vision of national culture and shared values. Goldberg argues that official multiculturalism (which he refers to as integration in the American context) creates a dichotomy between private ethnicity and public citizenship. "The new model of integration that emerged left cultural groups (including races) with effective control of their private autonomous cultural determinations and expressions at the sociocultural margins, while maintaining a supposed separate and, thus, neutral, set of common values (especially, but not only, economic and legal ones) to mediate their relations at the center" (Goldberg 1994:6).

In Ontario's system of liberal education, this has been played out by revising the old curriculum to render it more effectively neutral by weeding out some of the more blatant racism. However, this kind of revision to render the curriculum more sensitive and add some new voices does not address fundamental issues about inequality and oppression (McCarthy and Crichlow (1993:xxi). This allegedly neutralized core curriculum was complemented by the development of new heritage programs literally in the margins, outside of core school hours. Space is thus created to pursue heritage language and culture on the side, while the public core curriculum supposedly soars above cultural difference on the wings of great books and science.

Indeed, this can reinforce Eurocentrism as it implicitly constructs what is taught in the core curriculum as objectively superior to the work in the margins. The liberal curriculum at the core is cast as universal, in contrast to the particularistic knowledge of specific cultures and heritages which is to be learned on one's own time as a private act. Wendy Braithwaite (1996:200) describes this succinctly in reflections on her own high school experience: "The Black experience is still considered an 'extra-curricular' activity in the education system." Paul Beatty offers an incisive portrait of official multiculturalism from the perspective of Gunnar "the only cool black guy at ... Santa Monica's all-white multicultural school" in his novel *The White Boy Shuffle*. First, Gunnar describes the gaps between the teachings in the classroom and the practices in the playground. "My early education consisted of two types of multiculturalism: classroom multiculturalism, which reduced race, sexual orientation, and gender to inconsequence, and schoolyard multiculturalism, where the kids who knew the most Polack, queer and farmer's daughter jokes ruled.... Like most aspects of regimented pop-quiz pedagogy, the classroom multiculturalism was contradictory, though its intentions were good" (Beatty 1996:28).[11] He then describes what he sees as the hypocrisy of this multiculturalism: "Everything was multicultural, but nothing was multicultural. The class studied Asian styles of calculation by learning to add and subtract on an abacus and then we applied the same mathematical principles on Seiko calculators. Prompting my hand to go up and me to ask naively 'Isn't the Seiko XL-126 from the same culture as the abacus?' Ms. Cegeny's response was, 'No, we *gave* this technology to the Japanese after World War II. Modern technology is a Western construct.'" (29-30).

The Ontario education system is grounded in the perspective of the European settler in North America. Aboriginal people are racialized and inferiorized in this perspective (see Ng 1993:53-54). Even the introduction of small amounts of curricular material offering an aboriginal perspective could not balance off against the heavy weight of this Eurocentric settlement perspective. The Europeans are cast as the history-makers in North America (and around the world. They are the settlers who brought the continent into time and space and rendered it knowable.[12] The racialization of other non-European peoples is tied in to this history of imperialism and is integral to the settler-eye view. People of colour are characterized as outsiders to (real) knowledge. This implicit message has been backed up by practices, such as streaming, that push aboriginal and black students towards lower level and vocational programs (see James and Braithwaite 1996:16). Some of the black students interviewed by Dei et al. (1997:117-18) said that streaming was connected to teachers' stereotyping and low expectations of them.

In this context, it is not surprising to hear that "there is a persistent and well-founded belief among African-Canadians, especially the youth, that the formal education system itself cannot or will not accommodate itself to their needs" (James and Braithwaite 1996:13). This can produce a profound disengagement from the education system on the part of black students (see Dei et al. 1997). Yet too often the response of the system has been to define black and aboriginal students themselves as the problem. Carby (1983:183) argues that in the British context, black students have been constructed as the problem, to be addressed through specific "remedial, compensatory or coercive" practices. In Canada, school authorities have often responded in similar ways, which "shift the responsibility of addressing the situation from the school to the parents and the community" (James and Braithwaite 1996:15-16). Official multiculturalism in education for blacks in Canada reflects a complex combination of inclusion and exclusion. This is parallel to Paul Gilroy's characterization of the location of blacks in Britain. "The contingent and partial belonging to Britain which blacks enjoy, their ambiguous assimilation, must be examined in detail for it is closely associated with specific forms of exclusion." (Gilroy 1987:155)

Official multiculturalism was, then, a contradictory development that created certain spaces for resistance but did not challenge the inherent ethnocentrism of liberal education. In many ways, official multiculturalism was the highest stage of liberal education, its most powerful moment marked by the reduction of certain barriers to the successful incorporation of a variety of students. The new agenda of education reform has not formally renounced official multiculturalism, but it represents an important break from it. This will be discussed in the next section.

## Post-Liberal Education: Standards and Racialization

The right-wing education reform agenda is directed against multiculturalism as the highest stage of liberal education. Liberal education is in turn internally related to the project of social citizenship and the broad welfare state. Official multiculturalism extended the embrace of the state to its most expansive point, eliminating some barriers to the inclusion of certain groups of potential citizens within its illusory community. This was in large part due to the long-term struggle of various social movements to claim full citizenship rights for people of colour, aboriginal peoples, women, lesbians and gays and others. The end result was highly contradictory. One the one hand, it made the state look good, constructing exclusionary and hierarchical citizenship practices as inclusive and relatively egalitarian.[13] On the other, it opened up limited but real spaces for people of colour to create practices and to stake claims that in some ways challenged common-sense racism.

The education reform agenda aims to develop a post-liberal education system that is immunized against the claims of multiculturalism. The long-term trend towards inclusion within citizenship as a hegemonic strategy is being reversed. The education system is being retooled to fit in with the demands of a leaner conception of citizenship that exposes the population to deeper processes of commodification and new forms of discipline. The claim is that the market opens up realms of choice far greater than those promoted by state multiculturalism. In Chapter 6 I argue that the new orientation towards commodification is in fact internally related to a new emphasis on standardization and exclusion.

The broader context for this shift away from multiculturalism is the restructuring of the world order often referred to as "globalization." It is impossible to do justice in this text to the complex debates around globalization. Capitalism has tended towards the creation of a world market for a long time. It is arguable that the extension of capitalist processes around the world has now reached its full breadth. We are now seeing an intensification of these processes, so that commodification is sinking ever more deeply into daily life in different ways around the world. This has been accompanied by increased flows of investments and goods (see Wood 1998).

At some level, it might seem that the globalization of capital has made national culture less important as the market has overcome the partially decommodified character of "culture." There certainly is some degree of deregulation occurring with the restructuring of the welfare state, so that the whole matter of culture is becoming increasingly privatized. Official multiculturalism maintained a state-promoted and allegedly common public culture in combination with a tolerant nod towards various private cultural expressions. The current shift is towards the privatization of even the common public culture.

Yet there is an important countervailing tendency to this process of deregulation and privatization. Despite all the claims that we are in an epoch of globalization, the barriers to the free movement of people are actually increasing. The nation-state is, perhaps, being less defined by hegemonic processes of inclusion than by coercive measures of exclusion. Increased immigration controls and restrictions on refugee rights are deeply soaked in ideas of national uniformity and the naturalization of citizenship. The present moment is thus marked by a contradictory combination of elements of cultural deregulation and the intensifying mobilization of national chauvinism as a barrier to the movement of people. This is the broad context for contemporary moves against multiculturalism.

In Ontario, the shift to post-liberal education has not included much of an explicit attack on multiculturalism. This should not be taken as an indication that Ontario's education reform agenda is actually culturally neutral. Indeed, it is arguable that the Ontario government and the Canadian state more broadly, as relatively late arrivals to the lean state agenda, have been able to eliminate some of the "noise" of what is called in the United States the "social conservative" agenda to cut more directly to the core neo-liberal social and economic agenda. In other words, the attack on official multiculturalism may be more effective if implicit rather than explicit, at least at the present moment of restructuring. (Note that this is not a claim that these governments will not deploy a more explicit racist politic in the future.)

The attack on official multiculturalism in Ontario is currently being waged in the name of standards. As discussed earlier, standards occupy a central place in the contemporary agenda of education reform. They are presented as the crucial tool for constructing an educational system that is more accountable and relevant. The battle for standards is presented as the rallying call to challenge teacher laziness, educational aimlessness and the false egalitarianism of post-1960s schooling.

These standards are presented as scientific and neutral, the products of what an American report recently described as "modern assessment science" (see Arenson 1999:44). As described above, one of the themes of post-liberal education is the supersession of culture by science. Educational standards claim to be grounded in science (universal) not culture (particularistic) and thus soar above bias and inequity. This is, of course, a very old claim that has been around at least as long as I.Q. test debates (see Gould 1981). It has been rehearsed through the recent debates on *The Bell Curve*, a book that renewed conservative claims that educational and social inequities derive from measurable differences in intellectual capacities (see Hernstein and Murray 1994; Livingstone 1995b).

These allegedly neutral standards provide the crucial foundation for a neo-monoculturalist offensive in education. Traditional competences and knowledges are redeployed as immutable core measures of educational value, as "basics." Johnson argues that the new National Curriculum in Thatcherite Britain moved significantly against educational multiculturalism. "More generally the National Curriculum used traditional subjects, their common-sense definitions and canons (for example, 'English', 'a modern language') to override the cultural diversity of contemporary Britain and to privilege a particular version of Britishness (Johnson 1991:71-72). This emphasis on the "basics" casts other programs as peripheral and puts them at risk in the face of funding cuts. If many of the heritage programs in Ontario have survived the early rounds of cuts, they are always at risk in a situation where funding cuts are paired with a prioritization of certain areas of the traditional eurocentric curriculum as "basic."

The emphasis on standards is tied to the focus on measurement. The Harris government's action plan for the twenty-first century states that they must "continue setting standards of excellence for schools, with an emphasis on performance-based accountability" (Government of Ontario 2001:10). The measurement of accomplishment in the "basics" is read as a neutral way of assessing the progress of individual students and evaluating the effectiveness of teachers, schools and the educational system as a whole through testing regimes. Yet accomplishments such as English-language reading are highly culturally specific. More importantly, these measures are abstracted from the context of structural inequalities in society and treated as a fair assessment of individuals and institutions in very different locations. Ultimately the new standards construct "difference as deficit" (Giroux 1993:142). Testing for achieved competence at a pre-determined set of uniform tasks is then used to increase differentiation associated with a more hierarchical and competitive educational system, including a renewed emphasis on streaming. This increased streaming is certain to be racialized, given the longer-term trends discussed above. Yet this racialization will be naturalized. It will be presented as the result of different abilities rather than of inequality and oppression.

This neo-monoculturalism is in part founded on the assertion that we are in a post-racist society (see Kelley 1997:8). In a strange way, the egalitarian claims of official multiculturalism helped pave the way for an anti-diversity offensive. Campaigns against "political correctness," for example, stake their claims on the assertion that demands for equity in a context where fundamental inequities have already been addressed should be read as requests for special treatment by special interest groups. Whites are thus presented as victims of racism, disadvantaged as mobilized special interest groups (read people of colour) gain advantage by pressing demands for their own benefit (Giroux 1993:102).

Johnson (1991:38-39) argues that standards were located as part of a battle against educational disorder in Thatcher's Britain. According to this vision, the educational system has lost touch with its core mission and has ended up achieving too little in its efforts to do too much (something for everyone). Establishing standards for educational accomplishment in the "basics" is presented as a neutral exercise in providing goals for a system that has lost its way. Lurking under this emphasis on standards is thus a new uniformity in which racial and cultural difference is constructed as a threat (Giroux 1993:102).

This regime of uniformity extends beyond the curricular emphasis on the "basics" to include specific measures to suppress the expression of difference. School uniforms, which are to be introduced into individual Ontario schools where parents support a dress code, represent a specific attack on cultural difference and self-expression among young people. Young people can use personal appearance to express cultural solidarity and dissent.[14] Robin D.G. Kelley (1996) discusses the ways that young African-American men in Los Angeles dressed in particular ways associated with rap music as an act of cultural identification and protest, even in the face of increased police harassment. The fashion industry is, of course, an important part of commodified popular culture with all its contradictions and limits as a means of genuine self-expression. Indeed, there are some who support uniforms as a way to address the race among students to purchase designer labels, something that tends to stigmatize young people from households with limited incomes. Clothing nonetheless presents certain opportunities for dissent and self-expression, in contrast to imposed uniformity.

The post-liberal education agenda thus rolls back the limited gains made in the name of official multiculturalism. In this context, it is important to understand both the Eurocentrism of liberal education and the spaces that were created within those limits. One does not have to dig deep below the surface of the right-wing education reform curriculum to turn up a commitment to a new monoculturalism.

## Notes

1. Joy James (1997:176-81) is relatively unusual in the contemporary literature in her explicit recognition of the importance of activist movement-based counter-hegemonic education outside of the realm of formal education.
2. An article in the New York Times Magazine argued that the rise of B. Smith, a restauranteur and lifestyle purveyor along the lines of Martha Stewart, is a marker of the rise of the black professional class. The article notes that the number of black households earning $100,000 or more doubled between 1988 and 1998 (Reed 1999:26-29).
3. See Kelly 1997:16-19 for a powerful critique of the culture of poverty ideas.
4. See Reed 1997:141 for an important discussion of the role of notions of aesthetic culture in Gates.
5. The Fabians were middle-class social reformers in England in the early twentieth century who sought to use existing institutions to accomplish change on behalf of the workers. The mass of workers were always led in the Fabian vision, towards winning some sort of reformed capitalism that would regulate (but not eliminate) inequities to achieve a more harmonious society.
6. I am using "common sense" in Gramsci's (1971:325-26) sense here, referring to the often ambiguous and contradictory taken-for-granted understandings that tend to be shared within specific social groups at particular times. This conception of common sense is used to discuss everyday racism in the works of Bannerji (1995:45) and Ng (1993:53) among others.
7. Lazarus (1999b:90) argues that the imperial powers sought hegemonic relations primarily with the elite in colonized nations. It follows that liberal education in the colonial context was primarily aimed at the elite (see Bannerji 1995:56). The politics of the broad welfare state aimed to achieve broader hegemonic relations with the mass of the population, and thus access to liberal education was expanded. Liberal education is, then, specifically connected to hegemony.
8. I am including aboriginal education programs in Canada under the rubric of colonial education, given the relations of internal colonialism that have governed Canadian state relations with aboriginal peoples.
9. I am following Bannerji's (2000:5) usage of the term "official multiculturalism" to distinguish Canadian state policy from the counter-hegemonic conceptions of multiculturalism associated with anti-racist activists.
10. Jonathon Hyslop (1999) makes the important point that whiteness needs to be understood in the context of the British Empire and the self-creation of a 'white' imperial working class. Canadian whiteness would seem to map together this imperial white labourism with elements of American racism in a particular context of white bi-nationalism (anglophone/francophone).
11. Although the actual world of "schoolyard" multiculturalism is somewhat more complex and nuanced. Hatcher and Troyna (1993) argue that children deploy racialized categories in complex and contradictory ways. On the one hand, children use the racialized categories that are out there in the culture to make sense of developments in their own lives. On the other hand, there is an egalitarian tendency in children's play that can produce a countervailing perspective.
12. I am drawing on the characterization of Eurocentric knowledge in Dussel (1998:4) and the naturalization of concepts of race through long-term historical processes in Omi and Winant (1993:8-9).
13. Perhaps most disturbingly, official multiculturalism clothed English-Canadian whiteness in the smug garb of tolerance and "less racist than the United States."
14. Toronto anti-poverty activist Josephine Grey was quoted in *The Globe and Mail* as opposing school uniforms, in part noting the needs of different cultural groups to use clothing as a means of expression (Galt 2000b).

# Chapter 5

# Education: Gender and Sexuality

Chapter 4 discussed how liberal education has been based on universalistic claims for the partial perspective of bourgeois, heterosexual, European man. The education system encourages all students to aspire to see the world through his eyes, scaling the heights of his culture and looking down upon the world through the lens of his science. In this chapter, we will look specifically at the ways in which this perspective is gendered and sexualized.

Dorothy Smith (1990) has developed a powerful analysis of the gendered and partial character of the discipline of sociology, which claims to be inclusive and universalistic. Smith (1990:17) describes two basic modes of knowledge, "one located in the body and in the space it occupies and moves in, the other passing beyond it." Sociology focuses on the second mode, abstract knowledge that claims to transcend the body and grounded experience. This abstract mode is primarily associated with men, while women are generally the experts in the located, bodily realm due to the character of their work in the realms of caregiving and intimacy. This tendency to gendered modes of knowledge flows from the likelihood of very different life experiences given the dominant division of labour.

Women who seek to speak with academic authority as sociologists must cast aside the gendered specificity of their experience. "We must suspend our sex and suspend our knowledge of who we are as well as who it is that is in fact speaking and of whom" (Smith 1990:21). This analysis provides us with a way of making sense of the highly gendered character of educational experiences, even where overt gender segregation is not a central feature of the system. Liberal education is based on gendered ways of knowing that pretend to be universalistic.

The gendered character of the educational system does not stand still, but rather changes overall as social relations inside and outside of the classroom shift. At first glance, it might appear that gender has become less important in the organization of the educational system since the 1970s. There is no longer spatial separation by gender, as in the public school that I attended where boys and girls had to play on different sides of the schoolyard. Compulsory gender-streaming around courses like home economics (for girls) and shop (for boys) has been abolished. Statistics show that women's educational attainment now exceeds that of men up to the graduate school level.

This move away from particular forms of gendered education began during the welfare state period. The universalistic norms of education for welfare state citizenship did not sit easily with overt gender segregation (see Davies 1986:23). Liberal education, with its cultural emphasis, was not geared as specifically to the sexual division of labour in society. More importantly, the women's movement now organized to challenge gender discrimination in education.

## Education and Gender Equity

We have not seen a rise in the explicit gender organization of education as the shift to post-liberal education has gained momentum. At first sight this might seem surprising, given the new vocationalist emphasis of post-liberal education. As discussed above, earlier forms of "practical education" were highly gender-organized and segregated. It would seem to make sense that a more practical educational curriculum should mirror more closely the prevailing sexual division of labour. Yet there are few references to gender in the contemporary discussion of education reform and practical education.[1] Those references that do appear tend to argue for more equitable access for women. Firm advocates of practical education, such as the Task Force on Education and Training put together by the Canadian Chamber of Commerce (1989:15) mention gender only to advocate more attention to overcoming the stereotypes that limit women's access to science and mathematics.

It is quite easy to draw a rosy picture of these gender changes in education. That is certainly the message of the front-page headline in *The Globe and Mail* for 15 April 1998: "Women Jump to Head of Class." Women's educational achievement now outstrips that of men up to the university undergraduate level. The 1996 Census results showed that of those in the twenty- to twenty-nine-year-old age range, a higher proportion of women (51 percent) than men (42 percent) had completed a post-secondary degree or diploma, while a higher proportion of men (21 percent) than women (16 percent) did not complete high school (Statistics

Canada 1998:3-4). In 1991–92, women made up 52 percent of the post-secondary student population in Canada, up from 39 percent in 1970–71 (Goodall 1994:42). Women also made up a greater proportion of the graduate school population in 1993 (43 percent) than 1977 (37 percent), though men remained a majority at that level (Canadian Education Statistics Council 1996:123). A study of high-school students in the United States showed that girls had consistently higher educational and occupational aspirations than boys (Dennehy and Mortimer 1993:93).

It would be easy to see this pattern as the sign of a significant (though perhaps incomplete) move in the direction of a genuinely gender-neutral education. There have been important gains for women within the educational system but this does not mean that educational equity has been achieved. The educational system continues to be a crucial site for the reproduction of gender relations, which develop both in and against the official curriculum. The changes that are happening within the educational system reflect a broader reorganization of gender relations that Donna Haraway (1991:167) refers to as "a paradoxical erosion and intensification of gender itself." There is a diminution of certain forms of overt gender segregation at the same time as a reorganized gender division of labour is emerging.

This chapter includes a rather lengthy discussion of the shift in gender relations associated with the rise of lean production and the development of the lean state. It includes consideration of the hegemonic gender relations during the period of the broad welfare state. I contend that it requires a detailed discussion of the character of contemporary gender relations to be able to see the ways that post-liberal education is gendered.

## Gender in a Lean World

Lean production, as we learned in the Introduction, is founded on a particular organization of the relationship between paid and household labour. Women are disproportionately represented in the contingent workforce (Armstrong 1995:371). The combination of wage and household labour has forced women to participate in the paid labour market on a more "flexible" basis than men (Leach 1993:65). The intensification of paid labour, which consumes increasingly more of the time and effort of the core labour force, assumes domestic arrangements in which someone else has the time and energy to do household labour.[2] Of course, often there is not a "someone else," particularly given the intensification of domestic labour through cuts in the welfare state and the high participation of women in full-time paid labour. Many women are thus faced with a double intensification of time and effort that pushes beyond the absolute limits of the working day.

There is a tendency, then, for the lean workforce to be polarized along gender lines, with men more likely to be employed in the more secure full-time jobs and women more likely to be employed in contingent jobs while bearing the primary responsibility for household work. However, this division of labour is now more permeable than that of the previous period of mass production. There are women in core jobs and men who take considerable responsibility for household labour. It is in a very particular sense a "gender neutral" division of labour and not threatened by the defection of some women or men from gender norms. Indeed, one of the features of lean production is that it has brought more men into the contingent and flexible working conditions that women have faced for a longer time (Armstrong 1995; Leach 1993).

We face, then, the challenge of explaining this complex picture of gendered patterns emerging from the decline of the previous division of labour, including the breakdown of certain forms of gender discrimination. This appears in some ways to be a less overtly gender-polarized division of labour, at the same time as gender continues to serve as an important organizing principle. A brief discussion of the division of labour associated with the welfare state and Fordist mass production will help clarify this discussion, as the 1950s household/employment configuration continues to serve as an important reference point in contemporary discussions.

### Gender and the Broad Welfare State

The central feature of the household/employment configuration in the period of the broad welfare state was the construction of the norms of the male breadwinner and the female homemaker. This division of labour was never universal, but the norms were universalistic and those who did not fit were stigmatized. Even where women were employed full-time outside the home, they were not treated as free and equal members of society. For example, Joy Parr (1990:230) argues that women in Paris, Ontario were not treated as full citizens of the town, even though they were often the primary breadwinners in their households – many of them worked in a mill that functioned as the backbone of the local economy. Thus gender was not highly permeable and those who did not fulfill gender norms paid a price.

The construction of the male breadwinner and female homemaker equation was so economically and ideologically powerful that it was naturalized. The relative novelty of that configuration of household and employment tended to fade from view. Indeed, the combination of a male breadwinner, a female homemaker and dependent children is now regarded as the "traditional" family. Yet this family form developed among the middle classes and skilled workers only in the nineteenth century and spread more widely through society in the twentieth century. It is really only in certain places for certain periods of the twentieth century that this pattern was widespread enough in North American and Western European working-class households to be considered a standard (see Coontz 1992). Even then, many did not fit the pattern due to poverty, gender-specific employment practices in certain places or the interplay of ethno-cultural practices with the obstacles formed by immigration controls.

The dominance of this one model of the family required a number of social and economic factors to be in place. A considerable proportion of working-class men had to be able to earn a "family wage," an income large enough to sustain the whole household. This wage level was won through the spread of industrial unionism in the period during and after World War II (in Canada) and sustained by the long economic boom that lasted until the 1960s (see Palmer 1992:68). Not all households had a man who earned that kind of wage and a considerable proportion of women were employed outside the home even during the 1950s.

The "traditional" family rested on the ideological base of particular gender practices as well as the economic base of the family wage. The male breadwinner and female homemaker norms were built around particular conceptions of masculinity and femininity. These understandings of appropriate gender practices arose largely in the twentieth century as part of the "invention of heterosexuality" (Katz 1995). Heterosexuality combined particular gender practices with a specific organization of sexuality (separating sex from reproduction) and a certain family form. Specifically, a form of muscular working-class masculinity complemented a domestic femininity in a gender order that was integrated into the development of mass production, the welfare state and what is often described as the "traditional" family of the 1950s.

This is not a comprehensive examination of gender formation in the twentieth century, but it does sketch to provide a starting point for understanding contemporary changes. It is required in part to locate historically a process of gender formation that has been so thoroughly naturalized that it is largely taken for granted. Muscular masculinity and domestic femininity were not universal but they served as key reference points in the construction of gender as they fit with the dominant social relations of the times. These "hegemonic" gender constrictions can live alongside others, but are vested with a specific cultural prominence and authority at a given moment in the context of a specific set of social relations (see Connell 1995:76-81). Gender constructions work through the interplay between rigid dichotomies and "complicated, shifting and sometimes contradictory gender meanings" (Thorne 1993:158). A full examination of gender formation would require a richer analysis of gender meanings as well as a thorough examination of the dynamics of race/ethnicity and class in the construction of the gender order.

## Masculinity in Mass Production

One of the most important gender practices in the development of the male breadwinner norm was the masculinity associated with mass production work. The conditions of mass production work did not allow for the kind of pride associated with skilled craft production. The aim of Taylorism was to make workers interchangeable and to reduce discretion to a minimum. Lewchuk (1993) argues that a new kind of masculinity, formed in part through the management strategies, emerged in mass production that was based on pride in providing for the household and endurance through exhausting, noxious and tedious work.

This masculinity was very body-centred. Knowledge was not simply a mental comprehension, but also a set of physical capacities. Knowledge of the work process came through the experience of doing the work. Shoshana Zuboff described this as a "felt knowledge of materials and procedures": "It was knowledge that accrues to the sentient body in the course of its activity; knowledge inscribed in the labouring body – in hands, fingertips, wrists, feet, nose, eyes, ears, skin, muscles, shoulders, arms, and legs – as surely as it was inscribed in the brain" (Zuboff 1988:40).

The most important things a man knew he learned through his body. This was a muscular masculinity in which bodily prowess rated very highly. Muscular masculinity is defined by participation in sports, ability to fight, an endurance of pain and mastery over machines (see Connell 1995: 52-6, 64-6, 98-101). It did not emerge only from the workplace. It was also produced through the deliberate efforts of states to reproduce healthier populations to secure for the nation a competitive advantage in work or warfare. Beginning in the nineteenth century, the playing fields of elite English schools became the sites for the cultivation of an athletic masculinity required for the tasks of Empire. Sports developed not only the body but also a team spirit through which the individual became part of a struggle for a greater goal. "Games encouraged physical courage and self-reliance in a context which subordinated the self to the team" (Rutherford 1997:16).

In the early twentieth century, the promotion of a muscular masculinity in the national interest became a broad concern in state policy. The focus broadened from the elite to the working class, whose bodies were crucial to economic competitiveness or military effectiveness. State policy-makers in Britain were galvanized into action partly by the high rate at which men were rejected out of the military at the time of the Boer War on the basis of poor physical condition.[3] States assumed new responsibilities for the reproduction of particular forms of gendered behaviour, through programs that ranged from physical education or home economics in schools to public health home visitors (Sears 1995). This "nationalized" conception of masculinity was also highly racialized. Men were either included in or marginalized out of this gendered order on the basis of their racial/ethnic background and integration into the relations of whiteness. Some migrants, particularly from Asia and the Carribean, were permitted into Canada only under conditions that prevented the formation of families.

Muscular masculinity included a "national security" dimension, in which the body of every man was cultivated as a piece of military equipment. Muscular masculinity was cast as the crucial foundation of a gendered order that was less susceptible to subversion. This "national security" side to muscular masculinity culminated in the 1950s, where anti-communism was combined with the persecution of homosexuals to produce a specific conception of masculinity and deviance (see Adams 1997:23-25; Ehrenreich 1983:103). It included a vicious campaign of surveillance and persecution that drove many gay men and lesbians from their jobs in the federal public service in Canada (Kinsman and Gentile 1998).

The national security dimension of muscular masculinity was not only about militarization in the face of external threats. It was also about discipline, forging particular gendered subjectivities that answered specific ways of organizing production (especially mass production) and reproduction (a configuration of family, workplace and state). Masculinity was the meeting point for a multifaceted and interconnected set of disciplinary practices. Labour discipline concentrated on the problem of getting, "the human body to remain in one place, pay attention, and perform consistently over a fixed period of time" (Zuboff 1988:33). As discussed above, Lewchuk (1993) argues that masculinity played an important part in the reproduction of labour discipline by making the unpleasantness of industrial work a source of some pride in endurance and the sense of responsibility associated with providing for others.

Labour discipline in the workplace was complemented by breadwinner discipline which addressed the question of the disposal of wages and, particularly, the proportion that was actually handed over for the maintenance of the household. The development of breadwinner discipline was a major struggle as it was enforced primarily by women in the privatized realm of the household and contradicted established patterns of male leisure activities with other men (see Bradbury 1993:160-61). Of course, the other side of breadwinner discipline was the pride of place as "provider" and "head of household" (see Seccombe 1993:112-15). The 1950s family ideal encouraged men as well as women to form identities based on their family location (Coontz 1992:27).

The welfare state was central to the development of this form of masculinity. Here, we must understand "national security" in the dual sense of warfare (protecting the state from perceived threats, whether external or internal) and welfare (providing citizens with some measure of protection in terms of income support and social programs). Indeed, the welfare state provided the highest level of protection to employed wage-earning citizens. The contrast between the security offered to employed men and that offered to women, particularly homemakers, is strking. In this gendered pattern, the benefits offered to veterans after World War II were an important prototype for the welfare state to follow (see Wrigley 1992:6).

## Domestic Femininity

Muscular masculinity had its counterpart in the development of domestic femininity. This regime of femininity was grounded in the reorganization and standardization of domestic labour. It also involved changes in the patterns of women's participation in wage labour, new models of consumption and leisure and a new role for the state in the regulation of women's work.

Atina Grossmann (1995:5-6) argues that the period following World War I saw the development of the idea of "new woman" in Germany. The "new woman" was a highly rationalized worker who could handle the competing demands of employment, family and sexuality through hard work for limited returns. I would argue that the "new woman" complemented the breadwinner masculinity discussed above.

The early twentieth century, particularly the period just after World War I, was a time of intensive reorganization in the workplace in which new technologies were paired with a reorganization of the labour process. Claudia Goldin (1990:94) argues that such moments of change have historically been associated with an increase in female employment. Yet the emergence of the "new woman" did not reflect an increased orientation to paid employment associated with the rationalization of the labour process. Indeed, Lewchuk (1993:830) found that women's participation in paid employment at the Ford Motor Company decreased with the rise of mass production and rationalization. Grossman similarly argued that the development of rationalized mass production methods did not provide new openings for women. "In fact, far from precipitating a female invasion of modern labour preserves, rationalization tightened, indeed, institutionalized, the modern sexual division of labour" (Grossmann 1995:6).

There was, at the same time, a rise in the participation of primarily young, unmarried women in certain kinds of manufacturing, clerical and service work (see Strange 1995:4-5). Most women who married, however, either withdrew or were forced out of paid employment. The exceptions included women in the lowest income households, immigrant women or those living in specific localities with female-oriented labour markets, who more often continued in paid employment. There was a certain space for women who did not marry to find a degree of economic autonomy, which was important in the formation of same-sex relationships for women. This space was fragile, however, and economic downturns like the 1930s Depression could have a particularly dramatic impact on women's employment and personal autonomy (Faderman 1991).

Whether or not the "new woman" participated in paid labour, her life was crucially oriented around domestic labour. The domestic sphere was a place of great changes in the early twentieth century, being simultaneously increasingly privatized and more intensively regulated. A greater portion of working-class families were becoming increasingly settled in nuclear family units in improved housing conditions that afforded some sense of privacy (see Seccombe 1993) but, at the same time, state and philanthropic agencies were making new efforts to set and enforce standards for domestic labour (see Ehrenreich and English 1978; Sears 1995; and Valverde 1991). Home visits by school nurses, social workers, public health nurses and others were designed to regulate domestic labour in new ways.

Domestic work intensified in certain important ways, paralleling the changes in mass production. New technology and changing social relations created new expectations for domestic labour. More elaborate cooking and cleaning became a measure of love, commitment and competence (see Coontz 1988:350). As birth rates declined, the expectations for the mothering of each child increased (Seccombe 1993:130-31). Carolyn Steedman argued that the work of waged women employed in caregiving was used to set new cultural standards for mothering that revolved around everpresent watchfulness. "[W]e can see that in the classrooms, as in the middle class nurseries of the nineteenth century, the understood and prescribed psychological dimensions of modern good mothering have been forged – and forged by waged women, by working women – by nurses, nannies and primary school teachers" (Steedman 1987:122).

Beginning early in the twentieth century, and increasing with passing decades, was the shift in domestic labour from production for use to consumption (Seccombe 1993:130). More time was spent purchasing and transporting goods and getting people from place to place (Coontz 1988:350). This increased insertion into the market was somewhat contradictory for women. On the one hand it was simply a new kind of work, often complicated by poverty and disputed over the disposition of the wage. On the other hand, consumption offered a new space for forms of leisure activity for women, particularly those who were single and employed (see Strange 1995:117; Wilson 1991:10).

There were some alternative visions of possibilities for the "new woman" in domestic labour in the early twentieth century. Dolores Hayden (1981:3) argues that some American feminists challenged the privatization of domestic labour and developed conceptions of its socialization. This socialist and feminist notion of the "new woman" was defeated in the post-World War I period and largely faded from view.

Sexuality was a highly contradictory area for the twentieth century's "new woman." The 1920s saw the development of a new "sexual liberalism" that separated heterosexual intercourse from the goal of procreation and redefined sexual satisfaction as an important aspect of personal fulfilment (D'Emilio and Freedman 1988:241). Sexual liberalism offered some new opportunities for women in the area of sexuality, but it also imposed huge burdens. Christina Simmons (1993) points out that the new ideas of "sexual freedom" that circulated in the 1920s were in part directed at improving men's sexual pleasure by reducing the moral boundaries around sexual activity without increasing the social power and sexual autonomy of women. At the same time, it was primarily the responsibility of women to separate intercourse from pregnancy, particularly as working-class people were choosing to have smaller families. Women had to exert new forms of control over sex in marriage (for example, by limiting frequency of intercourse) to regulate family size, particularly given the limited access to contraceptives (Seccombe 1993:158-70).

Domestic femininity grounded in the household reached its pinnacle during the era of the broad welfare state. To reiterate, this was partly based on the increases in wages and job security for men that resulted from the spread of industrial unions in the period around World War II. The "family wage" actually became a reality for a greater proportion of men, meaning that more women could work full-time in the household after marriage. A combination of higher incomes and more limited family sizes increased working-class consumption capacity in the 1950s and early 1960s (see Palmer 1992:272). However, this was far from universal and many married women, particularly those in immigrant and lower-income working-class households, continued to be employed outside to home (Sangster 1995:99-100). Overall, however, domestic labour became a vocation for women in an intensified way in the 1950s. Stephanie Coontz (1992:27) argues that there was an element of "makework" in this as the amount of time women spent on domestic labour actually increased despite the increased consumption of ready-made products and labour-saving appliances.

The welfare state played an important part in reinforcing the domestic location of women, offering benefits in a form that increased dependency on the male wage. Mimi Abramovitz (1992:30) states that social programs in the United States "rewarded the two-parent, one-earner, heterosexual family unit and punished those families that did not follow this idealized version of the family unit." Welfare state benefits for women linked to domestic labour were generally at a lesser level and more highly stigmatized than those directed primarily to men on the basis of paid employment. The broad welfare state was organized around the family wage ideal to promote a particular household structure (Gordon 1990:182-83).

Women were not militarized in the same way as men were through the Cold War national security state. The female contribution to national security was primarily through domestic efficiency. This has been a theme in the regulation of women's domestic labour since the beginning of the twentieth century (see Davin 1978). Women were affected by the ways in which the 1950s national security regime was organized around a shoring up of the gender order as the first line of defence against subversion. Gary Kinsman and Patrizia Gentile (1998:18) describe this as a "gender anxiety" in the administration of the Canadian federal public service. The public service administration sought ways to neutralize any "threat" to the gender order, such as that posed by the increasing feminization of the public service clerical sector. The response was to create highly feminized ideals for women employed in the public service through, for example, the "Miss Civil Service" beauty contests (Kinsman and Gentile 1998:20-21).

This gender anxiety was linked to a broader concern about the family in general in the post-war world. The 1950s family is often viewed in retrospect as a virtually natural phenomenon based on a deep consensus about values. Yet at that time the family was viewed as problematic, requiring deliberate attention in the face of various threats. Mary Louise Adams argues, "The fact that families were being formed by more people more often than at any other time in this century did little to counter a pervasive sense that 'the family' as a social institution was under threat" (Adams 1997:25). The 1950s was at once the high point of the "traditional" family and the beginning of its end as marked by, for example, increased rates of divorce and teenage pregnancy (see Adams 1997:26-27; Coontz 1992:38-40). The increased commodification of the household pushed women towards various forms of paid labour to contribute to their family's consumption capacity at the same time as domestic labour expectations were increasing.[4] "The family wage system and protective legislation were only fragile gatekeepers in the growing conflict between woman's roles as guardian of the family hearth and contributor to the family larder" (Coontz 1988:350).

There was a contradictory pull between wage and domestic labour, but domestic femininity was rooted in women's caregiving duties. Women developed a particular embodied sense of femininity through domestic labour, just as industrial work was a standard for muscular masculinity. Household work is marked by its seamlessness; every individual is a generalist performing all the discrete tasks (child care, cleaning, cooking, laundry) (see Luxton 1981:18). It is also marked by a contradictory "privatization," on the one hand atomized into separate households and individual responsibilities while on the other hand regulated by state agencies to establish and enforce particular "standards" (see Coontz 1992:122-48; Sears 1995). It involves particular kinds of body work.[5] Mothering, for example, involves various combinations of lifting, feeding, soothing, breastfeeding, healing, washing and dressing. The physical and emotional aspects of caring are expressed through the body. At the same time, children often stake claims on their mother's bodies as a refuge, climbing device, source of nourishment and pleasure.[6] This is a very different kind of bodily experience than that of industrial work.[7] This experience is often taken for granted when women work in paid employment, where their caregiving has largely been taken for granted (Armstong and Armstrong 1996:101-2).

National security gender relations also saw women's bodies sexualized in a way that men's were not. Barrie Thorne (1993:141,170) noted in her study of gender in the schools that girls tended to be treated in a different, more sexualised, manner as their breasts grew in puberty. As that happens, there is an increased pressure on girls "to define themselves and other girls in terms of their positions in the heterosexual market." The sexualization of the woman's body was seen as a crucial aspect of shoring up femininity in response, for example, to the gender anxiety of the federal public service during the national security regime (see Kinsman and Gentile 1998:20-21).

This sexualization of the women's body as an object for others (that is, men) was complemented by a subjective experience of disengagement from the body and its possibilities. Janet Holland et al. (1994:23-25) argue that women often experience a passive embodiment, which involves a detachment from their own sensuality and distancing from their physical bodies. Carolyn Steedman argues that there is a direct relationship between the bodily experiences of caregiving or mothering (in her case as a teacher) and a sensual disembodiment. "My body died during those years, the little fingers that caught my hand, the warmth of a child leaning and reading her book to me somehow prevented all other meeting of bodies" (Steedman 1987:127)

## Childhood and School in the Welfare State

The national security gender order was founded on the distinct and complementary constructions of muscular masculinity and domestic femininity. The final feature of the order was the changing role of children in the family system. The core of this change was the extended dependence of children within the family and the growth of extra-familial regulatory agencies centred around the state. The shift towards the welfare state involved a contradictory privatization and nationalization of children through most of the twentieth century.

The early twentieth century saw children move out of the labour market. Craig Heron (1995:224-25) argues that important changes in work processes and employment practices reduced the requirement for the labour of children in Hamilton factories in that period. In 1921, the age for compulsory school attendance in Ontario was raised from fourteen to sixteen (Axelrod 1982:9-11). The participation of children in paid labour was also restricted in various ways by a succession of Factory Acts dating back to 1884 in Ontario (Guest 1980:40). Child labour was not suddenly eliminated by a single act, rather it diminished over time in the face of new regulatory controls, changing labour processes and a reorganization of the family system.

Children were pushed out of the labour market to become the "private" responsibility of their parents. This reversed historic patterns as extended dependence meant that children increasingly became a drain on, rather than a contribution to, family income (Seccombe 1993:109). At the same time, the rise of new agencies ranging from children's aid societies to school nurses established new regulatory standards for child-rearing and domestic labour more broadly (see Guest 1980:30-31; Sears 1995; Valverde 1991). The spread of compulsory education was one part of a broader social reorganization of childhood.

The extension of dependent childhood contributed to the shift towards having fewer children. The decline in the number of children was associated with a shift in the ideology of parenthood, leading to an intensification of the expectations for mothering as children became increasingly valued for their emotional rather than economic contribution to the household (see Seccombe 1993:183). Indeed, the family system became increasingly child-oriented, particularly at the high point of the "traditional" family in the 1950s (Adams 1997:27-28; Coontz 1992:27).

The 1950s family marked the consolidation of a regime of gender and sexuality in formation underway from the beginning of the twentieth century. One important characteristic of that regime was that schools became a pivotal place in the development of gender relations. Reformers were clear about this and sought to use the schools to prepare students for their place in the sexual division of labour, whether in paid or domestic work. As discussed above, gender-specific schooling was seen as crucial to the development of appropriate subjectivities for a divided world of work. This included specific forms of bodily discipline through physical education and standards for comportment on school property.

It was not only through the official curriculum that schooling contributed to gender formation. The secondary school provided a key focal point for the development of a gendered youth culture. John D'Emilio and Estelle Freedman (1988:257) describe the American secondary school in the 1920s as a place where, "adolescent boys and girls encountered one another daily, with casual interaction throughout the day that often continued into evening social activities." In this setting, forms of masculinity and femininity developed both in and against the school. These gender relations were both a product of the system of education and a reaction against it.

The 1950s family form was highly racialized. Aboriginal people and people of colour were often denied access to this kind of family. Children were taken out of aboriginal families and communities on a massive scale, either to residential schools or foster families. Women of Chinese origin were not allowed to immigrate to Canada through the first half of the twentieth century and so male Chinese could not produce Chinese families. Immigrants from the Carribean were (and are) often admitted either as domestic workers or as temporary workers in fields such as agriculture but could not bring family members with them. There is much more that could also be said about the tremendous variation in culturally-specific family forms. Suffice it to say here that the broad welfare state project included highly differentiated access to family formation.

## Shifting Gender Relations

The reach of the national security gender order was never universal. Further, the foundations of this gender order began to shift almost as soon as it was consolidated. The male breadwinner/female homemaker norm was undermined in part by the massive entry of women into paid employment. As significantly more women have entered paid employment, domestic femininity has been gradually eroded. This began in the latter half of the broad welfare state period and continued through the shift towards lean production. The proportion of women participating in paid labour increased dramatically, from 24 percent in 1951 to 44.4 percent in 1975 to 58.2 percent in 1991 (Phillips and Phillips 1993:34). The most important increases have been in the participation of married women, including women with children. Women's rate of participation in paid labour is now close to that of men (Philips and Philips 1993:34-40). However, this does not mean that the sexual division of labour in paid employment has vanished with a wide-scale entry of women into jobs previously held by men. Women have been employed primarily in the vastly expanded services sector (Clement and Myles 1994:34).

Domestic femininity has also been attacked politically. Changes in the conditions of women's work have been accompanied by the ideological challenge of the women's and lesbia and gay movements. These movements mobilized explicitly against the sexual division of labour, hegemonic gender practices and regulation of sexuality that were central to the national security regime. Women have fought for access to contraception and abortion, a shift in dominant modes of politics, gender equity in employment and education, and a cultural redefinition of gender practices. This political challenge has had an important impact on gender consciousness in contemporary society. "Men still rule the most of the world, but the contemporary women's movement has seriously challenged both the naturalization of gender differences and the assumed necessity of the subordination of women to men" (Livingstone and Luxton 1996:100).

While some aspects of gender relations have changed very rapidly, others have proved remarkably resilient. Perhaps the most important of these is the unequal distribution of domestic labour, which continues to be performed primarily by women. Women's work has been intensified with the combination of paid and domestic labour, although this has been obscured in part by the concentration of women in flexible and part-time employment (Ursel 1992:236-37). The amount of domestic labour performed by men in heterosexual households does increase where women are employed, but it remains substantially below that of women (Livingstone and Asner 1996:86-87). This unequal distribution of domestic labour is particularly problematic given the reorientation towards the lean state. There is a thorough-going intensification of domestic labour under way as social programs are cut back (Luxton 1997:22). Health care cutbacks, for example, force more people to rely on unpaid labour primarily performed by women: whether inside or outside of a hospital;

whether as domestic labour for kin or as formal volunteer work (Armstrong and Armstrong 1996:137-46). The reorientation of the state also has an impact on women's employment and impoverishment. Janine Brodie stated, "Given that women are overrepresented among the ranks of both welfare recipients and state workers, these cuts have a disproportionately negative effect on them" (Brodie 1995:55).

Women's domestic labour is also intensified by increased impoverishment, which requires more work and creates more stress in the struggle to survive. Indeed, attacks on welfare are in many ways an attack on domestic femininity. Women receiving welfare are now being punished by benefit cuts and forced workfare programs precisely because they had concentrated on child-rearing and domestic labour. There has been a highly contradictory approach to women's "dependence," where women receiving welfare payments are castigated by the same people who insist on the centrality of unpaid domestic labour in women's lives. As Linda Gordon (1990:177) argued, "women's dependence (e.g. their unpaid domestic labour) contributed to men's 'independence'." Workfare has reinforced this contradiction, forcing women into labour for benefits. Indeed, the development of workfare has included a particular ideological attack on single mothers (Shragge 1997:25-26).

As part of the lean agenda, gender relations are being restructured in complex and contradictory ways. Women are being irreversibly pulled or pushed into social labour (paid labour or workfare in the "public" realm under the control of employers or administrators) while continuing to bear the primary responsibility for domestic labour as it is being intensified. The combination of the political mobilization of the feminist movement and economic changes has provided many women with more ability to exert control over their bodies and their lives. There have been important developments of new services such as day care centres and abortion clinics, yet these are inadequate and under threat. It is arguable that at least some women have won increased control over their heterosexual relations, whether measured by the increased proportion of women initiating divorces[8] or reports that at least some younger women have a new sense of their own capacity to engage in sex for their own pleasure (see Segal 1994). At the same time, women who divorce men often face impoverishment and women's sexual agency is still undermined by harassment, violence and silencing. There may be some shift in women's sense of embodiment, but the transition towards an active sense of self in the body is very difficult given the impossible standards that dominant models of femininity continue to impose for every woman (see Holland et al 1994:24, 33).

The "traditional" forms of domestic femininity have been undermined by many of these changes, yet domestic labour continues to be a defining factor in the lives of many women. Gender relations are becoming more covert, yet they remain central to the organization of paid and unpaid labour. Blunt gender discrimination has been discouraged in much public discourse due to the gains of feminism. Schools, for example, do not employ overt gender streaming as they did up until the 1970s but girls and boys still acquire a gender-differentiated view of themselves and their places in education and in society. Femininity, then, continues to be defined in relation to domestic labour, but it is no longer exclusively domestic in itself.

Gender is always a set of relations and so, before we can define contemporary femininity any further, we need to look at changes in masculinity. Muscular masculinity has been undercut by changes in three areas of life: the restructuring of labour markets and work processes; shifts in family/household organization; and the new place of men in consumer markets. Yet this is not leading to gender equity. Instead, new forms of hegemonic masculinity seem to be emerging.

Muscular masculinity was in part rooted in particular forms of body work in which skills were expressed as bodily prowess. These forms of body work have not been completely replaced, but are yielding in at least some work environment to the "intellective" skills discussed above. Zuboff described this change which, she argued, is tied to the spread of new information technologies. "Immediate physical responses must be replaced by an abstract thought process in which options are considered, and choices are made and translated into the terms of the information system" (Zuboff 1988:71).

The old skills are not worth as much in work environments where the relation to the labour process is increasingly mediated by the information technology. In this context, there is some shift towards an emphasis on literacy, problem-solving and communications skills. Body-oriented muscular masculinity may actually serve as an obstacle to men developing these skills. School ethnographies, for example, show the ways in which some working-class boys develop a defensive masculinity in response to a school system that has no place for their knowledge, outlook or prospects (see Connell 1995 and Willis 1977). The intense valuation of physical prowess and the disparagement of mental skills can be an important part of this masculinity. This may be part of the reason that fewer men than women make it through high school, even though the prospects for people without at least a secondary education are bleak.

At the same time, the labour market is being restructured in ways that push some men towards employment conditions more like those of women. "But women's and men's labour-force experiences have become increasingly similar not simply because some women now have the kinds of good jobs traditionally held predominantly by men, but also because the labour-force work of a growing number of men has become more like that traditionally done by women and because fewer women have alternatives to labour-force work" (Armstrong 1996:30). Indeed, Leach (1993) suggests that some of the novelty in the discovery of labour force flexibility is that men are now facing conditions that women have confronted for a long time. Some men are facing a convergence with the situation of women in paid employment that also undercuts the male supremacist ideology of muscular masculinity.

Muscular masculinity also faces the erosion of the breadwinner norm in the household. There is still provider ethos among many men in heterosexual couples. Bonnie Fox (1997:147) found that men in heterosexual couples who became parents often responded by "becoming more serious about breadwinning." But fewer and fewer men are now acting as sole providers. Furthermore, male control over the household is being challenged by women's increased access to divorce and the public exposure of issues of violence against women (see Rutherford 1988:24).

Finally, muscular masculinity is incongruent with the ways in which men are increasingly inserted into relations of consumption and the marketplace. Shopping for necessities continues to be largely women's work, but the idea of gratification through commodity consumption has crossed gender boundaries. Barbara Ehrenreich (1983:45-49) argued that *Playboy* magazine marked the emergence of a more consumerist male ethos in the 1950s as a revolt against the rather dreary structures of the breadwinner norm. This consumerist masculinity has distinct feminizing aspects. "What had been understood as masculinity, with its implications of hardness and emotional distance, was at odds with the more feminine traits appropriate to a consumer-oriented society; traits such as self-indulgence, emotional lability and a soft receptivity to whatever is new or exciting" (Chapman 1988:234).

One of the key aspects of this change driven by consumerism has been the aestheticization of the male body. Muscular masculinity was rooted in a sense of the male as subject (actively looking) but not as object (being looked at). Now the muscular male body is a central feature of advertising, movies, television and music videos, challenging masculine positioning. Not only are men given new physical standards to live up to, their bodies also become legitimate objects of attention (see Simpson 1994:4).

Muscular masculinity has been weakened by these changes, but the impact on male power is less clear. New forms of hegemonic masculinity are emerging in the context of restructuring. Rowena Chapman (1988) and Johnathon Rutherford (1988, 1997) tend to portray the emerging forms of masculinity largely as the same old thing but with better manners. For example, Rutherford argues that Hugh Grant's role in *Four Weddings and a Funeral*, "epitomises a masculinity which has adopted the social tactics of niceness, compliance and liberal tolerance in response to the rising aspirations and assertiveness of women" (Rutherford 1997:140).

This was the core of the 1980s conception of the "new man." Chapman describes the "new man'" as "an attempt to resolve some of the obvious contradictions of the Classic Macho, to recognise and make peace with the feminine within itself, in response to feminist critiques" (Chapman 1988:227). The "new man" is defined more by his place in consumer culture and the specific market niches that have emerged around him (see Mort 1996:15-22). Fatherhood is more central to his identity, even if it is not clear just how much more he engages with children or domestic labour (see Chapman 1988:228-29 and Rutherford 1988:32-36).

It is difficult to establish the trajectories of masculinity and femininity at a time of serious restructuring. The conception of a new masculinity picks up some important changes, but leaves out other important aspects. To understand these changes, we need to return briefly to a more nuanced look at Fordist masculinities. I argued above that muscular masculinity was a central reference point for working-class men through much of the twentieth century and had important resonances throughout society. Connell (1995:193-94) argues that a second form of hegemonic masculinity, based on technical expertise and rationalization, co-existed with that based on dominance. This "expert" form of rationalizing masculinity was largely the purview of the professional and the manager. Rationalizing and muscular masculinity are not separate and mutually exclusive categories that apply to the lives of different men, but often imply one another and co-exist in complex relationships within and between men (see Connell 1989:295).

It is arguable that we are seeing a shift in the balance between muscular and rationalizing masculinity. Rationalizing masculinity has become more important as muscular masculinity has been weakened.[9] This has occurred in two ways. Insofar as there has been some shift towards "intellective" skills at work, those skills have been masculinized. Certainly skilled computing work has been masculinized as it has become more highly valued, although this has mainly affected middle-class experts and some highly skilled workers (see Connell 1995:55-56).

I would argue that there is also a second, more subtle, aspect to this rationalizing masculinity. Lean production represents yet another wave of workplace rationalization in the tradition of scientific management and in this context masculinity may be distinguished from femininity by, in part, the susceptibility to rationalization. Belinda Leach argues that managers have employed an implicitly gendered strategy as they have strategically increased their use of overtime and part-time work. "Women can fit part-time work around their domestic responsibilities, where those same domestic responsibilities make overtime practically unfeasible, even where women work a regular industrial day" (Leach 1993:76).

Thus the polarization of paid working time, with more people working either longer or shorter hours, is an important part of the reorganization of gender. Masculinity is defined in relationship to rationalization, both as its subject and its object. The man is both the key rationalizer (employing formal logic such as cost-benefit analysis with alleged disinterest) and the worker without limits, ever available for rationalization and intensification. From the point of view of the employer, there are obstacles to the intensification of women's paid labour posed by responsibilities for domestic labour, particularly in a situation where that unpaid work is also being intensified by cutbacks. Femininity, then, is "irrational" insofar as it continues to be rooted in caregiving relations that limit susceptibility to rationalization and intensification.

In this context, then, femininity is defined by an ability to reconcile the competing demands of paid and domestic labour, while masculinity is defined by an unencumbered availability for paid labour. These gender relations are less ideologically driven than those in the Fordist era, and thus considerably more permeable. Some women can and do take their place in the rationalizing or rationalized sector, providing that they can free themselves from the unpredictable requirements of domestic labour. At the same time, a minority of men now takes considerably more responsibility for domestic labour and child-rearing, including time as full-time homemakers. This gender order has more play in it than the one it is replacing, and thus can accommodate some crossing over without disruption. This is one factor that has created new space for the spread of lesbian and gay rights and the visibility of lesbian and gay images in popular culture.[10]

This also sheds a different light on the male "flight from responsibility" (Ehrenreich 1983). Perhaps men are not so much flying from responsibility as being rendered incapable of it by the intensification of work and falling wages. Hedonistic consumerist masculinity may help ease the psychic blow, but empirical work would be required to assess its real impact on the lives of working-class men. This is not to deny that men have privileged access to "good" jobs or that they underperform in the realm of domestic labour even where they are not caught in the overtime bind. But it is important to understand that rationalization and intensification are limiting possibilities for both women and men, albeit to different degrees and in somewhat different ways.

This, then, is a more supple gender order shorn of some of its ideological baggage yet still deeply naturalized to the point of being relatively invisible. The place of children has also been affected by the restructuring of gender and the family system. First, the increased participation in post-secondary education and the tuition increases associated with the spread of user pay, in combination with chronic youth unemployment, have in effect extended the dependence period of younger people far beyond their childhood. At an economic level, young people need ever-increasing amounts of "assistance" either in the form of repayable student loans or financial subsidy from parents to complete their education. The number of adult children residing with their parents has also increased, developing what some sociologists describe as the "crowded nest syndrome" (Boyd and Norris 1999).

Yet this dependence is combined with new forms of independence expressed through commodified child and youth cultures. Children of various age groups are being increasingly treated as independent market niches (Renzetti 1999). Economic dependence combines with new forms of consumer autonomy as children and young adults either earn their own money or exert an influence on household income to ensure that specific goods are procured. The Spice Girls, for example, found a market for themselves among girls six to eleven years old (Delap 1999). Not only did girls in this age group want Spice Girls paraphernalia, they also wanted to dress like members of the group. This combination of extended dependence and cultural segmentation in many ways simply extends trends that were already under way previously.

The intensification of adult lives, whether in paid or domestic labour, also impacts on children. The constraints of time-discipline are now forced into the lives of the youngest children as parents rush from daycare centres to jobs to lessons or activities in the context of their own efforts to juggle paid and domestic labour. It is arguable that childhood itself is being "leaned" as unstructured play time (particularly with others) gets trimmed to fit into complex schedules (see Chapter 6). It may also be that unstructured play time is looked upon with suspicion in a lean world where time is money and doing nothing is cast as parasitic and unhealthy.[11]

Young people are being increasingly constructed as dangerous in the context of restructuring. This is exemplified by a statement that Toronto police officer John Muise gave to a newspaper after one high-school student was murdered by another one. "You talk to people in the kid business, like teachers, and I think the vast majority will tell you that they see a lot more explosive problems, a lot more discipline problems, than they did 15 years ago" (Galt 1998a:A10). This resonates with a common-sense conviction among right-wingers that young people are committing more crimes and constitute a growing threat to the social order (see Chapter 6).

The right wing has begun an offensive against young people on the basis of the alleged problem of indiscipline. This offensive has consisted of a campaign for tougher laws and increased provision for treating young people as adults in the criminal system; the development of new forms of harsh incarceration for young people convicted of offences, such as boot camps; the use of curfews; strict anti-drug measures; the censorship of pop music; street harassment of young people, particularly young people of colour; legislative and police crackdowns on "squeegee kids" cleaning windshields; and efforts to keep young people from congregating at specific sites.[12] It has taken a particularly frenzied form in parts of the United States. "As a result of the war on drugs every non-Anglo teenager in Southern California is now a prisoner of gang paranoia and associated demonology. Vast stretches of the region's sumptuous playgrounds, beaches and entertainment centers have become virtual no-go areas for young Blacks or Chicanos" (Davis 1992:284).

At the core of the right-wing agenda lies a specific gendered construction of the "problem" of young people as a deficit of masculine authority. This is quite explicit in the "culture of poverty" analyses of African-

American single parent families. But it extends beyond this and is a central theme in the offensive against young people. The right wing repeatedly insists that young people just need a bit of old-fashioned discipline. Quite clearly the idea is to deploy the masculinized authority of the state to supplement or replace the diminished family patriarch. This requires that the state undergo something of a sex change, from the maternal "nanny state" of the welfare era to the masculinized "let them eat boot" state for lean times.[13]

The reorientation of the state towards a brutalizing masculinity of dominance is taking place in a context where that kind of masculinity is being undercut through a variety of social changes ranging from the reorganization of work to the mobilization of the feminist and lesbian and gay movements. For example, a committee to investigate sexual harassment and abuse in Canadian hockey decried certain excesses associated with masculine discipline: players pushed beyond the limits in practice until they vomit; ethnic and religious slurs; forced beer drinking and rewards in the form of pornographic materials for a good performance (*The Globe and Mail* 1998a:S2). These have been the underpinnings of a muscular masculinity founded on: team spirit forged through adversity, measuring the man by whether he can "take it" and the use of slurs (ethnic, anti-woman or anti-gay) to form an identity based on the exclusion of others. The reorganization of masculinity is reaching deeply as it extends (however partially) into the hypermasculinized realm of team sports.

Even the military is not immune from this gender restructuring. In May 1998, *The Globe and Mail* reported the assault and harassment that women have faced upon entering the Canadian armed forces. Maurice Baril, the Chief of Defence Staff, argued strongly that the military would have to change. "We certainly do have a problem, a problem of attitude in integrating women in the Canadian Forces…. Those who cannot quickly change their attitude are in the wrong uniform and the wrong profession" (Sallot 1998:A6). Of course, the actual changes in the masculine authority structure in hockey or the military remain to be seen. It is important to note that certain masculine methods are under scrutiny even in institutions founded on muscular masculinity. Yet at the same time, the right wing is summoning up these methods (for example, the boot camp) as a foundation of a new disciplinary apparatus for youth. It would seem that the shift to masculinized discipline is likely to involve elements of both muscular and rationalized masculinity. It is quite possible that muscular masculinity is being marginalized and relegated to the status of punishment for transgressors. Rationalized masculinity is being generalized in the form of a disciplinary structure focused on standards, competition, cost/benefit analyses and the deployment of market forces.

## Gender and Post-Liberal Education

The reorganization of gender in society has important implications for the way we examine the place of gender in educational restructuring. The emerging gender relations are somewhat more supple and permeable than those of the Fordist period. At the same time, a gendered division of labour is central to the organization of lean production and the lean state. There is good reason to assume that the shift to a new vocationalism and the reassertion of masculinity as disciplinary authority should have important implications for the gendered organization of education. However, this may take quite subtle forms given the character of contemporary gender relations and the extent to which they are obscured by their naturalization.

School is a crucial site for gender reproduction, although the official curriculum plays only a limited role in this. Girls and boys work out gender relations for themselves in the context of family relations, official teachings and interaction with peers in and around the school. Barrie Thorne (1993:3-4) describes this as "gender play," a term that captures both the agency of individuals and the variations in the experience of gender. Yet gender play occurs in an environment already structured by broader social relations.

One of the obvious ways in which gender is structured into the educational system is through the divisions of labour in the teaching workforce. As discussed above, teaching was feminized at the beginning of state education. The general tendency has been for the proportion of women to diminish as one goes higher in either the administrative hierarchy or the level of education (from elementary to secondary to postsecondary). Gender reorganization has had little impact on the feminization of teaching. The proportion of women in teaching declined slightly in the early 1980s, but then began to increase again. "Despite a mid-decade increase in male participation, the most recent available figures indicate that teaching in both elementary and secondary schools is now much more female- dominated than during any other recent period" (Robertson 1993:6). The proportion of female Canadian teachers was higher in 1989–90 (59.2 percent) than it had been in 1975–76 (58 percent), although it had dipped lower to 55.3 percent in 1984–85 (Macleod 1988:8; Robertson 1993:6).

However, there have been some changes. The proportion of women in school administration has increased. The status of women faculty in universities has increased modestly (see Ornstein, Stewart and Drakich 1998). But teaching remains largely women's work, particularly insofar as it involves caregiving. Even where both women and men are teaching there is some tendency for them to have different pedagogical approaches. Heather-Jane Robertson (1993:64) found that women tended to emphasize student effort, social skills and behaviour while men tended to focus on comparative achievement and the evaluation of final products (tests, projects). While these findings are affected by the concentration of men in the later years of schooling, Robertson argues that women teaching at higher levels also had some tendency to fit into the gendered pattern.

This gendered pattern is clear even in the selection of teaching as a career. Female teachers were more likely than males to say that teaching was their "first career choice" (Robertson 1993:53). Cecilia Reynolds (1989:31) noted that women teachers found it easy to get support from their social networks in their decision to become a teacher, but difficult to find support if they expressed an interest in becoming a principal. This was reversed for men. Their networks tended not to support the decision to become teachers but did reinforce the choice to enter administration. The gendered organization of teaching resonates with a web of taken-for-granteds that are so "obvious" they barely need to be mentioned. Carolyn Steedman reflected on her own experience of teaching, noting that she had been unaware of the implicit gendered expectation that she would become maternal as she entered the profession. "I didn't know about a set of pedagogic expectations that covertly and mildly – and *never* using this vocabulary – hoped that I might become a mother" (Steedman 1987:125).

These covert and mild expectations are a crucial component of the gender organization of schooling. Indeed, the gender relations are naturalized to such an extent that they are often too familiar to be easily recognized (see Delamont 1996:5-8). Thus teachers are often unaware of the ways in which they employ gendered categories in their interaction with students. Katherine Clarricoates (1980:32-34) did a comparative study of four primary schools in England with various degrees of gender segregation. In the most gender-integrated school, the teachers believed they were not treating boys differently than girls, and yet they did so. They tended to see boys as the more creative, imaginative and high-achieving students, even though girls were achieving the highest marks. They tended to regulate the behaviour of girls more closely, restraining them from aggressiveness or bad language that they would accept from boys.

In these often subtle and unselfconscious ways, teachers help shape children's gender play. Madeleine MacDonald wrote that "schooling transmits a specific gender code whereby individuals' gender identities and gender roles are constructed under the school's classification system" (MacDonald 1980:22). The gender code need not even be built into the actual content of classroom teaching to have an impact. Thorne (1993:34-35) argues that the generalized use of the term "boys and girls" when teachers address students implies that gender is important. "By frequently using gender labels when they interact with kids, adults make being a girl or boy central to self-definition, and to the ongoing life of schools."

One of the places where gender coding commonly occurs is in the scrutinized play activity of the schoolyard. Hunter (1988:40-41) argues that the early architects of the English state school system saw the supervised yet unstructured play activity of the schoolyard as an important feature in the development of the self-disciplining pupil. "It is the playground which mediates most visibly between the norms of the classroom and the ungoverned life of the streets: enclosing the latter within a simulacrum of itself, but one organised in such a manner that the environment itself subjects each child's activities to constant moral superintendence" (Hunter 1988:60).

This scrutinized play in the shadow of the school picks up elements of the school's social organization. Play in the schoolyard is far more age-stratified and gender-segregated than in the neighbourhood (Seccombe 1993:110; Thorne 1993:49-50). The contrast between play in the schoolyard and play in the neighbourhood indicates that this gender coding is not simply "natural," but is in part produced through the "classification system" of the school.

Gender coding through the schools can be highly contradictory. The official curriculum of classroom teaching may favour gender-neutrality and equity while the "hidden curriculum" of gendered and racialized stereotypes in stories combined with differential behavioural expectations and attention patterns reinforces gender codes as well as those oriented around race and ethnicity (Thorne 1993:51). Indeed, gender relations seem to develop both in and against the official curriculum of the school.

Muscular masculinity, for example, is often taken on as part of a reaction against the school system. Paul Willis (1977) described the ways in which some working-class boys formed a masculine identity around the rejection of a curriculum that denigrated their knowledge, offered little chance of success and was irrelevant to their futures. Connell noted similar patterns: "The reaction of the 'failed' is likely to be a claim to other sources of power, even other definitions of masculinity. Sporting prowess, physical aggression, sexual conquest may do" (Connell 1989:295). This is a highly contradictory process that accommodates elements of a rebellion against the authority structure of the school within a masculinity that is itself partially sustained by the school. Physical education classes and the arena of male competitive sports are, for example, officially sanctioned activities that tend to be deeply imbued with the values of muscular masculinity.

Schools remain a major site for the reproduction of muscular masculinity and this poses challenges in the struggle for equity. The sexual harassment of girls and women is often a way of gaining status within groups organized around muscular masculinity (Larkin 1994:96), posing a serious obstacle to women's participation in education, particularly in male-dominated areas.[14] If school authorities do not address this problem they contribute to the reproduction of the power imbalance (Larkin 1994:33). The fear created by this atmosphere of sexual harassment and anti-woman violence affects women in the teaching profession as well as female students (Robertson 1993:45-49).

Muscular masculinity is also deeply implicated in an aggressive heterosexism that moves between name-calling and violence. Blye Frank (1994:47) argued that many of the boys he interviewed expressed an awareness that their standing in the social relations of the school were integrally related to their placement in the social scale of masculinity. Prowess at sports, success with girls, the ability to deploy violence and avoidance of any hint of homosexuality were crucial to this placement. As one participant put it, "Sports is probably the biggest thing to prove you're a real man, besides not being a fag" (Frank 1994:49).

Although muscular masculinity may be losing some of its hegemonic power in society as a whole, it continues to be reproduced in school. This not only threatens gender equity in education, it also tends to push the boys themselves towards marginality. It is quite possible that the anti-scholastic codes of muscular masculinity contribute to the demonstrably lower educational achievement of men. Yet, educational restructuring in

Ontario will not challenge the reproduction of this masculinity. Indeed, as I will discuss below, educational policy is tilting distinctly towards masculinity through this process of restructuring.

Femininity is also constructed in and against the school system. Angela McRobbie described the oppositional feminine identity that working-class girls developed when they did not feel they had much of a chance within the official structures of the curriculum. "A class instinct then finds expression at the level of jettisoning the official ideology for girls in the school (neatness, diligence, appliance, femininity, passivity, etc.) and replacing it with a more feminine, even sexual one" (McRobbie 1978:104). The activities of boys jostling for their place in the scales of masculinity certainly increased the pressure on girls to adopt a heterosexualized femininity but they have also acted for themselves. McRobbie summed this up elegantly: "They are both saved by and locked within the culture of femininity" (108). The increasing educational achievements of girls and women undoubtedly open up new spaces for some women, but the constraints of a more passive heterosexualized femininity remain. There is still a strong tendency for girls to develop a sense of their future that includes domestic responsibilities, despite expectations of paid employment (see Dennehy and Mortimer 1993:93-95).

Gender relations, then, are reproduced in and against the schools through contradictory and often covert processes. There is every reason to believe that a simple shift to a fully gender-neutral curriculum would give only a limited impact on the transmission of gender codes through schooling. The most favourable interpretation of contemporary educational restructuring is that it is gender neutral inasmuchas gender issues tend not to be discussed and the process does not involve a return to gender-streaming. By not addressing gender inequities, the restructured educational system is certain to reproduce them.

I would argue, however, that the current process of educational restructuring is not gender-neutral. Instead, the educational system favours masculinity in a number of important ways. First, the emphasis on standardized testing means that the measures of accomplishment are being recalibrated to favour males, given that, statistically, boys tend to perform better on standardized tests while girls do better on report cards (see Gaskell, McLaren and Novogrodsky 1989:18; Sadker, Sadker and Steindam 1989:47). Further, this emphasis on standardized testing and measurable outcomes reinforces pedagogical methods associated more with male than with female teachers (see Robertson 1993:63, cited above). The tendency towards a gendered division of teaching labour between orientation to the student (women) and orientation to the outcome (men) will be enmeshed in a system that reinforces the masculine approach.

The educational system will also be skewed to the masculine by the emphasis on male-dominated subject areas in the government's strategic plans. It would seem that areas of educational endeavour are being devalued as they are feminized (arts and social sciences), while the value of areas that remain male-dominated (science and engineering) is being dramatically enhanced. The Ontario government has clearly favoured science, technology and engineering in discussions of post-secondary education, as discussed above. Patterns of course selection remain gendered and men continue to heavily outnumber women as students in university programs in the areas of engineering and applied sciences, as well as mathematics and physical sciences (Statistics Canada 1998:5). Not only are these areas numerically dominated by men, they also fit ideologically with the emerging rationalizing and rationalized forms of hegemonic masculinity. While the "human" in liberal humanism was never truly inclusive of women in its heyday, it has ironically been feminized by default at the moment of its historic defeat by technical-rationality.

The shift towards masculinized technical-rationality in education could contribute to the continued reproduction of elements of muscular masculinity. Rationalized and muscular masculinity often co-exist in quite a complementary fashion (for example, in engineering schools). It remains to be seen whether the prioritization of male areas and masculinized pedagogies will have an impact on the relationship between muscular and rationalized masculinity. Hegemonic masculinity may take more supple forms given the societal influence of rationalized masculinity, but it will continue to reinforce male access to institutionalized power. "A man who can command this power has no need for riding leather and engine noise to assert masculinity. His masculinity is asserted and amplified on an immensely greater scale by the society itself" (Connell 1989:298).

The restriction of access to education through the development of user pay systems is also likely to harm women more than men. Single mothers who are welfare recipients have already lost their benefits while attending university, thus impairing their access to affordable childcare. It is likely that the combination of rising tuition fees and loss of access to childcare and other services will have a disproportionate impact on women's access to education.

Finally, the restructuring of education will itself contribute to the intensification of domestic labour. "School choice" is itself a labour process, requiring time and effort both to become an informed consumer and to transport children to the selected institutions. The impact of education cutbacks on preschools, after-school programs, childcare centres in school buildings and school bus programs remains to be seen as the cuts work their way through the system.

The Tory educational agenda has clear implication for gender relations. I am not sure whether this is motivated by a direct desire to reassert male power or if it is the unintended outcome of the shift towards the lean state. It is clear, however, that we cannot simply accept the evidence of women's increased educational achievement as a sign that all is equitable in the halls of our schoolsT process of restructuring is reshaping gender relations in ways that open up new spaces for women, yet at the same time intensify the inequities of the division of labour. It would seem that education reform fits well in that broad framework.

## A Note on Schooling for Sexuality

I do not want to omit the issue of schooling and sexuality, although I cannot examine it comprehensively here. I want to briefly discuss sexuality in the high school, although some of the issues raised here also apply to other levels of education. The school atmosphere combines official asexuality with an aggressive, indeed punitive, heteronormativity. Schools are often highly hostile environments for lesbians, gays, bisexuals and transgendered people (LGBT) ( Frank 1994; Owens 1998) even though this hostility is not (necessarily) taught in the curriculum. I want to discuss briefly the relationship between the anti-sex politics of the school and heteronormativity.

The disembodiment that takes place in the classroom (discussed above) requires a suppression of sexuality. A classroom is an asexual place, where even sex education is reduced to a technical science lesson. This is particularly emphatic given that the dominance of an ideology of childhood and youth that insists on the "protection" of young people from exposure to any form of sexuality (including their own). The actual desires and practices of students or teachers must be shed at the classroom door.

Yet the high school as a whole is far from asexual. On the contrary, it is a coercively heterosexual environment, marked by key social events (such as dances) which are not part of the curriculum but are part of the official school culture. Mary Louise Adams (1997) traces out the historical development of a heterosexual youth culture in the schools and the leisure times and spaces of youth after World War II. This culture was constructed through a combination of forms of moral regulation that aimed to create "normal" young adults and a self-created "transgressive" heterosexuality grounded in an increasingly autonomous commercialized youth culture (see Adams 1997:48-50, 79-80). The supervised school dance, then, combines both the official chaperoned moral regulation that aims to accomplish a normative heterosexual social environment and the unofficial "get drunk and do it" heterosexuality of young people flouting the rules.

In the everyday life of the school, the official chaste heterosexuality and the unofficial sexualized version coexist in a contradictory whole. Together, these ideas and practices produce a pressure cooker of sexuality in which young people are encouraged to participate in official heterosexuality while being deprived of any space to have sex. In this atmosphere, heterosexuality becomes a test that must be passed through acknowledged sexual activity and gender normative behaviours. This creates a viciously heteronormative environment in which young people suspected of any gender deviation are brutally persecuted as "queers." Terms associated with homosexuality are a standard currency of abuse meted out in the halls, locker rooms and school yards (see Frank 1994; Smith 1998). This reign of terror is seldom challenged and gains official sanction through the chaste official heterosexuality of the school.

Heterosexuality is desexualized to make it safe and official school culture, reduced to safe social intercourse between the sexes in the context of a set of gender norms. Lesbian, gay, bisexual or transgendered life is reduced to sexuality and excluded as such. The sexual repression of official school culture has particularly strong implications for same-sex sexuality, which is obliterated while heterosexuality is magnified through the pressure cooker of its desexed official form and sexually charged outlaw culture. This combination produces a toxic environment for young people who are lesbian, gay, bisexual or transgendered and others who are non-conformists or outcasts.

There seem to be two steps that would remedy this situation. First, the discussion of lesbian, gay, bisexual and transgendered lives must be opened up at all levels of the educational system so that the real diversity of our social experiences can cross the threshold. We must resist the reduction of homosexuality to sex, even as we champion pro-sex attitudes. Second, the high schools need to be a site of struggle for real sexual liberation. That must include the right of young people to control their bodies and lives: to consent to sex or to refuse it; to have access to free contraception and abortion services; to have the space for sexual practice that is not limited to back seats of cars under the influence of alcohol; and to free discussion of sexuality.

There have been some important steps in these directions, although a much wider struggle is required. The lesbian and gay movement has made some difference in the schools. The Toronto Board of Education developed some important programs in the 1980s and 1990s before the restructuring that created an amalgamated mega-board in 1998. The Triangle Program, started in 1994, is an alternative high school for LGBT youth who are driven out of their schools by hetereosexism and homophobia. The program also hosts a prom dance for LGBT youth from across the Toronto school system (Nelson 2001:A16). The old Toronto Board also developed an equity program that included important interventions when forms of racist, sexist or homophobic harassment were reported. These programs are currently at risk, due to a combination of a changed political climate in the amalgamated Toronto school board that now includes the more conservative suburban boards and the province's funding formula that pushes towards standardized patterns of space and personnel usage that alternative schools cannot meet.

There are some inspiring models developed in local experiments in the United States that could be introduced here. The documentary film "It's Elementary: Talking about Gay Issues in School" aired on the PBS network in the United States on 20 June 2001. It showed valuable examples of teachers who have chosen to open up the discussion of lesbian and gay life with elementary school students. The film documented heartening classroom discussions about discrimination, diversity in family forms and the meanings of pride. The San Francisco School Board has been a pioneer in introducing various forms of anti-homophobia education in the schools.

One of the foundations for this kind of change is the protection of LGBT teachers from discrimination. The combination of gays and young people is particularly explosive in the homophobic imagination. Lesbian and gay teachers are bound to feel vulnerable without very strong protections that are actually enforced. Ontario's publicly funded Catholic school boards continue to harass and fire lesbian and gay teachers under provisions that exempt them from certain forms of anti-discrimination law. In public boards, it depends a great deal on the political climate and the practices of the teachers' union. It is clear that important progress has been made when a contingent of teachers marching with union flags could be seen in the Toronto Pride Day on 24 June 2001. Yet there are still many more teachers with understandable fears, and who might feel particularly exposed when dealing with lesbian and gay issues.

The most inspiring breakthrough in this area over the last few years has been the activism of some queer youth standing up for their rights. In 2002, we saw the brilliant example of Marc Hall, the Oshawa-area young separate (Catholic) school student who successfully challenged his principal and the school board to win the right to take a male date to the prom. Many fellow students supported him, as did a broad coalition including the Canadian Auto Workers (CAW) union and many community and lesbian and gay organizations.

It seems that the high-school atmosphere helps contribute to the formation of an intense heterosexism and gender normativity. At the same time, certain university programs seem to undercut heterosexism. A recent study at a Canadian university showed that liberal arts students in their fourth year were notably less heterosexist than those in their first year. Science, engineering and business students showed higher levels of heterosexism at the first-year level but the fourth-year students in these disciplines did not demonstrate the same pattern of decreased heterosexism (Schellenberg, Hirt and Sears 1999). It would require further research to explain these patterns and to evaluate the possible impact of such factors as: specific gay-positive course content, the general humanist ethos of the liberal arts and the preservative effect of male-dominated university programs may have on the aggressive masculinity associated with the high school. This is an important reminder that the education setting does matter.

## Notes

1. Sadker, Sadker and Steindam (1989) found very little discussion of gender issues in a survey of American debates about education reform. I have been unable to turn up any discussion of gender in contemporary Ontario government documents about educational restructuring.
2. This comes from a discussion with Anne Forrest.
3. The link between imperialism and social policy breakthroughs is the specific subject of works by Semmel (1960) and Davin (1978). The impact of imperialism on British public health and social policy is also discussed in Thane (1982:58-59) and Gilbert (1976:72-91).
4. Seccombe (1993:182) argues that married women with older children represent the first "breach in the floodgate" in the pull towards paid employment.
5. I took cues for this discussion from Armstrong and Armstrong's (1990:32-3) call for more work on mothering in the context of bringing women's bodies back into socialist feminist theorizing. I also extended Zuboff's (1988) discussion of the labouring body into the household.
6. This idea comes out of a discussion with Sue Ferguson.
7. This is not to imply that women did not participate in industrial work or experience particular forms of embodiment in paid labour. I am emphasizing the experience of work in the household here as it was the basis for the construction of this particular form of femininity.
8. See Rutherford 1997:142 for a discussion of British trends and Luxton 1997:12 on the diversity of family forms in Canada.
9. I am not arguing that muscular masculinity has disappeared – the ability to take the punishments of mass production are now even more in demand in the lean workplace with its relentless speed-up and high incidence of repetitive strain injuries.
10. Other factors include the rise of a lesbian and gay movement and the role of individual legal rights in an increasingly marketized economy (see Hennessy 2000).
11. This is the great transgression of the near-criminalized recipients of welfare and other forms of benefits in the lean era.
12. The Toronto Transit Commission started playing classical music at the Kennedy Subway station in the spring of 1998 to try to keep young people from congregating there.
13. This is a bit of a simplification, of course. The coercive authority of the police and the military always hid beneath the skirts of the welfare state.
14. The Committee on the Status of Women in Ontario Universities (1988:7) argued that the climate created by harassment and similar assertions of gender dominance would need to be addressed if women were to be recruited to, and retained in, science and engineering programs.

# Chapter 6

# Children of the Market

The front section of Toronto's *Globe and Mail* newspaper on 3 June 2000 had two articles on education. The first covered the commerce and enterprise orientation of the new high-school curriculum introduced by the Ministry that week, under the headline "Ontario students to study e-commerce" (Galt 2000c:A9). The second focused on the new student code of conduct also introduced that week. This was a more analytical two page spread, announced by the heading: "Teenage Breakdown? Canadians are worried about the drugs, drink and disaffection. This week Ontario introduced legislation to impose a student code of conduct. Are the kids all right?" (Gray 2000:A14).

The coincidence of these two articles being in the same front section sets up the central argument of this chapter. The commercial enterprise orientation and hardline disciplinary approach of the post-liberal education reform agenda are internally related, they are two sides of the same coin. These directions might appear to be rather contradictory. The reorientation of education towards the market is often couched in the language of choice, innovation and relevance. Yet it is integrally connected to a new disciplinary regime that emphasizes compulsion, uniformity and retrenchment.

This chapter analyzes the links between the market orientation of post-liberal education and the harsh disciplinary regime of standards that accompanies it. I begin with a look at the way play is being squeezed out of childhood in this lean era. Childish notions of play in a protected land without time do not conform to the lean principles of continuous improvement and economic self-reliance. Education reform contributes to the remaking of childhood by steering schools towards an apparently utilitarian market ethos linked to a tougher code of discipline. The second portion of this chapter focuses on the analysis of the market orientation of post-liberal education in the light of Marx's theories of commodification. I concentrate specifically on the relationship between the market ethos and strict discipline in the education reform agenda.

## Childhood in a Lean World

The shift away from the broad welfare state has been in large part driven by the imperative of engineering people for the emerging regime of lean production. This lean regime requires a population with highly differentiated expectations and capacities to meet the needs of an increasingly polarized labour market and intensified labour processes. Existing fault lines of gender, race/ethnicity, employment status and age are crucial to the naturalization of this process of social polarization.

It is not surprising that a reorganization of childhood should be a central priority for policy-makers interested in re-engineering the population. Childhood is often seen as a crucial time for the development of abilities, expectations and practices. I will argue here that the modes of childhood development associated with the period of the broad welfare state are increasingly seen as a barriers to the creation of a lean ethos. One central goal of the education reform agenda is to create a new conception of childhood.

The conception of childhood varies over time and across cultures, even if it is naturalized in ways that make it appear to be fixed and unchanging. Ariès (1962) is often credited with launching the study of childhood as a historically specific phenomenon with his claim that the idea of childhood as a distinct way of life did not exist in medieval European society. It was only in the period between the fifteenth and eighteenth centuries that children in Europe came to be seen as a distinct group whose development needed to be nurtured, in part through separation from the adult worlds of work and leisure. At first, only the upper classes could afford to offer their children this kind of separate realm, although this model of childhood was gradually generalized with the development of various institutions, ranging from the school to legal regulations (Stephens 1995:5). Indeed, one of the first goals of state social policy in Britain, Canada and the United States was to make possible a working-class childhood, in the sense of constructing a separate realm through protective legislation and state schooling. Social policy was highly gendered from the outset so that the construction of a separate realm of safety for children was accomplished in large measure through the regulation of women's paid and domestic work (see Thorne 1987:97; Ursel 1992).

Early social policy focused, as we said earlier, on creating the possibility of a working-class childhood. But the goals of the broad welfare state went even further, seeking to eliminate social problems by preventive interventions aimed at children. The social policy of the broad welfare state was based on the assumption that children were highly plastic, so that even "bad" children could be fixed if the appropriate agencies were in place. The key was the development of the correct form of social policy intervention to solve particular social problems (see Clarke 1980:74). This was very complicated as the "badness" of any given child is often not reducible to a single social problem. The highest stages of the broad welfare state saw the attempt to develop "child-centred" approaches with the flexibility to capture the complex interrelations of factors that led individual children astray (see Clarke 1980). The prioritization of consent in welfare state social policy was reflected in an orientation towards making children participants (albeit never fully enfranchised partners) in their own "civilization," so that individuals would come to understand their own needs as harmonized with the national interest (see Davies 1986:22-23). At the same time, in much of the "third world," the broad welfare state period saw state-centred modernization projects that contributed to the "complex globalizations of once localized Western constructions of childhood" (Stephens1995:8).

Over the past twenty years, a number of writers have argued that this modern conception of childhood as a separate realm is at an end.[1] Neil Postman (1982) argues in *The Disappearance of Childhood* that the emergence of childhood as a distinct realm of existence was connected to the extended training period required to attain adult literacy. The development of radio and television reduced the need for literacy as a means of gaining privileged access to the adult world of information, and so the distinctness of childhood is giving way to a more homogenous child/adult culture. While the book seems to lean too heavily in the direction of cultural explanation, it does represent an important argument that we are at a moment of significant change in the character of childhood.

Sharon Stephens (1995) offers a rich account of this moment of change, setting the contemporary reconception of childhood in the broader context of David Harvey's (1989a) account of a transition in the regime of accumulation. The education reform agenda is designed to consolidate the conception of childhood that is emerging organically through a broader process of social and economic change. Harvey (1985:12) argues that crises act as the "irrational rationalizers" in capitalist societies, forcing the pace of rationalization at the level of production, exchange, distribution, consumption and institutional structures including the state. I am arguing here that the profitability squeeze that began in the early 1970s (see Introduction) has created an intensive process of restructuring that includes the rationalization of childhood.

One of the vehicles for accomplishing this rationalization is a post-liberal pedagogy that shifts away from welfare state optimism about the plasticity of children. In some ways, it represents a return to early twentieth-century ideas of a hardened residuum, an anti-social layer who cannot be improved and who act as a downward pull on those around them (see Chapter 3). The aim of the emerging educational regime is to identify and remove this layer, deploying standardized teaching and testing to expose differences in ability and character. Rather than a child-centred pedagogy that is in principle oriented towards each individual child, the aim is to create a uniform learning style. There is a tilt towards compulsion here, as students are seen as incapable of knowing what is good for them. At the core of this post-liberal pedagogy is an emerging effort to create "leaner" version of childhood and youth, more compatible with the world of lean production, through continuous improvement, greater polarization and increased compulsion.

## Continuous Improvement

As discussed in the Introduction, "continuous improvement" is one of the central principles of lean production, focusing on ongoing changes in production processes to enhance efficiency and eliminate "waste." Workplace restructuring influences the realm of social reproduction directly through the diffusion of technology, changing requirements for paid labour time and fluctuations in the security of employment. It also serves as an indirect point of reference for common-sense conceptions of waste, productivity and fairness. One central goal of the social policy of the lean state is to systematize the influence of workplace restructuring on society as a whole. Although the language of lean production is not necessarily directly mobilized at the level of social policy, the core principles have become part of the taken-for-granted framework of state programs.

Childhood poses a real challenge to the rationalization processes that underlie the principles of continuous improvement. The playful, non-instrumental character of modern childhood could be looked at as so much waste, exaggerated by the relative absence of time-discipline. Further, labour-intensive processes of parenting govern childhood. In this sense, modern childhood could be seen as inherently subversive in an era of lean production, a current of radical resistance to rationalization. It is a barrier to intensification in the workplace (particularly of women's labour) and an ideological obstacle to the generalization of the lean ethos. Education reform aims to constrain childhood and to develop a more instrumental and rationalized approach to young age.

Time is one of the key battlegrounds in efforts to eliminate 'waste' in childhood. Many households with children currently face a severe time crunch.[2] People who work full-time are working longer hours, while part-time workers often face unpredictable schedules. The services required to accompany women's entry into paid employment, such as flexible and accessible childcare, are dramatically underdeveloped. In fact, cuts to health and social services have intensified the unpaid labour performed mainly by women in the household, whether that is in the form of caring for sick relatives released from hospital or organizing fund-raising events to maintain school activities (Armstrong and Armstrong 1996). Parents (particularly mothers) are often at their absolute limits handling the combination of paid and domestic labour.[3]

As a result of this time crunch, many parents must bring their children into the regime of time-discipline from an early age. Child time has its own rhythms, at once open-ended and rich with the immediacy of experience. Parents facing the time crunch often do not have the luxury of allowing their children to move at the pace of child time. There are places to be and things to accomplish. Thus, child time becomes "waste" to be overcome through a regime of time-discipline that subjects all activities to the rigours of the clock. Thompson's pioneering work on time-discipline discussed the importance of the school in the development of time-discipline. "Once within the school gates, the child entered the new universe of disciplined time" (Thompson 1993b:388) In the era of lean production, more children are forced into the regime of time-discipline more completely and at an earlier age.

The increasing place of time-discipline in the lives of children is connected to a broader erosion of the space for play. This erosion is happening at a literal level, with public sector cutbacks that actually reduce or degrade the public spaces that had once been used for play (Katz 1998:135). In Toronto, public swimming pools were threatened with closure due to budget cuts.[4] Other facilities are now charging user fees.

At the same time, the cultural space of play is under threat. Play is a non-instrumental activity, done for its own sake. Activity without purpose is increasingly considered waste in a period of intensification and rationalization. To understand this, we need to step back a bit and locate play in the web of capitalist social relations. Stephens (1995:6) argues that modern childhood can be understood as a specific location within (at least some) capitalist societies that is marked by "spontaneity, play, freedom and emotion" in contrast with the adult world that is characterized by, "discipline, work, constraint and rationality." The development of the welfare state included provisions that exempted (at least some) children from aspects of work discipline and market discipline, to contribute to the formation of the healthy, disciplined and productive adult. The idea that children should be exempted from certain aspects of capitalist social relations is increasingly problematic in an era of capitalist intensification. Ellen Wood (1999:87) argues that one of the characteristics of the current period of restructuring is "the penetration of the capitalist logic deeper into the societies of advanced capitalism." Childhood is one of those areas where the logic of capitalism is intensifying.

Childhood is therefore becoming serious work. This conception is captured even in a well-intentioned advocacy report on the state of children in Canada. "More than anything, today's environment requires people who can think creatively, adapt readily to change, master new technologies, work well with a wide range of people and continue learning through life. Children who don't have a good start in life and in school will find it tougher than ever to complete sufficient education to get a job beyond one in the minimum wage service sector" (Guy 1997:xiv). This is presented as part of an overall argument for an increased investment in children. Yet there is also a message here that childhood cannot be wasted in the current environment of rapid social, economic and technological changes. It is thus being viewed in increasingly instrumental terms as a time of preparation for extended education and the world of work. "It is vital to recognize that today's children are tomorrow's workers. That is increasingly important as society places ever greater requirements for education, training, innovation , and flexibility on its workers" (Guy 1997:22).

At one level, there is nothing new about the idea that children must be prepared for their place as workers in the adult world. Liberal pedagogy, however, was connected to a view of childhood that suggested a fairly indirect route to this goal, using play and exploration to develop a self soaked in a culture of citizenship and discipline. In the current period, the instrumental orientation to a location in the adult world is becoming much more direct. Childhood is increasingly cast as a serious business, where everything from the choice of music (Mozart for IQ stimulation) to enrolment in lessons to the selection of toys is governed by the imperative of preparing the young for the competitive struggle of adult life. Norma Field (1995:55) provides examples of advice books for Japanese parents that suggest education should begin with the fetus and continue from the moment of birth.

As in the workplace, the regime of continuous improvement of childhood has important technological dimensions. The home computer is presented as a crucial tool for children's learning. Television has operated as a means to slightly reduce the labour-intensiveness of childcare by providing a diversion to occupy children and thereby to free up bits of time for care takers to complete other tasks. Cellphones, pagers and other portable communications devices are marketed as childcare devices that extend the supervisory gaze of caregivers to wherever the child goes.

Education reform also seeks to consolidate the conception of childhood as serious business. Childhood is being subjected to the standards of continuous improvement and the waste is being squeezed out. Field's examination of the Japanese educational system presents a portrait of a leaner, rationalized childhood. She argues that the educational system has essentially become a place of child labour, where children are driven to work extraordinarily long hours to secure adequate results in competitive exams (Field 1995:54-56). These children suffer increasingly from stress-related diseases generally associated with adulthood (53). Fields argues that in Japan, "labor, or the instrumentalizing logic of production, [has] ... taken over all of society, including early childhood and schooling" (61). An important example of this in the new Ontario curriculum is the heavy loading of homework onto even elementary school pupils, ensuring that children have less time to "waste" on play.[5]

Middle-class households have generally gone the furthest in making childhood a serious business. The middle-class families in Annette Lareau's American study "had a hectic, at times frantic, pace of life" (Lareau 2000:161). Children in these families tended to be accompanied by adults to a variety of scheduled activities (such as lessons and organized sports) outside of school hours. In contrast, children in working-class families tended to have less formal schedules and spent more time without adult supervision (159-66). The parents in working-class and middle-class households are undoubtedly all working very close to their absolute limits, but this may be reflected in somewhat different ways at the level of childcare.

The education reform agenda in Ontario pushes increasingly in the direction of education as child labour in preparation for work in the adult world. I will discuss below the impact of new testing regimes and the emphasis on the development of a career-oriented portfolio from the youngest age. Indeed, the orientation of education as serious business for children and youth is present is reflected in the whole emphasis on a rationalized core curriculum that is "back to the basics" (as opposed to wasteful studies in the arts, leisure or other courses related to self-expression).

## Inequality and Polarization

The creation of a more polarized and competitive environment is one of the key factors in the development of a leaner childhood. The need to mobilize all available time and resources for competitive placement provides a major incentive to avoid "wasteful" play. Toughening up the conditions of childhood is connected to the broader shift towards a more polarized society, as discussed in the Introduction and Chapter 3. Indeed, there is good reason to expect children's status to fall and their lives to become more driven at a time when the overall trend towards social inequality is increasing. The subordinate status of children needs to be understood in relation to social inequality more broadly, as adult/child dualisms are often invoked to justify other forms of domination (Thorne 1987:96). The status of children thus serves as an index of polarization in society, as the ideological and material conditions for the domination of the young are internally related to other forms of social inequality.

New regimes of standardized testing play a central role in the development of a more competitive atmosphere for children. As discussed above, the intensive testing regime has had a profound effect on Japanese childhood (see Field 1995). Indeed, it is not so long ago that Ontario had a stress-inducing standardized exam in the final year of high school (Grade 13) which was required for graduation. This exam system plagued the final year of high school and focused teaching on exam preparation (Ontario DE 1964:15). The 1967 Revision, which eliminated the Grade 13 exam, stated that "External standards requiring uniformity of achievement are unrealistic at best and cruel at worst" (cited in Fleming 1971b:269, see also 155-64, 287).

Standardized testing regimes purport to evaluate students' abilities objectively and to rank them against an overall scale. Along with I.Q. tests and other quantitative measures of "intelligence," they train the eye of the teacher to view the classroom in terms of a hierarchy of abilities. Carolyn Steedman ably summed up this process: "It is almost impossible for a teacher to look at a room full of children and not to see them in some way as being stretched out along some curve of ability, some measuring up to and exceeding the average, some falling behind. This is the historical inheritance we operate with, whether we do so consciously or not" (Steedman 1982:5). Further, this hierarchy of ability ties "intelligence" to other forms of social inequality, drawing on a deep taken-for-granted knowledge of differential abilities. Steedman continues, "and it has become a matter of 'common sense' ... that children of class IV and V parents [lower socio-economic status] are going to perform relatively badly compared with children of higher socio-economic groups" (5).

Of course, teachers will develop common-sense expectations for students' performance based on class, gender and race/ethnicity even in the absence of standardized testing. However, the testing regimes sharpen this tendency, as the teacher becomes the personification of the exam standards. This is particularly likely given that exam results are taken as measures of the performance of teachers, schools and the whole school system (see Field 1995:58-59; John 1995:116). "Bad" students, and indeed potentially "bad" students (as identified by taken-for-granted class, gender and racial/ethnic stereotypes), become problems for the teacher, who is likely to reflect that in her or his behaviour towards them.

The heavy homework regime also reproduces forms of social inequality. Many homework assignments require parental assistance. Working-class parents with less formal education, and non-anglophone or single parents are less likely to have the time and resources to assist their children with these assignments. Further, children who are having more trouble at school will end up more loaded with work as unfinished assignments are turned into homework. This is likely to be stigmatizing and could easily turn children with difficulties against education all together.

## Fear the Children
For the past two decades, state policies in Britain, Canada and the United States have increasingly constructed children as a danger, to be controlled through harsher measures. The system of law enforcement has developed a more punitive orientation towards children at the same time as the media focus tremendous attention on "problem" of "bad" children. Young people face tremendous scrutiny these days, whether the focus is on all-night parties or school violence. The brutalization of children is

also becoming a public spectacle. *The Maury Show* (an American daytime talk show) had a recurring theme of airing footage of children's trips to boot camps. The episode that aired on 23 May 2000 included film clips of ten-year-olds at a boot camp, breaking down and crying in the face of intensive yelling by large adults in military uniform. The audience applauded loudly at the end of each clip.

Social policy is increasingly treating children as, "the dangerous classes that the state must tame"(John 1995:125-26). It is not new for the state to regard children as a threat. Children have been regarded as both a vulnerable population in need of special protection and a danger to society throughout the history of social policy (Thorne 1987:90). The location of childhood as a special realm set apart from the everyday rigours of adult working life invests it with a certain subversive character. Children are not held to the same standards of discipline or industriousness as adults are and are therefore in the contradictory position of being socially sanctioned rule-breakers.

The social policy of the broad welfare state emphasized the distinctness of childhood and the requirements that it be governed by a separate set of rules. In contrast, the emerging lean state is eroding some of the distinctness of childhood and increasingly subjecting children to adult-like rules. The lean state is oriented to intensifying the subordination of labour to capital, eliminating alternatives to wage-labour and ideas of entitlement that developed with the welfare state (see Introduction). The socially sanctioned rule-breaking of childhood stands out as a threat to the consolidation of a leaner capitalist order.

One of the central features of the shift towards the lean state, as discussed in the previous chapter, has been a crackdown "dependence." Social policy is being reoriented to reduce barriers to independence which, in practice, is defined as reliance on wage-labour for subsistence. Social programs that created a limited alternative to wage-labour under specific circumstances are being dismantled. In this context, the dependence of some children becomes a problem. The dependence of children in wealthier families is not a concern for public policy, but is rather a private issue internal to a self-reliant economic unit. The dependence of working-class children is, on the other hand, very much a social policy issue.

As discussed above, the development of a separate and protected realm for (at least many) working-class children was only accomplished through the intervention of social policy. Without state programs, many working-class families could not afford to keep their children out of wage-labour or to provide them with the protected domestic spaces associated with a separate realm. Mass unionization has undoubtedly had some impact on this and a greater proportion of working-class families are now "self reliant" at least some of the time (although this can be rapidly eroded with job loss, illness or the end of a relationship). Working-class households with higher incomes, better benefits and more secure jobs might be able to manage the privatization of childhood in a way that unemployed, low-income or single-earner households will not.

The offensive against dependence is a way to free the state from its obligations to children and women. The domestic work of women and the dependent status of children was never fully recognized during period of the broad welfare state. The top tier of programs and services was accessible only to wage-earners, who obtained benefits in proportion to income. In contrast, the assistance to women working in the home and to dependent children was always at poverty levels (see Fraser 1989; Gordon 1990; and Ursel 1992). Now the poverty-level services are being cut dramatically and tied to workfare (forced work) programs, generally without adequate childcare provisions. The "dependence" of women and children is thus constructed as a social problem to be remedied by making any alternative to the wage unsustainable (see Gordon 1990).

The attack on children's dependence has created what Giovanni Sgritta (1997:386) describes as the "'golden age' of child poverty." More children are being driven deeper into poverty around the world, in both the wealthier industrialized nations and the Third World. Children have faced an overall deterioration in living standards since the mid-1970s, a disproportionate fall that has been greater than any other population group (387). In Ontario, the proportion of children living in poverty conditions almost doubled between 1989 and 1997, while the overall rate of child poverty in Canada increased by about 50 percent (CCSD 1999:18). Further, impoverished children and their families are falling deeper into poverty (18). At the same time as images of idealized materially privileged childhoods circulate increasingly in the media, austerity programs that have slashed subsidies and social programs have badly affected children in the Third World (Stephens 1995:20).

Yet, as the actual life conditions of children have deteriorated, the official commitment to "children's rights" has been ratcheted up (Sgritta 1997:378). In 1989, the United Nations General Assembly approved the Convention on the Rights of the Child, which commits the participating states to "recognize the right of every child to a standard of living adequate for the child's physical, mental, spiritual, moral and social development" (United Nations 1995:343). That same year, the Canadian House of Commons unanimously approved a resolution to eliminate child poverty by the year 2000 (CCSD 1999:18). The very same governments that are making policy decisions that directly increase child poverty are also formally committing themselves to recognizing the economic, social and cultural rights of children. It would seem that the legitimacy of children's dependence is being recognized rhetorically at the same time as government policies and practices move in the opposite direction.

Contemporary social policy approaches to children's dependence are highly contradictory. Both dependent and independent children can be constructed as social problems, providing that they are poor. Hungry children in the Third World are often presented in the media of the more developed capitalist countries in terms of dependence, as mouths to feed rather than hands to work. They are often constructed as the cause of poverty and environmental degradation, placing endless demand on limited resources as their numbers increase (Stephens 1995:13). At the same time, "street children" whose work makes them more independent, face hostility in that their visible presence transgresses the boundary that relegates children to the private realm (see Apetekar and Abebe 1997). In Ontario, there has been a sharp crackdown on homeless youth, including new levels of police harassments and legislation (the so-called "Safer Streets Act") to punish those who wash car windows for money.[6] Children, then, are presented as a threat insofar as they leak out from the private sphere, either as dependents in need of public assistance or as independents working in the streets.

The broad welfare state created an extended period of childhood and youth in order to incorporate children as citizens who were sufficiently disciplined and self-regulating. Children were confined to a separate realm, which suspended certain expectations and tolerated a level of non-instrumental activity that, in adults, would be categorized as lazy, dependent, rule-breaking and time-wasting. In exchange for this tolerance, children were excluded from the rights of citizenship (see Roche 1999). There is less room for this tolerance of children in the intensified lean state. Children are to be broken out of their subversive childishness at a much younger age through a more punitive disciplinary regime.

As discussed above, the welfare state approach to childhood was premised on the assumption that children were highly plastic and that, in the right hands, any one of them could be formed into a good citizen. In contrast, the harsher lean regime is connected to the assumption that there is a hardened layer of children who cannot be reformed. An example of this comes from a *Globe and Mail* article: "The majority of Canadian teenagers are just fine.... But there is 'a hardening underclass' of young people who are disengaged from school and veering off-course, say professionals who work with youth and track social trends. These youngsters are more inclined than their successful classmates to drink, use drugs, skip classes or drop out entirely" (Galt 2000b:A15).

The new punitive regime is particularly harsh in its orientation to this supposedly hardened layer, particularly young people who come into conflict with the law. Here, the attack on the separate realm of childhood is particularly clear. Through the welfare state period, the Canadian criminal-legal system developed a set of processes (focused particularly in the Young Offenders Act) to deal with young people charged with or convicted of crimes differently from adults (Caputo 1987). This shift reflected a conviction that younger people were more likely than adults to be successfully rehabilitated as they were less hardened into patterns of anti-social behaviour. At the same time, young people were seen as less capable of forming criminal intent than adults and therefore less culpable. Right-wing critics regard this separate realm for young offenders as dangerously lenient and egal reforms have begun to erode it, subjecting some young people to adult courts and harshening the punitive orientation to others.

The focus of the young offender system has shifted from treatment to punishment. The adoption of boot camps and harsher discipline in other facilities for young offenders in Ontario is an important example of this trend (see Armstrong 1997). At the same time, police are adopting harsher tactics in the context of legal changes that criminalize many of the activities of young people on the streets. The racialized orientation of policing means that black, Asian and aboriginal youth are much more likely to be criminalized in this new disciplinary regime. The criminalization of black youth has certainly been a prominent feature of the harshening criminal-legal regime in Britain (Sivanadan 1985:8). A study of street youth in Saskatoon revealed that aboriginal street youth were arrested more than those who were not aboriginal (Schissel 1997:83).

Bernard Schissel (1997:9) argues that "Canada's war on crime, like the war on crime in many other countries and in other eras, is quickly becoming a war against youth." This war against youth is not aimed exclusively at the supposedly hardened layer of young people who come into conflict with the law, even if they are the most prominent target. Rather, the harsher regime aimed at young offenders serves as the anchor for a broader continuum of punishment to control children. The recent crackdown on raves in several Ontario cities represents an explicit attempt to control young people's access to unregulated public spaces for enjoyment (see Tackaberry 2000).

The Harris government has brought this tougher law-and-order agenda into the schools. A Toronto School Board program to engage students who had been expelled from school was ended by the new "zero tolerance" approach that excluded any funding for services to expelled students (Galt 1999). Instead, the province introduced "strict discipline" programs for expelled students (OMET 2001). A new Code of Conduct was introduced in 2000 as part of the Safe Schools Act. This Code emphasizes responsibility, respect for those in authority and acceptable behaviour.

Students are to be treated with respect and dignity. In return, they must demonstrate respect for themselves, for others and for the responsibilities of citizenship through acceptable behaviour. Respect and responsibility are demonstrated when a student:
- comes to school prepared, on time and ready to learn;
- shows respect for themselves, for others and for those in authority;
- refrains from bringing anything to school that may compromise the safety of others;
- follows the established rules and takes responsibility for his or her own action. (OMET 2000:8).

In the end, the Code of Conduct did not include a compulsory citizenship oath to be recited every day, although Education Minister Janet Ecker proposed this, she backpedalled in the face of a negative reaction (see Coyle 2000; Galt 2000a). It did, however, include an automatic suspension for swearing at a teacher or another person in authority (OMET 2000a:13). The Code also mandates school boards to establish protocols that specify, amongst other things, the conditions upon which police must be involved in school disciplinary matters (Brennan 2000; OMET 2000a:4). There is an articulation between schools and police in the creation of an atmosphere of intensified coercion.[7] Indeed, Bob Runciman (a Conservative Minister) called for a much greater presence of uniformed police in the schools, but Premier Harris rejected this (*Windsor Star* 1999).

The disciplinary orientation is also reflected in the policy that allows parents to establish dress codes for individual schools. School uniforms can be seen as an antidote to the raging consumerism that is particularly hard on children from lower-income families.[8] Yet they can also be a severe restriction on personal and group self-expression, thus imposing conformism. Minister of Education Janet Ecker explained the introduction of the new dress code regulations in fairly disciplinary terms. "Today we are taking another step forward in ensuring our schools are safe, respectful places for learning and teaching" (OMET 2000a). The emphasis on safety and respect reflects a coercive conformism. A student named Ibay who had too many piercings to meet the dress code requirements at his Hamilton school was quoted in the news as saying "I think it goes against my rights. I think it's my body and I should be able to do what I want" (Oosthoek 2000:E3). School dress codes are a way for someone else to claim that body and to prove that students cannot "do what they want".

The harsher regime of youth punishment represents a partial erosion of the separate realm of childhood. Yet this process has been quite contradictory. Youth is being extended at the same time as it is being eroded in certain ways. Increased participation in post-secondary education has tended to extend the time of youth, in combination with a youth job market marked by low pay and insecure employment. More younger people are residing with their parents for longer periods of time (CCSD 1999:15). The blurring of the boundaries of childhood and youth seem to be producing a more extended childhood for many, but it is one that is less distinguished from adulthood.

As I will discuss below, the greying of the adult/child distinction is in part connected to the extension of commodification processes deeper into everyday life and the construction of childhood and youth as market niches. As elsewhere in society, the marketization of childhood carries with it elements of deregulation. Specifically, we are seeing a limited moral deregulation of youth as market forces increasingly shape the immediate cultural environment. The right wing is in a very contradictory position here. They are restructuring education to promote marketization that brings with it a certain amorality. The panic over internet access, rock music lyrics and the television v-chip represent attempts to handle this contradiction through censorship and self-censorship by cultural producers. Yet this does not seem to be having the intended impact. If anything, the self-censorship of American commercial television seems to have relaxed over the past fifteen years.

Marketization, then, is associated with a moral deregulation that does create certain spaces for younger people to win some autonomy, particularly in areas of sexuality. This space is not simply the result of marketization, but also of the struggles of the women's movement (for reproductive freedom and women's control over their bodies and lives) the lesbian and gay liberation movement (for sexual liberation) and AIDS activism. As a result of these changes, sexual regulation among younger people is eroding at the very time when the right-wing punitive agenda is being introduced into the schools. In the past, the containment of sexuality has been at the core of youth discipline in capitalist society. It remains an open question whether the new disciplinary offensive will attempt to deploy new forms of sexual regulation to strengthen the subordination of the young. It seems likely that issues of youth sexuality will be a key battleground for questions of sexuality in the foreseeable future in light of the contradictions of youth consumerism and the right-wing drive to discipline the young.

It is not my intention here to counterpose an analysis of the leaning of childhood against a nostalgic and idealized version of welfare state childhood. State programs and benefits were never enough to provide a decent childhood to all, as they were always bracketed by wage-labour on the one hand and unpaid domestic labour on the other. Benefits were kept below subsistence level to reinforce the imperative to wage-labour and services were organized around women's domestic labour. At the same time, welfare state childhood was premised on the exclusion from citizenship and highly restrictive on children themselves.

Yet a comparison with welfare state childhood does provide us with insights about the depth of contemporary education reform. The aim is to transform childhood so that it fits with the economic and social realities of emerging systems of lean production. The space of play is being constricted by new disciplinary imperatives. Compulsory education has always squeezed the play out of children to prepare them for the internalized disciplinary regimes that mark adulthood. The new leaner education will do this in new ways, deploying competitive testing, uniforms, punitive rule books and user pay to prepare children and youth for a world where the balance is shifting from the discipline of citizenship to market discipline.

## The Market Orientation

The harsher disciplinary regime of post-liberal education is associated with an increased market orientation. The neo-liberal equation of marketization with laissez-faire does not do justice to the contradictory nature of contemporary changes. Rising market forces are associated with certain forms of moral deregulation, but at the same time bring with them new dimensions of coercion and subordination. At the most basic level, the market itself is a disciplinary apparatus that regulates activity by restricting access to resources. Market discipline is necessary, but not sufficient in itself, to sustain capitalist societies. Throughout the history of capitalism, the market has required various forms of state regulation to discipline the population and channel capitalist competition.

We need to push a bit further into Marx's analysis of the commodity in capitalist society to understand this particular configuration of market and state. A commodity is a human product made for exchange on the market. Marx begins *Capital* with an analysis of the character of the commodity, which he believed to be a crucial point of entry into the workings of the capitalist system. Every commodity has two sides, which Marx identifies as "use-value" and "exchange-value." The use-value is based on the characteristics of the thing that allow a particular person to make use of it in a specific way. Use-value cannot be quantified, as it is based on the needs and desires of particular individuals. The use-value of thong underwear, for example, will vary from person to person depending on their taste and shape. Exchange on the basis of use-value takes the form of barter, in which individuals strike a particular deal based on their own qualitative assessment of the relative worth of specific objects or services. In contrast, purchase and sale on the market is based on exchange-value, which is a quantitative measure.

Marx argued that this quantitative exchange-value was not arbitrary but was, rather, the measure of something specific. Every commodity contains some amount of the one ingredient they all share in common, human labour. Goods are therefore exchanged on the market on the basis of their value, the quantity of labour they contain. Of course, people will not pay more for an identical item simply because it is made by a particularly slow and incompetent worker or a very old-fashioned labour process. The value of a commodity is therefore based on the socially necessary labour time required on average to produce the item, given existing levels of technology and work organization (Marx 1954:46).

If all commodities exchange at their value, it is not immediately obvious where profits come from. There is, however, a unique commodity that actually adds value during the process of production: labour-power, or the capacity to work. Labour-power, like every other commodity, is exchanged on the basis of its value, in this case the socially necessary labour time required to keep the worker alive. The key to profits is that, during the working day, the value the worker adds to products exceeds the wages she or he receives, which are based on the costs of keeping her or him alive, the value of labour-power.

Marx's analysis of the commodity therefore leads him to identify the basis of profits in surplus-value: the measure of the amount that the value workers add during the process of production exceeds the value of labour-power. It also leads him to specific conclusions about the gap between the appearance of things in a capitalist society and the ways the system actually works. In his discussion of commodity fetishism, Marx discusses the particular process through which things take on the appearance of being the active agents in society and people the passive objects. Things interacting with each other on the market seem to dictate the terms of our access to them, so that hunger or homelessness appear to be the result of market conditions that establish the price of homes or rice. Market fluctuations seem just as outside of our control as the weather. "These quantities vary continually, independently of the will, foresight and action of the producers. To them, their own social action takes the form of the action of objects, which rule the producers instead of being ruled by them" (Marx 1954:79).

The operations of the market are therefore naturalized, taking on the character of impersonal forces that shape the conditions for human existence. A real understanding of capitalist society requires an analysis that goes beyond the obvious and apparently self-explanatory operation of market forces. The deeper workings of the system are obscured, not by some clever ideological ruse but by the very character of commodity exchange.

Labour-power is a unique commodity and not only because it alone can add value. It can only be actualized when real flesh and blood workers put their minds and bodies to work. Labour-power is the only commodity with a mind of its own. Specific disciplinary processes are therefore required to induce potential wage-labourers to actualize themselves on the market under prevailing conditions (see Aumeeruddy, Lautier and Tortjada 1978). Labour-power is the one commodity that must be disciplined to find its way to the market. In the period of the broad welfare state, the mediation of citizenship was central to the reproduction of labour-power. The leaning of childhood represents a crucial reorientation of that disciplinary process towards a relentless emphasis on self-commodification.

## Closing Extra-Economic Space

One of the central projects of the lean state is to shut down some of the extra-economic spaces associated with welfare state citizenship. The idea of citizenship rights and entitlements runs up against the market ideology that individuals have the right to whatever they can afford to purchase. Yet at the same time as it is eroding the semi-decommodified spaces of citizenship, the lean state is also intensifying other forms of extra-market discipline. Market discipline is being complemented by new mechanisms to promote and enhance market-oriented identities. The entrepreneurial self is to be made through the marketplace, through a combination of acts of consumption (buying the goods and services to locate oneself) and self-commodification (the sale of labour-power, one's capacity to work).[9]

The deeper penetration of market relations into everyday life has had a profound impact on childhood. Children are increasingly located as consumers and targeted as a niche market. The breakthrough development of the youth market in the 1940s and 1950s was an important harbinger of this process of commodification (see Adams 1997:42). Since then, these processes have extended deeper, reaching down the age scale to capture ever younger children and tightening the grasp on the lives of youth. Fashion for children is gaining in importance at the same time as computer and video games are being developed to commodify the imagination. The centrality of the mall in many versions of youth culture is an important indication of the deeper commodification of youth. Indeed, the youth niche in the labour market and the youth market for consumption often overlap in the service sectors of the economy.

Processes of commodification and sexualization are interconnected, as sex is mobilized to sell products and desire is reflected through consumer goods. At the present time, we are seeing the increased sexualization of children through the fashion and entertainment industries. Yet this is paired with panic about child pornography and sexual content that is reflected in legislative and regulatory crackdowns. The lean world is very hypocritical about child sexuality, condemning it loudly while enthusiastically drawing children into the sexualized worlds of fashion and leisure.

The market is often presented as a realm of choice, and yet it is often about standardization. A quite finite range of highly standardized goods serve as the raw material for consumer identities. At the same time, workers themselves must be standardized to conform with pre-established labour processes.

## Commodifying Education Space

One important way in which the education system is being realigned to fit with this market emphasis is the commodification (or, in some cases, pseudo-commodification) of the space of education itself. Educational institutions are being openly commercialized through, for example, sponsorships of various types that mark space as corporate. Administration methods are being reoriented towards competitive market models at every level. New regimes of user pay and testing are reversing educational entitlements that developed during the period of the broad welfare state. Finally, the content of education is being reoriented towards more practical and market-directed outcomes.

The education reform agenda revolves around a central shift in the goal of state schooling, from the development of self-regulating citizens to the formation of self-commodifying individuals. This shift requires a multi-dimensional reorganization in the content and form of education. Liberal education aimed to form self-regulating citizens through strategies of inclusion that sought to locate students in an illusory state-centred community bound together by national culture. Contemporary education reformers reject this emphasis on citizenship, which is seen as a fetter on the leaning of the social order in the context of capitalist restructuring.

A self-commodifying individual must be freed up from some of the baggage of liberal education and self-regulating citizenship. Any sense of entitlement (to an education, to a job reflecting educational accomplishments, to certain services and resources) must be shattered, so that individuals understand that their rights extend only to whatever they can afford to purchase on the market. The largely decommodified spaces of education must be stripped away to leave the individual more fully exposed to the market. And the non-instrumental and abstracted character of the liberal arts and science education must be replaced by a more functional and concrete curriculum.

The education system is being refitted to prepare students to take their place as commodities in a world of commodities. Self-commodification is accomplished when the individual is seamlessly integrated into the market, both as seller of labour-power (one's own capacity to work) and as buyer of consumption goods and services to fulfill needs and wants. The welfare state promoted self-commodification through rather different means, relying on the mediation of the state to create the ideological and material conditions required to accomplish the sale of labour-power in the face of working-class resistance. Self-commodification is necessarily a complex and contradictory process, as labour-power is the unique commodity that has a mind of its own. State action was required to contain resistance by meeting workers' demands (for example, for dignity, security and a decent standard of living) in a limited and often distorted form.[10] The welfare state complemented market forces to create the conditions of inclusion in society that seemed to create orderly work and social life.

The shift to the lean state reduces that mediation, drawing on the deeper insertion of the working class into the market both as a result of workers' own gains and the greater penetration of commodification into everyday life.[11] It relies more directly on market forces themselves to create the conditions of inclusion, depending on both the thrall and fatalism of commodity fetishism.[12] This is certainly not a foolproof strategy from the perspective of capital, as larger sections of the working class are facing exclusion under present circumstances and even those who are included face insecurity and an inability to meet their needs.

The reorientation of the educational system towards the preparation of self-commodifying individuals requires changes at many levels, including curriculum, pedagogy, institutional structure and labour relations. It will require change at all of these levels to squeeze liberal education out of the system. A set of institutions developed around one educational regime are being refitted to suit another one. This thoroughgoing reorganization might ultimately open up questions about the need for these institutions to exist at all.

## Teaching Enterprise Culture

In Chapter 4 I discussed the shift away from a liberal education curriculum oriented around key forms of cultural and scientific knowledge. This shift is required so that the educational system can contribute to the formation of the entrepreneurial self. Liberal education located the citizen-in-training in relation to the state, which was identified with the pinnacle of national culture and of technical expertise. The entrepreneurial individual does not necessarily need all that esoteric learning to find her or his place in the market. She or he is more concerned with knowledge that offers market advantage; skills or competencies that are immediately saleable, or at very least help the individual navigate the marketplace.

Michael Apple (1995:xvii) argues that the shift towards a more entrepreneurial focus in education is a cultural as well as an economic project. The aim is not simply to prepare students for the realities of a changing workplace, but to contribute to the development of a way of life that is oriented around the market. The entrepreneurial self focuses on obtaining a return through buying and selling. For most people, this will mean first and foremost selling themselves (their labour-power or capacity to work) for a wage or equivalent. In Ontario, the centrepiece for this emphasis on selling oneself will be the portfolio that every student will keep from the youngest grades to relate their learning to their post-schooling goals (see Chapter 4).

The Thatcherite education reforms in Britain emphasized the development of an enterprise culture (Tasker and Packham 1994:151-54). This revolved specifically around core values of risk, independence and self-reliance (Deem 1994:30). The British Conservative government developed their educational policy over a long period of time, beginning in the 1960s (before Thatcher led the party) right into the 1980s. Johnson (1991:38) points out that one of the key aspects of this development was the complex and shifting balance between neo-conservative (order) and neo-liberal (market) elements. The Harris government's education reform agenda in Ontario has attempted to reconcile these elements, presenting the neo-conservative elements (order through standards) as if they were the necessary product of a neo-liberal orientation to the market.

The shift to an enterprise culture shifts the standards by which the usefulness of education is assessed. The idea that the student must graduate into citizenship with a certain cultural and social foundation has been quickly overtaken by an emphasis on job preparation. However the Economic Council of Canada argues that this reorientation stems largely from the preferences of students and their parents. "Many of them [young people] and their parents judge the quality of the education system by its success in preparing students for the labour market" (Economic Council of Canada 1992:4). There is a real constituency for a more instrumental labour market focus in education, particularly at a time when the bottom is falling out of the labour market for people without a great deal of formal education. Satu Repo argues that there is another constituency that has essentially been silenced. "It seems at times that the clamour for making schools tougher and more practical – the complaints of the impatient and important Dads – has silenced all those who actually know about children: mothers, childcare workers, teachers, child psychologists" (Repo 1999:15). Yet we have to be somewhat cautious about dismissing the constituency for a more practical education, even if we seek to understand the particular material and ideological circumstances that have contributed to its development and the inherent contradictions that mean these ideas can shift rapidly. At the very least, we need to recognize that mobilizing these silenced constituencies (as well as others, particularly students themselves) means going against the current of contemporary changes in common sense and economic developments (see Jones and Hatcher 1994:258).

Certainly, the experience of teaching university students at the present time has made it clear to me that a significant portion of my own students has a fairly instrumental approach to their own education. They are tolerating economic hardship, overwork, long-term debt and deferred adulthood in exchange for a practical advantage in a difficult labour market. It seems to me that we need to recognize that this orientation cannot simply be wished away by liberal educators who want to carry on teaching as they once were taught. This does not mean, however, conceding the ground to the right-wing education reformers. On the contrary, there is a great deal of room to enter the debate about practical education and the capitalist marketplace. This does mean, though, going beyond the defence to liberal education to a broader agenda for social justice.

At its core, this market-oriented education takes as neutral the task of shaping students to slide easily into the slots that employers might have for them. From this perspective, students and employers might both seem to benefit from a system that shapes graduates to the needs of the labour market. Yet, as Avis argues, this "assumption of an inherent unity of purpose between learners and capital glosses over very real points of antagonism" (Avis 1996a:116). Difficult questions about the character of the workplace and the capacity of workers to contest management control are left aside. Students as potential workers might have an interest in contesting employers' ideas of suitable jobs, the relation between work and leisure, decent pay, appropriate comportment, personal dignity and autonomy (or the lack thereof). The entrepreneurial orientation excludes such "political" questions at the same time as it casts the employer's definition of the ideal graduate as "neutral."

Reports by employers' organizations give us some sense of the way they see the ideal graduate and potential worker. The Canadian Chamber of Commerce Task Force on Education and Training (TEFT) (1989:15) argued that youth unemployment was connected to the inadequacy of the preparation for the workforce that young people receive. The report cites a series of concerns about preparation, including a lack of basic skills (reading, writing, analysis and interpersonal), an overly academic (vs. vocational) education, insufficiently developed work habits and a lack of knowledge about work opportunities. The ideal graduate, from this perspective, has certain skills, is work-habituated, is occupationally (not academically) oriented and can navigate the labour market, finding the opportunities that are out there. The TEFT (1989:37-46) argues that the solutions to these problems include more active business partnerships in education programs to ensure that relevant skills are developed, a wider range of vocational programs and more co-op placements for work experience.

There is nothing "neutral" about this assessment – it reflects the employer's perspective on the workplace. From this vantage point, the ideal graduate is prepared for the regime of work-discipline and their expectations of the workplace align closely with the real possibilities that are out there for them. A survey of employers conducted by the Canadian Federation of Independent Business (CFIB) (1996:27) that "character qualities" (such as "discipline" and "reliability") ranked at the top of the list of attributes valued in young employees.[13] The TEFT (1989:45) stresses the ways that co-op programs can contribute to the development of such character qualities: "Even in the simplest jobs, students learn dress and behaviour standards and how to work with other employees." Thus, employers' desire for compliant employees is built into the mission of the educational system as if there were no alternative.

I would consequently agree with Tasker and Packham (1994:152) that the enterprise orientation in education is "blatantly ideological." I might perhaps nuance this by stressing at the same time that the liberal education model from which we are departing was itself far from neutral and might be characterized as "discretely ideological." The citizenship orientation in liberal education placed a premium on claims of disinterest and neutrality (see Chapter 4). Realigning the educational system more directly around employers' goals puts some of that guise of neutrality at risk. However, changes in common sense have restored some of that sense of neutrality, as the idea that the interests of business correspond to those of society as a whole have gained increasing currency. Apple argues that the right-wing project of shifting common sense towards a more market-oriented direction has met with some success. "[T]he project of changing our common sense so that freedom equals the market, so that failure is only the result of individual character flaws, and so that democracy is simply guaranteeing the unattached individual a choice among consumer products has been more than a little successful" (Apple 1995:xvi). Certainly, when the next wave of social mobilization hits, the educational system is likely to have a harder time claiming neutrality. Indeed, corporations are now branding educational institutions directly with their marks, rendering the issue of neutrality less ambiguous.

## Knowledge As a Commodity

This alignment of the educational system with employers' goals is associated with a crucial shift in the valuation of learning. The blunt entrepreneurial orientation uses market criteria to measure the true value of learning. Thus, knowledge itself becomes commodified in new ways, it becomes a thing that can be broken down and accumulated (Apple 1995:139). The entrepreneurial learner is thus oriented to the accumulation of marketable knowledge. Apple argues that success in this situation is marked by "the possession and accumulation of vast quantities of skills in the service of technical interests" (139).

The shift to a commodified model of knowledge requires important changes in pedagogy. Liberal education, particularly at its highest stage during the welfare state period, aimed to cultivate citizens. Cultural knowledge was worthy in itself in that it contributed to the improvement of the individual by locating her or him in community established in relation to the state (see Chapter 4). In fact, the lack of market value was an important characteristic of this cultural knowledge as it abstracted these ways of knowing from the immediate realm of competing interests and therefore provided an allegedly neutral bond for the state-centred community. Pedagogical approaches were oriented more to the transformation of the individual than the transfer of specific items of knowledge. The emphasis was more on the process of learning than on what was actually learned (Avis 1991:115). If these goals sound lofty, it is important to bear in mind that the goal of this transformation was to create the self-regulating citizen who had deeply internalized discipline and habits of subordination. Further, this is an ideal model of liberal education that does not necessarily represent the actual teaching in real classrooms.

In contrast, the commodified model centres on the transfer of bits of knowledge, which students can accumulate and then summon up for "objective" testing to certify their possession of it. Paolo Freire (1972:58) describes this as the "banking" model of education, which casts students in the role of passively receiving, storing and then handing back ("using") the precious bits of knowledge the teacher hands to them. I would like to push this economic analogy a bit further than Freire, to relate the banking model of education to the logic of commodity exchange in a capitalist society as outlined by Marx (1954). Not only does the commodified model reduce knowledge to exchangeable bits of information, it also subordinates the "use value" of these bits (their practical utility to the person learning) to their "exchange value" (the quantified measure of their worth relative to others). Grades, then, mimic the role of money as the universal equivalent, the quantified measure for all relative worth on the market.

In the commodified model of education, what matters most is the grade a student is assigned and not what she has actually learned for herself. The co-operative and active labour process of learning combines physical and mental dimensions and varies tremendously between individuals depending on their own interests, skills and resources. The intrinsic value of these highly diverse learning processes to the students are themselves obscured by the quasi-commodified character of the education system, which sees only classroom learning and grades. David McNally (2001:44) argues that capitalist commodification produces "a unique kind of fetishistic thinking which 'forgets' the concrete labors that go into producing things." This fetishistic thinking is present in liberal education and even more prominent in the emerging post-liberal model.

The proliferation of performance goals centering around measurable outcomes therefore accompanies the commodification of knowledge.[14] This new pedagogy is more individualized than the liberal model, in that it focuses on personal accumulation and not location in a community. Yet it is also less individualized in that it rejects the "child-centred" model of liberal education in favour of an approach that presumes that everyone learns in the same way (Aronowitz and Giroux 1985:29). For example, Canadian education reform advocate Mark Holmes (1998:156-60) argues for de-individualized teaching, favouring direct instruction ("which means the teacher teaches the ideas or skills to be learned, as distinct from giving students individually or in small groups the opportunity to find them out for themselves") oriented to the class as a whole (as opposed to individual or small group teaching).

The commodification of knowledge in this fashion makes teaching more amenable to scientific management, including the introduction of new technologies. Liberal pedagogy, particularly in the form of child-centred learning, cast teachers as highly skilled workers who required great discretion and control over the labour process so they could fine-tune the curriculum to meet the needs of the various individuals in the classroom. Teachers were professionalized as skilled workers with "multiple knowledges, negotiating skills and intuitions" (Livingstone 1995a:37). The post-liberal system opens up teaching to new forms of Taylorist scientific management, where tasks are broken down, performance is measured and conception is increasingly separated from execution (see Dickson 1991:110-11; Esland 1996:33). An important example of deskilled teaching is provided by new forms of prepackaged curricular materials that have been developed in the United States, including tests for specific outcomes (Apple 1995:130-31). The teacher becomes the relatively interchangeable deliverer of a standardized curriculum that is developed elsewhere, without consideration of the specific needs or attitudes of individual students.

Technological change plays a prominent role in the deskilling of teaching, just as it does in other industries. Bromley (1997:55) argues that we should regard new technologies as neither neutral nor deterministic. Technologies are not neutral, they are developed and deployed in the context of specific social relations. At the same time, they do not have inherent powers, but rather are instruments in struggles around social power. Computers can be very useful educational tools and can also be used to intensify teaching labour and transform knowledge into bits of information. It seems clear that standardized packages of computer-based self-teaching are being deployed to increase the productivity of teachers and professors, so that each instructor will be able to process a much greater number of students.

We therefore have to wonder about the absolute commitment to teaching technologies in the context of contemporary education reform. The question has not been whether to use computers or when they are useful, but how to make the most intensive use of them throughout the whole educational system (Arnold 1996:237). It is crucial to bear in mind that this commitment to the use of computer technologies comes at a time of cost-cutting, outsourcing and work intensification (Friese-Germain 1999:56). Computer technologies provide a useful set of tools for tying together a leaner labour regime with the commodified model of knowledge by mechanizing information transfer. This is not the only way computers can be used in educational setting. The issue is not the specific character of information technology, but the way it is being used in the context of contemporary education policy. However, given the present context it is safe to assume that there will be a bias towards the mechanization of information transfer in the deployment of new technologies.

Information transfer always played some role in schooling, but it leaps to the top of the list of educational priorities in the high technology model (Postman 1995:73). The claim that the computer opens a window into a whole world of information is presented in alluring terms.[15] Yet the problem that students face is less one of access to information than it is of learning to make sense of it, to evaluate it critically and use it for their own ends (Postman 1995:74; Robertson 1998:138). Arguably, the combination of skills and judgement required to make sense of information cannot be learned by individuals working on their machines in isolation. L.S. Vygotsky (1978:90) wrote that "learning awakens a variety of internal developmental processes that are able to operate only when the child is interacting with people in his environment and in cooperation with his peers." Individuals can perform at a higher level with some combination of guidance and peer co-operation, nurturing budding abilities that are in the process of the development.

Livingstone (1995a:37) argues that teachers who do not immediately endorse the use of new technologies in education are not necessarily doing so out of ignorance, but rather out of "a knowledge of the intangible human dimensions that they and their students could be losing." These "intangible human dimensions" are in fact integral to learning processes. Children learn with their whole beings, their bodies and minds, emotions and intellects (Repo 1999:16-17). Indeed, this is not only true of children. Learning processes require a variety of forms of engagement: doing things physically, interacting and reflecting. Working alone with a machine can certainly play a useful part in this, but it cannot substitute for other kinds of activity. Information technologies in education are being used to make learning more individualistic, more commodified and "radically less discursive and dialogical" (Arnold 1996:238).

Information technology is a crucial tool in reshaping education into a business. At the most obvious level, the educational use of these technologies contributes to the marketing of computers, particularly to students and their parents (Robertson 1998:127). The spread of computer technology in education has also been associated with new kinds of modularization in which a learning process is broken down into a number of discrete elements (for example, specialized software) that can be produced for the market. Over time, this commodification will favour more heavily capitalized corporations who will be able to invest in research and development. Wotherspoon wrote, "Particular groups and companies, which have the resources to prepare, promote and distribute course-ready materials have an advantage in capturing the education 'market.'" (Wotherspoon 1991:27)

The rapid expansion of the educational marketplace is indicated by the annual trade fair for the Canadian "education industry." The trade fair, "Canadian Education Industry Summit 2000 – Making It Happen: The Bridging of Education and Private Finance" was held in Toronto in October 2000 (see *National Post* 2000). Sponsors included *The National Post*, Air Canada, HSBC Securities, KPMG, Yorkton Securities and Canaccord Capital. The conference was described as "a platform for education industry leaders and the investment community to discuss unique opportunities in this emerging industry." Its website notes the expansion of the industry. "This year's summit deals with the continued rapid growth of the education industry evidenced by revenues reaching US$98.5 billion in 1999 according to Eduventures, a US education market research company." The particular technological dimensions of this growth are reflected in the testimonial of John Chambers, the CEO of Cisco Systems, who proclaimed that the "next big killer application for the Internet is going to be education. Education over the Internet is going to be so big it is going to make e-mail look like a rounding error."

Industrializing education makes the teacher a content entrepreneur and the student an individualized consumer (Arnold 1996:238-39; Bowe and Ball 1992:36). The student as consumer may seem to gain a certain element of control ("choice") over her or his education, although it falls far short of full democratic participation. At the same time, the student-consumer is produced as a consumable by the entrepreneurial educational system. Indeed, in many ways it is business that acts as the final consumer for the educational system, buying the labour-power of the self-commodifying students as they graduate.

The regime of standardized testing that is being introduced as part of education reform also fits the entrepreneurial orientation. One characteristic of commodification is that quality is reduced to quantity so that everything can be measured against everything else. The regime of standardized testing provides quantitative measures of the accomplishments of individuals students and of educational institutions. The emphasis, then, is on "quantitative measures of performance in instrumentally defined areas of competency" (Arnold 1996:240). This relentless quantification establishes the performance of every student in relation to all others. Apple (1996:32) describes this as "a system in which children will be ranked and ordered as never before." The commodification of knowledge is expressed in the quantification of learning and in the competitive individualism created by the testing culture and increases the opportunity for failure.

## Market Mechanisms in Education

The institutional structure of the educational system is being reorganized to fit with the new entrepreneurial orientation. It is not only the content but also the form of education that "speaks" to students, locating them within a regime of administration.[16] Institutions organized along public administration lines are unlikely to produce the entrepreneurial culture required for the formation of self-commodifying individuals. New methods of private sector management are replacing the methods of public administration, both within the educational system and within the state more generally (Shields and Evans 1998). The educational system is now being restructured to incorporate market mechanisms, direct corporate participation and lean management strategies.

These new management strategies are important for achieving the goals of education reform. In the next section, I will discuss the resistance this new educational regime has met in Ontario. In Thatcher's Britain, it took a long period of policy adjustment to develop the variety of free-market strategies that made neo-liberal education reform acceptable (Johnson 1991:39). Private sector management methods cloak the ideological character of education reform in the impersonal garb of market mechanisms, lending the aura of inevitability to a specific political agenda.

The development of market mechanisms at all levels of the educational system is a crucial element in this restructuring. The Ontario government is fostering competition throughout the system. Direct commercialization and fictitious market mechanisms are being deployed to create market-like pressures on administrators, educators and students.[17] These market mechanisms seem to bring a certain democratic accountability to an educational system that has been marked by bureaucratic control (Avis 1996a:111). The left must be careful here not to get trapped in the defence of bureaucratic regulation, arguing instead for genuine democratic control that points forwards to a revolutionized educational system rather than backwards to the liberal state.

Mark Holmes argues that the introduction of parental choice in schooling is the crucial foundation for systemic change. "What reform has to do is to set conditions where parents can choose the kind of education they want and make it difficult for those supplying the service to resist" (Holmes 1998:223). The agents of choice in this model are clearly to be the parents rather than the children. "We should reject the idea that the state must endow all children with significant educational choices in the classroom" (15). Indeed, this model privatizes the responsibility for education and lays more on the shoulders of parents, which in actual practice is likely to mean primarily mothers (see Delhi 1995:113). This model is founded on a particular construction of parenthood. "The parent who owns his child, the parent who consumes education" (Johnson 1991:75-76). The mechanisms that claim to increase accountability will also reduce the control of students over their own education.

The idea of choice sounds appealingly open-ended. Holmes said that he favoured providing "parents with choices, many of which will be opposed to my own" (Holmes 1998:15). Yet the rhetoric of choice disguises the extent to which government policy has already shaped the range of available options. In Ontario, school choice is to be based on standardized test results that will be central to the new school "report cards" to be issued to parents (Mackie 2001). Indeed, the medium-term fallout of the new funding formula in Ontario schools is likely to lead to a much narrower range of schooling, with fewer neighbourhood and alternative schools. Meanwhile, at the post-secondary level the provincial government is using its funding power to favour particular programs and institutions.[18] The actual terrain of choice, then, is determined in advance by the shift to post-liberal education (except perhaps for those who can opt for private schooling).

Further, the focus on parental choice is tied to the ideology of consumerism that reduces freedom to the act of choosing between commodities on the market. It leaves aside the real limits in market mechanisms, where profitability determines the limited variety of products that are actually available for consumption and structured social inequality dramatically limits access to market goods. The actual "freedom" of choice has to be considered in the light of the social forces that influence acts of consumption. Parents (and students) make educational decisions on the basis of their own material circumstances (including actual limits on time, financial resources and access to information) under the influence of shifting conceptions of common sense in light of political and economic changes (see Bowe, Ball and Gewirtz 1994:43-47). Consumerist ideology isolates the moment of choice from the broader plane of social, political and economic interchange and therefore provides an impoverished idea of freedom.

Remaking the educational system around the idea of consumer choice sets educational institutions up as businesses in competition for students (Deem 1994:27). The introduction of charter schools (autonomous institutions within the public system distinguished by a specific mission) is one tool to create a competitive environment. Thus far, Alberta is the only province in Canada to have introduced charter schools (see Dobbin 1997; Robertson et al. 1995). In Ontario, a competitive environment is being fostered without the introduction of charter schools through the use of published school rankings based on student achievement in standardized tests (see Kidder 2001).

At the post-secondary level, educational competition is being intensified at every level. Departments and disciplines are pitted against each other in a Darwinian dance for resources in which the losers are marked for extinction. The primary criterion for success in this dance seems to be student enrolment. The survival of disciplines that seem less directly "practical" is clearly threatened by this competition (see Engell and Dangerfield 1998). Universities and colleges are marketing themselves as never before in order to compete for the student enrolment that is crucial to their funding base. Finally, this competition will be heated up by the introduction of new private institutions, some of which will operate on a highly marketized model. The Ontario government is in the process of recognizing certain private institutions, most importantly the for-profit University of Phoenix that has introduced a highly standardized curriculum, delivered almost exclusively by contract teachers who are not responsible for course design (see Traub 1997:114; *Windsor Star* 2000).

Directly commercializing education relations is an important part of the shift to a market-like regime of administration. The commercialization of education is to be accomplished through privatization of certain functions, user pay, corporate sponsorships or partnerships and the opening up of spaces in the education system for commercial participation. It seems likely that the government will encourage the development of private institutions at the post-secondary level. Private schools already exist in Ontario and the government is promoting them through the introduction of a tax credit for parents who send their children for private education (see Urquhart 2001). Private tutoring is growing dramatically in Ontario, given the pressure of the new curriculum and standardized test requirements (see Fine 2000). Beachheads of privatization are also being opened through the outsourcing of certain services and activities, ranging from food services to curriculum consultants.

The principle of user pay is a crucial feature in this commercialization, particularly at the post-secondary level. Students fees across Canada increased by 62 percent in real terms over the period 1990–95 (Little 1997). Canadian university tuition fees increased 126 percent in 1991–2001 (up 140 percent in Ontario), while college fees went up 200 percent (McIlroy 2001:A7). By 1997–98, tuition fees provided 31.6 percent of the costs of running Canadian universities, up from 13 percent in 1979–80 (Tudiver 1999:159). Students who have to cover an increasing portion of the costs of their education are drawn into a more entrepreneurial orientation, in part because their own increasing debt forces them to focus very specifically on the employment opportunities that will follow their graduation. The average student debt was more than $25,000 by the year 2000. Further, user pay teaches students that they have a right to nothing that they cannot purchase (albeit with credit). At the primary and secondary levels, user pay is currently most likely to take the form of relentless fundraising for activities and facilities. While this stops short of the radical disentitlement created by fee paying, it is certainly creating a generation of chocolate bar entrepreneurs who are focused on selling as the means to almost any end.

The commercialization is intensified by a dramatic increase in the presence of corporations within educational settings. Barlow and Robertson (1994:79) argue that corporations have three major goals for their participation in the education system: to gain the ideological allegiance of the young to the free market system; to obtain access to young consumers; and to train a suitable workforce. Certainly, the opportunity to meet these goals is increasing as the direct corporate presence in educational institutions expands.

Educational policy in Ontario now actively promotes corporate participation, particularly in the form of partnerships.[19] Capital expenditures on university and college campuses in Ontario are funded through the "Superbuild" program that stipulates that government contributions be matched through fundraising (Ibbitson 2000b). The major contributors to such funding are corporations and wealthy individuals. Institutions are therefore most likely to embark on projects that appeal to potential sponsors and fit with the orientation of the province's pro-business education policy. New capital projects in post-secondary institutions are thus heavily weighted towards commerce and high-technology. Another important form of partnership in post-secondary education is the commercialization of university research. Funding programs and university policies are being reoriented towards promoting research with direct market value. Tudiver wrote that, "Over the course of about 25 years government has replaced university grants with programs targeted for commercialization of research." (Tudiver 1999:152). Smaller-scale sponsorships are also creating a higher-profile corporate presence in schools, colleges and universities. Soft drink companies, for example, have offered financial contributions to educational institutions in exchange for exclusive marketing rights in those locations (8). These contracts sometime gear contributions to sales and thus may in effect give the institution an interest in higher product sales (Turk 2000:4). They also include projects aimed directly at the curriculum – teaching materials bearing corporate logos or "educational" television programs that include advertisements, for example. Heather-jane Robertson (1998:199-233) has written a chapter that examines a wide range of corporate strategies to gain access to the youth market and influence teaching.

Commercialization both provides direct marketing opportunities to corporations and changes the character of educational spaces. The erosion of non-commercialized public spaces reduces the social to the commercial. In other words, the possibilities for coming together with others are increasingly limited to commercial spaces. The common spaces at universities, for example, which had been used by a variety of clubs and associations to promote political and social activities up until the 1990s, are increasingly being displaced by on-campus malls and rent-paying commercial tables selling products. The next "free speech"struggle on campuses will likely have to confront not only institutional administrations but also the enterprises that have consumed the physical spaces for speech.

This is simply one feature in a broader commodification of childhood and youth. The development of a specific youth market in the 1940s and 1950s was an important condition for the rise of specific heterosexual youth culture in the secondary schools (see Adams 1997). The commodification of childhood and youth has since become more intensive (deeper implication in commercial relations) and more extensive (reaching a wider age range and more diverse population). Denby points out this shift in his examination of changes in the teen movie from documents of youth rebellion to representations of the autonomous commercialized spaces that teenagers inhabit. "It's a teen world, bounded by school, mall and car, with occasional moments set in fast-food outlets where kids work, or in the kids' upstairs bedrooms, with their pin-ups and rack stereo systems" (Denby 1999:96)

Children are being drawn deeper at ever-younger ages into the realm of commercialized culture. Indeed, commercial products that provide a specific ground for play and fantasy are being increasingly colonizing the imaginations of children. Giroux argues that we need to take seriously the cultural impact of children's films. "Unlike the often hard-nosed, joyless reality of schooling, children's films provide a high-tech, visual space where adventure and pleasure meet in a fantasy world of possibilities and a commercial sphere of consumerism and commodification" (Giroux 1994:26. The identification of pleasure, the fantasy world and commercial products is one crucial aspect of the extension of commodification processes deeper into everyday life, including that of children. The commercialization of education is naturalized in a world where pleasure and self-realization are increasingly tied to the consumption of commodities. Eroding non-commercialized spaces is one feature of a multi-dimensional process that increasingly locks the self into circuits of commodification. Of course, this process can never be completed as collective struggles always open up new possibilities for expression linked to action.

## Towards Lean Education

The shift to a more entrepreneurial orientation in education finally requires the adoption of private sector management strategies associated with lean production. The management of the educational system has particular significance given its high profile and formative mission. It is difficult to imagine that an educational system that is not itself "lean" would serve as the ideal place to transmit the lean ethos to a new generation. The education system was a "model" of public administration that communicated a state-oriented citizenship ethos to students. Now the aim is to transform it into a model of lean managerialism that can contribute to the development of the lean ethos.

As I discussed in the Introduction, the goal of lean production is to enhance productivity by deploying new technologies, eliminating "waste" associated with older methods and organizing work in new ways. These methods are being brought into the educational sector as part of a set of new managerial strategies. Wotherspoon (1991:17) stated that educational retrenchment in Canada has focused around four key strategies: organizational rationalization, downsizing, privatization and increased managerial control. These strategies are crucial to the project of creating a lean, mean educational system.

One of the first steps in the leaning of the educational system is to teach educational practitioners that existing practices are wasteful. Harry V. Roberts a firm advocate of lean methods in education, wishes to train our eyes to detect the waste in the current state of things. "These wastes are pervasive, but not obvious until faculty start learning how to look for them. Once faculty catch on to the idea of waste elimination, they will find that the potential for improvement is much greater than they would have imagined" (Roberts 1995:2). A central feature of the education reform agenda has been the redefinition of current practices as wasteful. The view that contemporary educational processes are wasteful has very influential advocates, such as the 75 percent of corporate executives who responded to a poll by stating that it is possible to cut costs significantly without harming the quality of education (see Barlow and Robertson 1994:15). The Ontario government has devoted considerable resources to the campaign to persuade the public that teachers are underworked in this wasteful system.

Roberts (1995) specifically argues for the use of Total Quality Management (TQM), one of the crucial strategies associated with lean production. TQM uses the language of "quality" to provide criteria for the evaluation of organizational efficiency in meeting a set of clearly defined (and measurable) goals. Influential bodies such as the Conference Board of Canada, now argue that TQM provides a model for restructuring the administration of education (Barlow and Robertson 1994:15). Part of the power of TQM as an administrative strategy is that it pretends to provide a set of objective measures of quality, even if in reality this proves to be narrow and partial (Hart 1996:51). The development of appropriate indicators for educational quality has been an area of tremendous interest in Canadian and international education policy (Gilbert 1994:44).

TQM is one tool that is being used to transform students into customers (Tasker and Packham 1994:155). One of its central ideas is that the most important measure of 'quality' is customer satisfaction. These standards therefore seem to bring some degree of accountability to bureaucratic educational institutions (Roberts 1995:243-44; Wideman 1995:4). For example, educational "consumers" in Ontario now have specific measures by which to assess schools, colleges and universities, including standardized test scores, post-graduation placement rates and the incidence of student loan defaults. This is supposed to function as a consumer guide to the "best buys"(Hart 1996:38). Yet these criteria are very narrow and may have very little to do with a particular individual's desires in the education area.

TQM also provides a transmission belt for generalizing education reforms between institutions in a competitive marketized environment. TQM scoring is used to identify "best practices" which are used to establish standards for all "competitors" (see Arnold 1996:234). Yet these standards often have an averaging effect. Hart (1996:42) argues that this regime of control tends to pushing all towards some central measure of acceptable quality that should be met yet not exceeded. For example, the development of a new provincial funding formula for education in Ontario has used the median school board as a benchmark for assessing space requirements and overall costs. The focus, then, is more on the measure of board against board than it is on the adequacy of educational funding to meet the actual needs of a given population in specific circumstances. The benchmark system does not factor in the greater costs that might be associated with a concentration of non-anglophone students or a disadvantaged population (Mackenzie 1999).

The emphasis on benchmarks represents an important instance of centralizing administrative control over the education system. The central authority (in this case, the province) establishes the benchmarks and hence gains tremendous control over the work of school boards. In Britain, education reform involved important elements of centralization combined with specific forms of decentralization – for example, granting greater autonomy to individual schools (see Arnold 1996:242-43; Deem

1994:29; and Johnson 1991:68). Similarly, a centralized regime of standards is being combined with a degree of decentralization – for example, through the creation of school councils. Kazolana (1996:104-6) suggests that parent or school councils in Britain, Canada and New Zealand have been associated with increased centralized bureaucracy, declining equality of opportunity, corporatization, privatization and an undermining of democratic accountability such as that represented by elected school trustees.

The commodification of education and the coercive turn of discipline fit together. The welfare state period represented the high-water mark for a moral economy of working-class childhood. This moral economy needs to be swept away to open up childhood to capitalist intensification. The contemporary attack on childhood is in many ways parallel to the destruction of the moral economy of the working class to establish the normalcy of wage-labour relations (see McNally 1993; Thompson 1993a). The suppression of alternatives to wage-labour, and the eradication of ways of life and expectations that impeded the full assimilation of adults into the regime of wage-labour was a crucial historical task for capitalists, achieved through considerable coercion and violence (Corrigan 1977; Thompson 1968). Capitalist intensification now requires the destruction of the moral economy of childhood that solidified through the welfare state period. The contemporary education reform agenda fits with the broader shift in the conception of childhood associated with the process of restructuring and an increased orientation to the market.

## Notes

1. This "end of childhood" literature is discussed in Stephens (1995) and Thorne (1987:91), who refers to it as a "wave of books with almost interchangeable titles."
2. This time crunch derives directly from the character of capitalist production, which has rationalized and intensified time from the outset (see Harvey 1985:37).
3. See Canadian Council on Social Development (CCSD)1999:14 and Guy 1997:157 for discussions of the stress on parents (particularly mothers) of combining paid and unpaid work.
4. School swimming pools that had been available through the municipal recreation system might now be closed to public use as the principle of user pay means that the school board is now charging the City fees for the use of the pools (Lawlor 2001).
5. This discussion of homework arose out of discussions with friends who have school-age children in Ontario. Their reports of a sharply increased homework load with the introduction of the new curriculum seem very consistent.
6. Charges brought under this legislation in its first year of operation were being legally challenged. Many charges were dropped as they would not stand up in court. However, some of the charges proceeded (Abbate 2001).
7. This parallels links between police, social service agencies and schools in the intensified criminalization of black youth in Britain in the 1970s and 1980s (Carby 1983:207).
8. See Galt 1998c for a discussion of the impact of consumerism on students from families with lower incomes.
9. One of the frustrations of the burgeoning literature on consumerism and identity is that much of it detaches consumption from production and ignores the relationship of wage-labour to processes of commodification. Featherstone (1991), for example, rejects a focus on production relations in the examination of consumer society.
10. Topalov (1985) reminds us that workers and other activists do not necessarily get what they want when they make demands on the state. A process of displacement occurs through the policy-making process so that demands in one area can produce outcomes in another.
11. The waves of industrial and public sector unionization in the Canadian state in the 1940s and 1960s–70s dramatically increased the proportion of workers who were active consumers (having choices in the market place). This contributed to the intensified commodification of everyday life, as did the post-1970 economic crisis that pushed capital to colonize new frontiers by extending deeper into everyday life. For a theoretical discussion of these processes that is not specifically Canadian, see Brosio (1991).
12. On the thrall and danger of commodity fetishism: commodity fetishism includes both the joy of desire and the fear of failure. The fulfillment of attaining the commodity is sharpened by the knowledge that it might not have happened and the threat that it might not last. I am drawing here on Benjamin's (1999a:511, 515) discussion of prostitution and gambling.
13. This quote is cited in full in Chapter 2.
14. For a discussion of this orientation towards measurable outcomes, see Avis (1991:119), Jackson (1992), Robertson, Soucek, Pannu and Schugurensky (1995:91) and Wideman (1995:4).
15. Chapter 13 in Volume 4 of the Royal Commission on Learning (1994) waxes very enthusiastic about the learning possibilities opened up by information technology.
16. Corrigan and Sayer (1985) argues that the form of the state "speaks." The institutional structure of the state is a crucial feature of regimes of administration.
17. Readings (1996:36) argues that what is occurring in post-secondary restructuring is actually "the highly artificial creation of a fictional market that presumes exclusive governmental control of funding."

18. See Ibbitson (2000b) for a discussion of the ways post-secondary funding is being used to change the character of post-secondary education, particularly the shift away from arts and social sciences towards high technology, information technology and life sciences.
19. This is not limited to Ontario. Weeks (1995:91) argues that the New Brunswick Commission of Excellence in Education was "preoccupied" with partnerships with businesses.

# Chapter 7

# Learning Freedom

In the preceding chapters, I argued that a new post-liberal regime of education is emerging in the context of a shift to the lean state that serves to promote the generalization of lean production methods. Liberal education reached its pinnacle during the period of the broad welfare state as part of the apparatus for the development of social citizenship – it contributed to the formation of citizens by teaching students to locate themselves in relation to the state. The very form of liberal education, including the space of the classroom itself, has been tied to the process of creating citizens. In the classroom, students developed their selves in relation to the state, as personified by the teacher at the front of the room. Liberal education inserted students into citizenship relations by rehearsing the appropriate norms and expectations for adult citizenship.

The lean production restructuring agenda driving the emergence of the lean state is hostile to the forms of social citizenship that developed during the period of the broad welfare state. Social citizenship is seen as an obstacle to restructuring as it creates a sense of entitlement outside of market relations. This sense of entitlement could be understood in E.P. Thompson's (1993a) terms as a "moral economy" of citizenship, the outcome of a long history of working-class mobilization around workplace, democratic and economic justice issues. The neo-liberal Harris government attempted to make a revolution in common sense by crushing this moral economy, just as their classical liberal forebears struggled to defeat earlier forms of moral economy to create a disciplined working class in the first place.

Education reform is aligned with the reorientation of social policy towards the lean state. The cultural dimension of liberal education is seen as a problematic mediation in a lean world based on intensified commodification. The education reform agenda aims to shift the emphasis of schooling away from the cultural orientation of liberal education. This is less about the content of education than the form, which is increasingly instrumental in its focus on teaching specific measurable skills and the transfer of specific information. The priority of post-liberal education is to equip students to market themselves in a world where there is nothing outside the market.

Post-liberal education attacks the moral economy of citizenship. It is tied to a logic of commodification without borders, in which the capitalist market reaches every corner of the globe and penetrates every crack of social life. Yet this unbound commodification still needs the mediation of the state. At the very least, all alternatives to the market need to be suppressed. But more than that, the workers' selves need to be aligned with the market. It is not true that the thrall of commodification spontaneously seduces all who catch a bright glimpse of its charms. On the contrary, the glow of the commodity is but a pale refection of suppressed desires for a better world, shining only in a world made dull by the compulsion of wage-labour and the stunting of all gratification save that to be had through shopping.[1]

Post-liberal education seeks to produce selves who seek commodification, in part because they know nothing else. It is therefore the appropriate mode of education for an emerging lean world, though not on the basis of meeting the technical requirements for ever-smarter high-tech production. Rather, post-liberal education aims to produce a disciplined and entrepreneurial workforce who will accept the highly polarized and insecure conditions of lean production.

The shift to post-liberal education seems to have acquired an air of inevitability given this fit with the conditions of a lean world. It has certainly become the platform of political parties of all stripes. But there is nothing inevitable about this transformation. Indeed, as the next section will discuss, there are powerful forces that can mobilize to challenge at least some of the features of post-liberal education. However, the likelihood of success at challenging the right-wing education reform agenda is much more limited if the horizons of the opposition are limited to changes within schools, colleges and universities. Instead, opposition to post-liberal education must go hand in hand with a broader struggle against lean production and the capitalist logic that drives it.

In the rest of this chapter I discuss the actual fight against the Harris education reform agenda in Ontario and offer some ideas about what education for real freedom might look like. The opposition to the Harris government's education policies was widespread, at times producing huge mobilizations such as the 1997 teachers' strike. This opposition had tremendous potential and yet did not succeeded in stopping the key aspects of education restructuring. I argue that part of the blame for this lies in the tactics of the opposition movements, tactics that have tended to be self-limiting.

I end on what might seem to be a rather utopian note, with a discussion of the ways in which education can serve the cause of real freedom. Specifically, I examine the ideas of teaching and learning that are contained in the works of the German communist writer Bertolt Brecht. I raise these ideas here because I think it is important to have a sense of what we are really fighting for in these struggles around education. We need to move beyond the defence of a flawed liberal education against the destructive right-wing education reform agenda. I believe that the opposition movements we build can provide important workshops for developing forms of education for freedom that align theory and practice.

## Fighting Back

The most important single factor in shattering the apparent inevitability of the shift to post-liberal education is mobilized opposition. Potentially powerful forces have been unleashed in the fight against aspects of the education reform agenda in Ontario. Teachers' mobilizations reached a pinnacle during a two-week teachers' strike in October and November 1997. High-school students participated in a wave of walk-outs leading up to that strike. University students have demonstrated against tuition fee increases and the restructuring of post-secondary education. Unionized teaching assistants have used their leverage as workers to win protection against tuition increases. Non-teaching education workers have struck back against the degradation of their conditions of work in the face of cutbacks and restructuring. Parents have fought against school closures. School board trustees have fought against legislation that ties their hands in budget processes.

The introduction of post-liberal education has been a struggle and the government has had to temper parts of its program and negotiate the terms of implementation. Yet the opposition to date has been far from decisive, despite its immense potential. Public opinion around education reform seems to be highly contradictory, shifting in complex ways depending on the state of the mobilization and the ways in which issues are posed. Many of the core elements of the post-liberal agenda, which will totally transform the education system over time, have been effectively implemented. The sense of resignation among the opposition forces is palpable and the political consensus among all political parties is quite solid. The sense that "there is no alternative" hangs over the education battlefield in Ontario. I want to argue here that it could have been different and still could be in the future.

The Harris government has met considerable resistance to its attempts to implement the shift to post-liberal education. Teachers, education workers, university faculty, teaching assistants, students, parents, school trustees and community members have fought back in various ways against aspects of the Harris government's education agenda. I will argue in this section that this resistance has been most effective when it has been most audacious in challenging the broader political direction of education restructuring. This audacity is important as it allows the opposition to pierce the aura of inevitability that the government has tried to construct around its educational, economic and social policies.

### Teachers on the Front Line

The high point of the resistance was the illegal two-week political strike by teachers in 1997 that challenged the government's agenda in the education realm. The Harris government reached its lowest point of popularity during its first term in office around the time of the teachers' strike (*The Globe and Mail* 1999; Ibbitson 2001). Once that strike ended, the opposition was limited largely to quibbling over the terms of the restructuring, a far less inspiring project.

The teachers' union called off the 1997 strike after two weeks, without having made any gains. This, together with the winding down of the labour-led Days of Action campaign against the Harris government, took much of the wind out of the sails of the opposition on the education front. As the time of writing, there are hopeful signs of a new wind in those sails, this time originating with the global justice and anti-poverty movements that have mobilized new forms of militant protest in (amongst other places) Vancouver, Seattle, Prague, Melbourne, Windsor and Quebec. The teaching and research assistants, and sessional faculty of CUPE Local 3903 at York University won a remarkable victory in a strike that was launched almost exactly three years after the great teachers' strike. A key layer of activists in that local was deeply involved in global justice and anti-poverty mobilizations. The CUPE Local 3903 strike showed some return to the audacity of the 1997 teachers' strike, linking specific contract demands to issues of quality, accessible education.

In 1997, Ontario's school system was totally shut down by a two-week political strike that united all five teachers' unions, representing 126,000 people.[2] This was the largest teachers' strike in Canadian history. It very successfully drew together the specific defence of teachers' working conditions with a broader resistance to the government's education agenda. The fight escalated when the government introduced Bill 160, the legislative core of education restructuring that changed funding processes, systems of governance and labour relations. The legislation centralized power over education, including aspects of labour relations. The provincial government adopted new powers to impose class sizes and working conditions (Lewington 1997). Local School Boards had already been merged and reorganized through an earlier piece of legislation (Bill 104). Bill 160 took away most of their powers. It eventually came to represent the whole agenda of education 'reform' in Ontario. A leaflet produced by the Ontario Education Alliance during this strike reflects the broad claims the opposition staked out at the time. "Teachers are standing up for our children. This isn't just a fight between teachers and the Harris Government. It's a fight by parents, students, communities and teachers who want a quality public education system that puts our children first. We are proud to stand with them" (Ontario Education Alliance strike leaflet n.d. [1997]).

The 1997 teachers' strike represented the end point of a longer term mobilization dating back to the social contract introduced by the previous NDP government. The social contract attacked the wages and working conditions of all provincial government employees and workers in the broader public sector funded by the province. Teachers played a leading role in the public sector mobilization against the social contract (Martell 1995).

Teachers had already established patterns of activism when the Harris government was elected in 1995. The new government's education reform agenda combined a general policy reorientation with specific attacks on teachers' working conditions as established by collective agreements. These were combined with a specific campaign of teacher-bashing (Walkom 1997) that reflected an animosity that seemed almost personal. See, for example, this response by Mike Harris to teacher resistance when preparatory time was cut: "I thought there was enough time left in their day and weekends and evenings and summer and Christmas and school breaks to do some preparation" (*The Globe and Mail* 1998b, A5).

## Teacher-Bashing and Education Reform

Attacking teachers and their unions is a necessary strategic feature of the contemporary education reform agenda. The strategic importance of politically defeating teachers is outlined, for example, in an American plan for education reform developed for the Rand Corporation by Hill, Pierce and Guthrie (1997). This plan is notable for its explicit strategic vision. I am not claiming that this specific plan influenced the Harris government, but rather that it provides an important example of the logic of the strategic calculation required to accomplish education reform in the current period.

The Rand Corporation report calls for the creation of a competitive market by contracting out the education system school by school. The central education authority would set performance indicators and provide core funding, and the contractors running a particular school would be responsible for meeting the established performance indicators within a specific budget. In essence the plan makes every school a charter school, opening up competition as parents could choose where to send their children (Hill et al. 1997:vii-ix). The study anticipates resistance. "Caution is called for when introducing market ideas and competition into public education, however. There is an obvious demand for and support of public schools. Schools produce services that are highly valued by most citizens" (78).

The study advocates coalition-building, particularly oriented around mobilizing parents, to accomplish change (Hill et al. 1997:191-3). Teacher unions (or specifically "leaders of teacher-union locals") are cited as likely opponents of this reform strategy, along with legislators dependent on teacher-union political contributions, other professional education groups, career administrators and school board members (196-97). The report lays out a systematic strategy to reorganize teaching, undermine teachers' unions and reconfigure the organizational structures of the education system.

The reorganization of teaching in this plan has three dimensions. First, Hill, Pierce and Guthrie (1997:158) call for a shift in the fundamental employment relations in education to create a "true labour market" so that teaching jobs are no longer "lifetime civil service posts." Current practices tend to standardize teaching as pay and conditions are based on credentials and seniority. This creates a "civil service mentality" that "discourages individuals who want to be regarded as true professionals and are willing to make the added effort necessary for high performance" (78). The report aims to establish a far more differentiated teaching labour force, in which lead teachers (rewarded with performance-based pay) would develop and organize the courses to be delivered by ordinary teachers and teacher aids (1997:18, 40, 78-79). The front-line teacher would be deskilled and have her autonomy reduced as control devolved towards a limited number of lead teachers.

At the same time, teachers' unions would be radically fragmented as organizing and bargaining would by conducted on a school by school basis (1997:6, 158). This fragmentation would dramatically reduce the ability of teachers to have an impact on education policy. The fragmented teachers' unions would face an administrative structure that was at once more centralized and decentralized than the current system. The state would have responsibility for setting standards, controlling quality and conducting standardized tests (1997:151-52). The rest of the administrative responsibility would devolve to the school.

As I stated above, this report is useful to us here as it is explicitly strategic, bluntly discussing the opportunities and constraints that shape the field of education reform. At this point, it seems safe to say that the specific choice of contracting out all schools is not on the map of education reform policy in Ontario. Yet this book is in many ways a visionary and politically explicit version of the education reform agenda that is guiding the transition to post-liberal education across Canada and in many other places. At the most general level, the project of education reform combines elements of standardization (standardized testing to measure the outcome of more standardized teaching), a shift to market model administration (whether through contracting out, state funding of private schools, intensified competition for students and resources, charter schools or vouchers) and a simultaneous centralization and decentralization of administration.

One of the key elements of this general project is the leaning of education work, restructuring along lean production lines to accomplish differentiation, intensification and work reorganization. Teaching is highly labour-intensive. Productivity gains in the education sector are difficult to accomplish and are likely to lag behind those in more technology-intensive sectors (see Vision 2000 1990:72-73). Throughout the period of the broad welfare state, increased productivity in the education sector was accomplished largely through administrative consolidation and increases in class sizes. The administrative consolidations included the merger of school districts, the creation of larger schools and the closure of smaller schools, particularly in rural areas. Barlow and Robertson (1994:4) argue that the post-World War II period saw a major focus on administrative efficiencies, including school and district consolidations. The period of the Robarts reforms in Ontario in the 1960s was one of consolidation in the face of pressing numbers (Fiorino 1978:41).

These consolidations sought efficiencies primarily outside of the classroom, by reducing the amount of custodial, administrative and service work per student. Increased class size was really the only method available to increase efficiency (as measured in capitalist terms by productivity per worker) inside the classroom. Yet increased class sizes conflicted directly with the learner-centred pedagogies that came to dominate high liberal education. There were some attempts to use closed-circuit television and other technologies to transform teaching in the 1960s and 1970s (to transmit lectures to more than one classroom at a time, for example) but with very limited results. The ghosts of these reforms continued to haunt some university classrooms for a long time, in the form of disused monitors hanging from the walls.

There are, then, two reasons that attacks on teachers and their unions are an important feature of the education reform agenda. First, the position of teachers as workers in the education system needs to be weakened to permit the introduction of leaner work processes. Second, teachers represent a politically powerful voice against elements of the emerging system of post-liberal education. A detailed analysis of the reasons that many teachers identify strongly with at least some of the elements of liberal education is not possible here but I would speculate that three factors are involved. First, a significant proportion of the current cohort of teachers was drawn into teaching at the highest point of liberal education in the 1960s and 1970s. Particularly given the political climate of the times, it seems reasonable to assume that many of those who chose teaching as an occupation identified with at least some of the values of the liberal education. Second, student-centred approaches to education require teacher discretion and autonomy in the classroom and therefore contribute to the professionalization of teaching. Finally, there is bound to be some conservatism among teachers who simply do not want to change what they have been doing for many years and how they have been doing it.

There is, then, a relationship between liberal education, the professionalization of teaching and an increase in the amount of power that teachers have in the classroom and in the system. Teachers must yield considerable ground if the education reform agenda is to succeed. The only way to avoid confrontation is if teachers' unions are in a concessionary mode from the outset, as has been the case in many other jurisdictions in the United States and Canada. In Ontario, however, the education reform agenda came up against a mobilized teaching community, linked to a broader activist response to neo-liberal restructuring. The mobilization against the Harris government included a campaign of city-by-city one-day shutdowns that included massive participation by teachers. The campaign against the Harris government's education agenda was integrated with a broader fightback against anti-union laws and cuts to social programs.

Ontario teachers were not willing to unilaterally cede ground that they had gained on a number of fronts over a period dating from the 1960s to the 1980s. Larry Kuehn (1995a:57) argues that management control over teachers' labour eroded during this period for three reasons: the professionalization of teaching, the increasing complexity of schooling and collective bargaining rights. Ontario teachers won the right to collective bargaining and full unionization in 1975, after a long struggle that culminated in a one-day illegal strike that largely shut down the province's school system (Smaller 1995:348-49).

The wave of activism that produced teacher unionization was still within recent memory when the challenges of the social contract arose. The Rae government hit teachers on three fronts: the social contract eroding public sector labour rights; the beginnings of a restructuring process aimed oriented towards developing a post-liberal system in Ontario, particularly represented by the Royal Commission on Learning; and significant cuts to educational funding (Martell 1995:1, 10-11). Teachers responded with substantial mobilizations, often forming the backbone of local coalitions to defend public sector workers (Martell 1995).

## Mobilizing Against the Harris Agenda

Teachers responded to the Harris government agenda by mobilizing. The response to a demonstration called by the Catholic teachers' union (OECTA) in January 1996 was a surprisingly strong showing of about 40,000 protesters (Galt 1996b). Teachers also played a key role in the Days of Action, city-wide one-day strikes to protest against the Harris government's policies. In city after city, teachers were the largest delegation in mass demonstrations. My own impression from the day, for example, would be that teachers made up perhaps half of the 100,000 protesters on the Toronto Day of Action. Teachers also closed down schools when one-day local general strikes were called as part of the Days of Action (Munro 1997). This activity drew teachers' unions closer to the rest of the labour movement. The major high school teachers' unions (OSSTF and OECTA) joined the Canadian Labour Congress in 1996. Doug Little (1996:17) found a "fighting mood" at the March conventions of those unions.

In the lead-up to the 1997 strike, teachers held rallies and meetings in cities across the province. In Toronto, 24,000 teachers gathered at Maple Leaf Gardens and then marched on the Legislature. Across the province, perhaps 100,000 teachers attended these meetings and rallies, according to Ontario Teachers' Federation head Eileen Lennon. The level of mobilization was high in the lead up to the strike and it climbed even higher, with remarkable participation at picket lines and protest rallies. The picket lines were solid and only tiny numbers of teachers crossed. In Toronto, the province's capital and largest city, tens of thousands of teachers gathered three times to protest outside the Legislature and once at the Ministry of Education. I was at all of these rallies and they were loud and spirited.

The second week of the strike actually started well for the union. The Harris government went to court to try to get an injunction to force the teachers back to work. On Monday 3 November the injunction was turned down. This was a surprise to many who had expected the courts would act against an apparently illegal strike undertaken during the life of a contract (or, in fact, many contracts as teachers across the province bargain separately with their own school boards).

The striking down of the injunction should have been a moment of strength for the teachers. Yet, the common front of their unions soon began to fall apart. The elementary school unions (OPSTF and FWTAO) and the French-language union (AEFO) announced on Wednesday 5 November that they were calling for a return to work on 10 November. Once the injunction bid by the government failed, these unions wanted to ensure that there was a strategy for ending the strike.

Many teachers were angered by the response of their union leaders. On Friday 7 November, a meeting at the Hummingbird Centre in Toronto called by the elementary teachers' unions to discuss the return to work was stormy. The hall was rocked by teachers chanting, "We won't back down!" This was the slogan that the unions had used to mobilize. It was now thrown back at the union leaders who were in fact backing down. The union was forced to call a vote on the return to work for 9 November. In the end, two-thirds of the Toronto elementary teachers voted to return to work, in part because it was clear by Sunday that the rest of Ontario's teachers were returning to work.

The last of the rallies was held on Saturday 8 November, after the leaders of three of the unions had called for a return to work. While the numbers remained high and the solidarity support of unionists was striking, it was heart-rending to hear leader after leader refer to the strike as over. CUPE Ontario leader Sid Ryan won the largest cheer of the day when he called on other unions to join his union to "shut the province down." Yet his rhetoric sounded hollow when everyone present knew the teachers were returning to work and no further solidarity action was forthcoming.

The support for the strike was thoroughly impressive. On picket lines, parents showed up with coffee, doughnuts and support. High-school students were a real presence at picket lines and rallies. The popularity of the strike increased as it went on. The teachers' union leaders sounded the retreat as the strike was gaining support, just after the province had suffered a serious setback with the failure to win a court injunction. They were interested in a symbolic protest but not a real challenge to the government. Such a challenge might have required solidarity from other unions and that might have been possible at the time given the mobilization around the Days of Action campaigns. There were important moves by rank and file workers to widen the strike. A meeting of branch presidents and picket captains from District 15 of the Ontario Secondary Schools Teachers Federation voted on 3 November to urge their union leadership to ask the Ontario Federation of Labour for solidarity action. About thirty local presidents and stewards in the Ontario Public Service Employees Union voted on 4 November to call on their union leadership to build for solidarity strikes. But these small steps were not enough to build an independent fightback.

Turbulent labour relations have continued to be a feature of Ontario's education system since the 1997 teachers' strike. Teacher strikes have developed against local Boards of Education around contract negotiations. I cannot do justice here to the complex picture of these local negotiations. The work-to-rule has been an important feature of high school teacher resistance, particularly in response to the increase in class contact time and forced participation in after-school activities that the Ontario government has insisted on adding to contracts. Teachers in two-thirds of the province's school boards worked to rule and boycotted after-school activities to protest against these contractual changes during the 2000–01 school year.

## Fightbacks by Other Education Workers, High School Students and Parents

Other school staff members have also been involved in strike actions. There have been prominent school staff strikes in, for example, Toronto (1999 and 2001) and Windsor (2001) since 1997. The government funding formula pressures school boards to squeeze the teaching assistant, clerical, housekeeping and groundskeeping staff (Heath 1999:23). The fear of layoffs and contracting out has made job security a major issue in negotiations between staff and school boards.

High-school student walkouts have recurred during this period of turbulent labour relations in Ontario schools. Many student walkouts took place in the lead up to the 1997 strike. Students also walked out and protested against the disappearance of extra-curricular activities dues to teacher work-to-rule campaigns. They have organized in defence of schools threatened with closure, such as Windsor's W.D. Lowe School in 1999–2000. This pattern of student walkouts requires much closer investigation than space allows here. These walkouts often have a multi-sided character, combining elements of an outburst against school authoritarianism, a break in the routine, a protest against government and/or board policies, and a criticism of teachers for withdrawing their labour.[3]

Parent activism in various forms has been another feature of the education struggles in Ontario over the last number of years. Above, I noted that Hill et al. called for a coalition with parents as part of the strategy for winning education reform. The Ontario education reform agenda has included a series of measures, generally focused around ideas of accountability, that might serve to cement a coalition with parents. Parent councils in schools, for example, can serve as a new source of pressure on teachers in the name of accountability. Parents have been given new decision-making powers. For example, in the area of school uniforms where a majority of parents are now in a position to enforce them on a whole school. New success measures, whether of individual students (in the new report cards) or of whole schools (through the posting of test results), might also encourage parents' support for the education reform agenda. The language of choice and accountability is oriented largely towards parents.

At the same time, parents have not simply lined up with the education reform agenda in Ontario. The 1997 teachers' strike received tremendous support on the picket lines and, as stated above, showed growing support in public opinion. School closures have pushed parents in many localities to mount fightback campaigns. Parent councils can also serve as vehicles for resistance, as when Dundas Road School in Toronto boycotted the Grade 3 test in 1998 (Galt 1998d). The balance sheet of parent response to education reform cannot yet be drawn. It certainly seems that at those moments where some sort of serious resistance seems possible, there is significant parent support for the opposition to education reform. Yet there has also been important parent backing for different aspects of the restructuring agenda. This has varied from exasperation at the disruptive labour relations in Ontario's education system (that may or may not contain elements of union-blaming) to enthusiasm for testing and other elements of the new curriculum.

## Fightbacks in the Post-Secondary Sector

The post-secondary sector has also seen some important struggles in the face of restructuring. This has included some important labour struggles as well as some significant student mobilization. I will look at three strikes here and briefly discuss the patterns of student activism. I will also look quickly at the difference between universities and colleges in the area of activism, pointing to the need for further work in this area.

The picture of labour relations at Ontario universities is a complex one. Each institution is an independent employer and so levels of unionization vary significantly from campus to campus and employees doing different jobs are generally covered by separate contracts. The three strikes that I have chosen to look at here are closely linked to issues of education restructuring: the 1997 strike by faculty at York University (unionized through the York University Faculty Association (YUFA); the strike by groundskeepers, housekeepers and cafeteria workers at the University of Windsor (Canadian Union of Public Employees CUPE 1001), also in 1997; and the strike by graduate assistants and part-time faculty at York University (CUPE 3903) in 2000–01. I will discuss each strike very briefly and then discuss some common themes.

The YUFA strike at York was a response to negotiations marked by high management pressure for concessions. As the strike continued, a political realignment took place within the union that provided the basis for a higher level of solidarity among strikers and better links with students and potential supporters. Strike activists highlighted issues of equity, emphasizing in particular the distortion of salaries caused by years of restraint, creating a situation in which a whole layer of faculty, disproportionately made up of women and people of colour, was relatively underpaid (see Briskin and Newson 1999). The strike also raised issues of control over the labour process and technological change in teaching (Tudiver 1999:183).

The CUPE 1001 strike at the University of Windsor was also a fight against concessions. Specifically, management sought to roll back the parity the union had won in a previous contract between the pay of full-time and part-time employees. The union also fought to strengthen job security language to protect against the threat of contracting out jobs. Although the strike ended with some gains in these areas, the union did accept a two-tiered wage system that protected existing part-time workers but brought in new part-timers at substantially less than parity with full-time workers.

One of the important features of the strike was the high level of solidarity activity, which included designated "days of action" on which the university was largely shut down. The "days of action" were largely possible because campus unions and student activists had established new ways of working together through mobilization against cutbacks, particularly in February 1996. Indeed, a unity group of campus unions established in the build-up to the 7 February day of action (called by the Canadian Federation of Students) continued meeting and served as a crucial vehicle for solidarity in the CUPE 1001 strike. CUPE 1001 had a good record of fighting on student issues and the status of part-time employees (who were largely students) was a central issue in the strike. There was also considerable resistance to the strike on the part of some students on campus, who even organized clean-up campaigns that got volunteers to do the work of striking workers.

Finally, the CUPE 3903 strike at York focused largely on access to education issues. The union sought to index wages to tuition increases, providing graduate assistants with some protection at a time when universities were shifting rapidly towards user pay. This strike was notable for its membership mobilization, transparent bargaining that made negotiations unusually accountable and high solidarity, particularly from the important segment of faculty who shut down their classes. The university administration tried to end the strike by forcing a vote on their most recent contract offer, but it was rebuffed by the membership. The administration then tried to force faculty back to work, but with little success. The strike ended with important gains for the graduate assistants.

This brief examination of three strikes reminds us that university strikes are highly political, particularly at a time of education restructuring. The need for solidarity is intense as student activism can make a big difference in these strikes. The link between working conditions, quality, accessible education and the education reform agenda can prove an important axis in building a successful strike in this context.

University student protest has risen and fallen during this period. The Canadian Federation of Students (CFS) called a remarkably successful day of action on 25 January 1995 that led to the shut-down of many campuses across Canada. The mobilization at the University of Windsor was fantastic, with over 3,500 students marching and a sizeable contingent of auto workers in support. The federal government was moving towards a substantial reduction in its contribution to post-secondary education and a system of income-contingent loan repayment tied to a dramatic increase in tuition fees. The reduction in transfer payments and sharp tuition fee increases went ahead, although the government did not proceed with the program of income-contingent loan repayment.

The next year, the CFS called a day of action on 7 February. The response was patchier. At the University of Windsor about 1,000 people marched in the protest demonstration, which garnered much stronger support from campus unions. Teaching on campus was very limited. The next CFS day of action was not until 2000, with the Access 2000 campaign. In Windsor, a few hundred people marched and much of the campus was shut down. Student anger is often close to the surface in universities in Ontario as fees have increased dramatically, class sizes have climbed sharply and employment success upon graduation has been highly uncertain except in certain fields. However, that anger is often combined with a potent sense of helplessness and a claim that protest does not work.

At the same time as there was some tendency towards a more limited activism on the part of a broader mass of students, a militant minority explored new forms of protest. The 1996–97 school year saw a wave of occupations at universities across Ontario. The militant minority on campuses has broadened as the movement for global justice has developed from the demonstration against APEC in Vancouver through Seattle, Washington, Windsor, Quebec and Genoa. There is a significant possibility of some larger fightback emerging.

Resistance at the level of community colleges has been less overt than in the universities. Between 1991 and 2001 there does not seem to have been much mobilization on the part of college faculty. Nor have college students mobilized in the way their university peers have. The political atmosphere is somewhat different at colleges than university, as the school day tends to be more structured with less free time and students have not won the same free speech rights through historic struggles. A serious exploration of the politics of the college sector in Ontario would seem to be an important project for future research.

At a general level, then, the introduction of post-liberal education in Ontario has seen a very important wave of struggles. This has involved the mobilization of both the workers and the products (students) of the mind factory, as well as important forms of community activism. These struggles have been successful when they have been boldest, as it is only at those times that they seem to offer any alternative to education restructuring. When the opposition is confined to bickering over the terms of restructuring, the horizons of possibility contract substantially.

## Towards Education for Freedom

The liberal education classroom is a constrained learning situation and post-liberal methods threaten to reduce learning potential even further. Social relations in the classroom are not about learning in the sense of people developing the resources to control their bodies, their minds and their lives. The role of the teacher, the disinterested expert who is in the room to profess her or his accumulated knowledge, undermines learning. Co-operative learning processes are impossible in a situation where students form a community only through the mediation of the teacher and are placed in explicit or implicit competition for grades. The illusory community of the classroom is founded on the supposed superiority of an allegedly neutral body of racialized, gendered, classed and sexualized knowledge (culture and/or science) identified with the nation and reproduced through a series of statified institutions. Nor is this a single body of knowledge, but rather a fragmentation of ways of knowing to create a series of separate and therefore relatively meaningless subjects or disciplines. Further, classroom knowledge is profoundly disembodied and rooted in the separation of theory from practice.

This critique of liberal and post-liberal education would be incomplete without some discussion of a contrasting perspective on learning and teaching. My starting point for this other view is the work of the

German communist playwright and theorist Bertolt Brecht. This represents a deliberate choice to examine a theory of teaching and learning that originates outside the realm of formal education as institutionally defined. I want to start with a perspective in which schools, colleges and universities are not taken for granted as the prime location of "education." It should be obvious from the arguments that I have made above that I do not believe that problems will be solved by simply adding good content or exciting teaching methods to the current educational system. Fresh insights and methods will either be captured inside the system or frozen out. The best efforts of those of us working inside these institutions too often simply broaden the grasp of the system or reinforce its claims to genuine openness and inclusiveness.

This is not to dismiss struggles for decent teaching and more inclusive content within schools, colleges and universities, but rather to point out their limits. I believe we need to look beyond these institutions for conceptions of education as it could be. We can then use these insights to help us figure out ways to orient our day-to-day struggles within and against the education system around inspiring conceptions of real teaching and learning as they might become. Further, we can attempt to use these conceptions to structure experiments in those precious but very limited spaces that exist for "'our'" education associated with social movements, trade unions, the arts and, perhaps, on the margins of formal education settings.

## Brecht on Teaching and Learning

Bertolt Brecht was one of the key practitioners and theorists of innovative left-wing cultural production at one of its highest moments (roughly between the 1917 Russian Revolution and the consolidation of a cold war "world order" after World War II). Brecht attempted to develop a new form of theatre that was "useful" to the project of changing the world.[4] This was not simply a question of offering up an aesthicized version of "the line" to teach the workers. On the contrary, the Marxist vision of liberation requires self-conscious agency so that workers develop their own analysis of events as they act to change the world. This kind of analysis cannot simply be handed over as a gift, but rather must be actively developed by workers themselves in the process of developing their ability to organize and act. Brecht worked on a specific form of political theatre that aimed to stimulate problem-solving and develop analysis. The song "Praise of Learning" from *The Mother* puts this very clearly:

"Don't hesitate to question things, comrade/Don't just accept then but/ See for yourself/ ... You must be ready to take over" (Brecht 1997:121)

The problem of pedagogy, strategies for teaching and learning, is therefore central in Brecht's own plays and in his reflections on the theatre. The starting point for his pedagogy is the identity of teaching and learning (see Brecht 1980:141; and Jameson 1998:98). The standard pedagogy of the classroom severs teaching from learning, casting individuals in either the role of the expert educator or the student with everything to learn. Brecht, in contrast, calls on teachers to learn and learners to teach. Scene 6 of Brecht's play *Life of Galileo* begins with the words "Things indeed take a wondrous turn/When learned men do stoop to learn" (Brecht 1980:50) Brecht argued that those performing his play *The Decision*, "have the task of teaching as they learn" (Brecht 1997:345)

Most importantly, this requires that learners take an active role (see Jameson 1998:4). Students in a classroom resemble a traditional theatre audience in that both are cast in the role of passive recipients of knowledge emanating from the front of the room. Brecht sought to create a new form of epic theatre that would challenge the audience to analyze. Traditional dramatic theater worked very hard to create a naturalistic illusion of realism and to promote audience empathy with the characters portrayed on the stage. In contrast, Brecht's epic theater distanced, jarred and disrupted.

> The dramatic theater's spectator says: Yes, I have felt that too – Just like me – It's only natural – It'll never change – The sufferings of this man appal me, because they are inescapable – That's great art; it all seems the most obvious thing in the world....
>
> The epic theater's spectator says: I'd never have thought it – That's not the way – That's extraordinary, hardly believable – It's got to stop – The suffering of this man appal me, because they are unnecessary – That's great art; nothing obvious in it.... (Brecht 1964:71).

Brecht worked to develop techniques that would give the audience responsibility for actively making sense of what was presented on stage. "The spectator must be given the possibility (and duty) of assembling, experimenting and abstracting." (Brecht 1964:60) He developed formal experiments to promote active audience participation including, for example, particular lines for the audience in the musical plays *Lindbergh's Flight* and *The Baden-Baden Lesson on Consent* (Brecht 1997:317, 319, 327).

His pedagogy aims to redeem learning, which has been spoiled by its association with formal education. Adults seek "pure" entertainment in their leisure time, in part as a response to bad memories of schooling experiences. "The man who comes to the theater for 'entertainment' refuses to be let himself be 'treated like a schoolboy' once again because he remembers the fearful torments with which 'knowledge' was hammered into the youth of the bourgeoisie" (Brecht 1964:61). The adult who is learning is infantilized in a society that uses graduation from formal education as the mark of entry into full adulthood. Graduation certifies the adult as fully competent to participate in paid and/or domestic labour. The audience member who allows herself or himself to be "caught learning" risks being marked as incompetent in a society where education is equated with childhood and youth (61). Students are also deprived of the joy of learning by the commodified form of formal education. "It is really a commercial transaction. Knowledge is just a commodity, it is acquired in order to be resold"(72).

"Pleasurable learning" (Brecht 1964:73) forms the basis of Brecht's pedagogy. Learning that is fun redeems both entertainment, which is then allowed to have real content, and education, which is allowed to be engaging (see 60-61). One of the important features of this pleasurable learning was that it overcame the separation between mind and body in educational processes. Brecht praised the actor Charles Laughton's interpretation of the character of Galileo. "His eyes were there to see with, not to flash, his hands to work with, not to gesticulate" (Brecht1980:139). This was in marked contrast to the standard views of the scholar as "an impotent bloodless, quaint figure, conceited and barely fit to live." The character Galileo makes a speech that associates the hunger for real scientific learning with manual labour. "Our new thoughts call for people who work with their hands. Who else cares about knowing the causes of things? People who only see bread on their table don't want to know how it got baked; that lot would rather thank God than thank the baker. But the people who make the bread will understand that nothing moves unless is has been made to move" (80).

Brecht presents learning as a passion, a tactile activity and a source of joy in the *Life of Galileo*. The character of the Pope describes Galileo to the Inquisitor. "He enjoys himself in more ways than any man I have ever met. His thinking springs from sensuality. Give him an old wine or a new idea, and he cannot say no." This is a vision of learning as a pleasure in this world, not a world-denying spiritual quest. Indeed, Galileo is a contradictory figure whose wisdom is integrally connected to lust, whether for wine or for knowledge (see Jameson 1998:82).

Learning is also presented as activity, as practice in the world. In Scene 9 of the play, Galileo guides his students through an experiment in which they seek to understand why things float or sink in water. Brecht discusses his particular pleasure with the "lightness and elegance" of Charles Laughton's interpretation of this scene. "Galileo's relationship with his pupils is like a duel in which the fencing master uses all his feints – using them against the pupil to serve the pupil" (Brecht 1980:149).

## Mind and Body

The educational system ascetisizes learning, severing the mental from the physical. In Brecht's adaptation of Lenz's play *The Tutor*, a young man who is hired as a private tutor for the rich literally castrates himself to put an end to the lust that keeps getting him into trouble and losing him clients. This is described in a poem by Brecht on the theme of Lenz's play.

His bread and butter, he soon recognizes.
Lift out of reach each time his member rises.
He's got to choose, then, and he makes his choice.
His gut may rumble, but he knows his station
He cries, groans, curses, opts for self-castration.
Describing it, tears break the poet's voice.
(Brecht 1976:311-12)

In response to the self-castration, the village school-master describes the young tutor as "a shining star of pedagogy." He goes on to say, "Now you have the highest qualifications of them all. Haven't you destroyed your rebellious spirit, subordinated everything to duty?" (Brecht 1972:44-45). Brecht's (340-41) notes on the play make it clear that the act of self-castration is simultaneously physical and intellectual. He argues that the fourth act of the play, in which the self-castration is performed, must be presented so that "the audience can transfer the self-mutilation from the sexual to the wider intellectual sphere."

This imagery is laden with a taken-for-granted masculinity that must be challenged. The equation of manhood with intellectual audacity is simply sexist. The predatory sexual politics of masculine power are not questioned in this discussion. Yet I believe that Brecht's association of the de-eroticization of pedagogy with its ideological neutralization is extremely important. This point is difficult to make in the context of contemporary sexual politics that have attuned us to the potential for and actuality of sexual exploitation in the educational setting, a context of unequal power relations marked by ambiguous boundaries between the personal and the professional. Yet we cannot simply leave it there.

In the contemporary context, bell hooks (1994:191) links the discussion of the erotics of teaching to the severing of mind from body and the repression of the physical in the classroom setting. Learning is thus presented as an ascetic quest of self-denial and control rather than a playful and experimental journey. The ways of learning and knowing that students have developed before they ever enter a classroom are pushed aside. Genuine curiosity develops as a complex combination of the quest to know with bodily exploration and the desire for sensation. The student arrives at the classroom door as a human being who needs to know, play, explore and feel. Yet once she or he crosses that threshold, her or his own need to know is subordinated to someone else's idea of what she or he needs to know. The potential for joyful, self-active education is radically reduced by the asceticism of the classroom.

## Making the Familiar Strange

Learning is to be made joyful and earthly, although it must still be a challenge. While at some level there is an obviousness to the critique of capitalism, it is not enough to teach the content. In the play *The Mother*, Brecht describes communism: "It is that simple thing/Which is hard to do" (Brecht 1997:116). It requires real work to move beyond the appearances of things, to develop emancipatory theory linked to revolutionary practice. The actual workings of the capitalist system are obscured by the very form of commodity exchange (see Chapter 6). Therefore, pedagogy must help people to develop the analytical skills required to move beneath the surface to understand the deeper processes at work. Jameson (1998) argues that Brecht's pedagogy was ultimately about learning a method of analysis, a way to learning and teaching about the world.

Brecht sought to stimulate the development of these analytical skills through the "alienation-effect," that "consists in turning the object of which one is to be made aware from something ordinary, familiar, immediately accessible, into something peculiar, striking and unexpected." (Brecht 1964:143) The "alienation-effect" represents an important pedagogical step that aims to teach people new ways of looking. "Before familiarity can turn into awareness the familiar must be stripped of its inconspicuousness; we must give up assuming that the object in question needs no explanation" (144). The aim is to teach people that there is always something else beneath the obvious, if one only seeks it out. Things that appear natural, eternal and fixed are actually historical, transitory and changeable. One of the key features of the alienation-effect is therefore to historicize. "The actor must play the incidents as historical ones. Historical incidents are unique, transitory incidents associated with particular periods. The conduct of the persons involved in them is not fixed and 'universally human'; it includes elements that have been or may be overtaken by the course of history" (140).

This historical approach is central to any way of knowing that seeks to overcome commodity fetishism. "Man's reflections on the forms of social life, and consequently, also, his scientific analysis of those forms, take a course directly opposite to that of their actual historical development. He begins, post festum, with the results of the process of development ready to hand before him. The characters that stamp products as commodities, and whose establishment is a necessary preliminary to the circulation of commodities, have already acquired the stability of natural, self-understood forms of social life, before man seeks to decipher, not their historical character, for in his eyes they are immutable, but their meaning" (Marx 1954:80). Historical awareness unfreezes those things that appear fixed before us, laying bare the specific process of development that led to this particular moment and opening up the possibility of a different future. The alienation-effect aims to teach a way of looking that is profoundly historical (see Jameson 1998:47).

Doubt is a necessary part of the critical perspective that the alienation-effect attempts to develop. The character of Galileo celebrates the doubt that marks the "new times" of his day. "For where faith has been enthroned for a thousand years doubt now sits. Everyone says: right, that's what it says in the books, but let's have a look for ourselves. The most solemn truths are being familiarly nudged; what was never doubted before is doubted now" (Brecht 1980:7). Brecht's pedagogy encourages people to cast doubt on the reality they think they see and to challenge established ways of doing things. In the second half of the play *He Said Yes/He Said No*, the character of The Boy dares to "say no" in violation of the custom of consenting to his own death when he is too sick to carry on with an expedition. "And as for the ancient Custom I see no sense in it. What I need far more is a new Great Custom, which we should bring in at once, the Custom of thinking things out anew in every new situation" (Brecht 1997:59).

It requires specific methods to teach doubt. This is one of the reasons that Brecht often favoured teaching through parables. "I show them in parables: if you act this way the following will happen, but if you act like that then the opposite will take place" (Brecht 1964:67). The spectators must develop their own active analysis to make sense of the parable and take from it what they will.

## Art and Science Together

Finally, Brecht called for the unity of science and art as part of his critical pedagogy. At its best, science is animated by doubt. In the words of the character Galileo, "The battle for a measurable heaven has been won thanks to doubt" (Brecht 1980:108). Doubt pushed the development of astronomy despite opposition by the Church hierarchy. Yet the radical edge of science was blunted as it was contained and rendered harmless. A few sentences later, Galileo remarks, "If the scientists, brought to heel by self-interested rulers, limit themselves to piling up knowledge for knowledge's sake, then science can be crippled" (108)." Science was domesticated when it allowed knowledge of the heavens to be separated from knowledge of the earth, and most importantly, the earthly practical knowledge crucial to the political mobilization of the downtrodden. "The movements of the heavenly bodies have become more comprehensible, but the peoples are as far as ever from calculating the moves of their rulers" (108).

Culture has similarly become domesticated under the slogan "art for art's sake." The arts are turned into something harmless and trivial by the very process that proclaims their importance as the official culture of capitalist society. Brecht (1964:196) disputed the claim that art was elevated only insofar as it did not sully itself with politics. "Thus for art to be 'unpolitical' means only to ally itself with the 'ruling' group."

The separation of art and science has been associated with the domestication of both. The healthy skepticism of science can help animate the arts, which are too easily frozen under the rubric of official culture. Similarly, creative cultural activity can connect scientific inquiry to the practices of peoples' everyday lives. Brecht argued that art and science could not thrive separately in the conditions of his time: "In the old days there was no more need for the artist to bother about science than for science to concern itself with him. But now he has to, for science has progressed much further" (Brecht 1964:67) The problem of making sense of the world demands a kind of knowledge without borders. "But in my view the great and complicated things that go on in the world cannot be adequately recognized by people who do not use every possible aid to understanding" (Brecht 1964:73).

## Social Movements and Ways of Knowing

This pedagogy offers an important example of ways of knowing grounded in social movements. Brecht (1964:76) argued that his theatre was possible only under certain social conditions. "It requires not only a certain technological level but a powerful movement in society which is interested to see vital questions freely aired with a view to their solution, and can defend this interest against every contrary trend." This idea of knowledge tied to mobilizations is reflected in Brecht's conception of "positive criticism," which moves beyond taking apart what exists towards building something new. "[T]his criticism of the world is active, practical, positive. Criticizing the course of a river means improving it, correcting it. Criticism of society is ultimately revolution; there you have a criticism taken to its logical conclusion and playing an active part" (146).

The ultimate goal of Brecht's pedagogy is the formation of the self-active, self-educating person, in interchange with others. This pedagogy offers a powerful challenge to both liberal and post-liberal approaches to education. To recap the key principles of Brecht's pedagogy, it is founded on the identity of teaching and learning, overcoming the separation between the expert who professes and the know-nothing student who absorbs. Learning is rather to be an active process of physical and mental work in the world. This kind of learning engages mind and body, combining pleasures with hard work in many activities that people undertake for their own fulfillment including sports, renovations, gardening or cooking. It is learning without borders, drawing together aesthetic experiences associated with the arts and instrumental knowledge associated with science.

Brecht's pedagogy disassociates learning from immaturity and job preparation in the narrow sense, making it rather a crucial activity for people at any stage of the life cycle. The expert and the novice, the old and the young, all have much to learn and must learn from each other. Even the person who has worked on a problem for years must learn as she or he sees the world anew when the familiar is made strange. Indeed, the novice can teach the expert by asking even the simplest question, provoking defamiliarization. The novice is also the expert at assessing her or his own needs and tastes, yet this self-expertise is totally neglected in an education system that locates knowledge outside the learner in the guise of the teacher.

Doubt must be a central component of an education that centres on making the familiar strange. The process of defetishization begins when we doubt the obviousness of the taken-for-granted worlds we inhabit. In this sense, the content of education is much less important than the form. The self-educating person asks questions about the world, probes for the reality beneath the appearances. Education must therefore teach learning rather than simply passing on bits of knowledge packaged as certainties. The development of the historical imagination is a crucial component of this process of education, as it allows the learning individual to locate herself or himself in a dynamic process of change. Perhaps the best way to defamiliarize the present is to show how different it has been, how it came to be this way and what it could become.

## Is Brecht Useful?

These are the key principles of Brecht's pedagogy. We must now ask whether these insights are useful outside of the theatre. Most importantly, there is an aesthetic dimension to this pedagogy that might be difficult to reproduce outside of the theatre. Even difficult learning can be pleasurable in the context of great craft and stunning beauty. This is one dimension of Brecht's pedagogy that might defy easy translation into day-to-day learning situations. In his notes on *The Tutor*, Brecht comments on the importance of "poetry and virtuosity" in the theatre. "For it is a peculiarity of the means employed by the theater that they communicate insights and impulses in the form of pleasures, and that the depth of the latter corresponds to the depth of the former" (Brecht 1972:345). The importance of the aesthetic dimension poses perhaps the most challenging stumbling block in translating Brecht's pedagogy out of the theatre.

I do not have any simple solution for this problem. It seems to me that at the very least we need to draw upon Brecht as a reminder that the aesthetics of learning do matter. Even settings that cannot match the beauty of a finely crafted theatrical production must be considered from an aesthetic perspective if they are to be a ground for pleasurable and difficult learning. The precise implications of the foregrounding of the aesthetic in educational processes need to be worked out in application. It is particularly important to think about ways that arts and culture can be used across the range of educational situations to stimulate real learning.

I believe the core of Brecht's pedagogy can be translated into other educational settings. Of course, it runs against the whole logic of liberal and post-liberal education and thus will prove rather difficult to import into the school, college or university classroom. Brecht can be used as the basis for some sort of emancipatory pedagogy that is bound to have a contradictory fit with educational institutions that are not in the first instance emancipatory. The most obvious spaces for Brechtian pedagogy are those associated with movements for social change. This is important as these spaces often use the classroom model in the educational activities. Any attempt to adapt Brechtian learning into formal educational institutions must be balanced against a realistic assessment of the contradictory character of emancipatory education in unfree spaces.

There are two dimensions of Brecht's pedagogy that I particularly want to emphasize in discussing its wider application. The first is defamiliarization, the process of making the familiar strange. I want to argue that the social movements of the second half of the twentieth century (anti-imperialist, anti-racist, women's liberation, lesbian and gay liberation, aboriginal, Asian and black nationalisms) provide us with a crucial contemporary approach to defamiliarization. One of the best ways to make the familiar strange is to make the strange familiar. The act of queering (to pick up the terminology of contemporary LGBT liberation movements) renders visible the taken for granted assumptions that govern the "normal." Heterosexuals, for example, tend not to name their own sexuality, it is simply taken for granted as normal. It is only the open presence of LGBTs that makes heterosexuality visible as a set of practices and choices that are not universal, eternal and natural.

One powerful application of the alienation-effect is therefore to expose people to a vision of the society in which they live from the perspective of the exploited and oppressed. Whiteness, masculinity, heterosexuality and a bourgeois perspective are most visible to people of colour, women, LGBTs and workers. Canadian history looks very different if told from an aboriginal perspective. A twofold purpose can be served by making the stories, experiences and theoretical expressions of the less powerful central to educational settings. For members of dominant groups, it defamiliarizes their world and hopefully exposes them to another way of looking. For members of oppressed and exploited groups, it can mean seeing their own experiences and ways of knowing reflected at the centre rather than at the margins of knowledge. Indigenous knowledges thus have an important role to play in learning freedom (see Dei, Hall and Rosenberg 2000).

Education from the perspective of the less powerful also requires that children be placed at the centre of the education that is aimed at them. The standard educational practice is for adults to teach and children to learn. And yet children contribute to defamiliarization through their everyday practice of asking questions. "Children make the best theorists, since they have not yet been educated into accepting our routine social practices as 'natural,' and so insist on posing to those practices the most embarrassing and fundamental questions, regarding them with a wondering estrangement which we adults have long forgotten" (Eagleton 1990:34). Liberal and post-liberal educational systems actually sap the theoretical orientation of children by shutting down spontaneous questioning, substituting instead certainties from the front of the room. The aim of existing educational institutions is familiarization with the world from the perspective of the powerful (adults, men, white people, heterosexuals). The insights of the less powerful tend to be marginalized.

## Active Learning For a Change

Along with defamiliarization, Brecht's pedagogy stresses active learning. Children's spontaneous learning is active, tactile and self-directed. Liberal and post-liberal education systems shut down this active, whole-body learning and replace it with a passive learning that severs mind from body (in part by freezing the body in a seat). Emancipatory education requires a shift away from disembodied and passive learning. Asja Lacis developed an approach to education through theatre that was then theorized by Walter Benjamin. Children developed their own plays with adult assistance and then presented them. Lacis wrote, "We set free the children's hidden powers through the process of work, and developed their capacities through *improvisation*" (Lacis 1973:26). Benjamin compared the final result to a carnival: "Everything was turned upside down; and just as in Rome the master served the slaves during Saturnalia, in the same way in a performance children stand on the stage and instruct and teach the attentive educators" (Benjamin 1999b:205). This is precisely the identity of teaching and learning.

Liberal education, even at its most child-centred, was never about turning the world upside-down in this way. Post-liberal approaches move even further in the direction of crushing spontaneous learning and crediting only the measurable outcome deriving from specific teaching exercises. Ultimately, the struggle against post-liberal education must take us beyond the limits of liberal education to a more emancipatory set of practices. This will develop not through any kind of education reform, but rather through mobilization for social change. Movements for change create the spaces for pedagogical experimentation associated with the knowledge people need to fight back. Education should not be about burying people beneath a new knowledge that suffocates what they have learned from their own experience. Instead, it should be about setting free their own curiosity and activity in the world. Benjamin wrote: "What is truly revolutionary is the *secret signal* of what is to come that speaks form the gesture of the child" (Benjamin 1999b:206)

## Notes

1. This is my interpretation of Walter Benjamin's (1999a) particular contribution to the discussion of commodity fetishism.
2. This section draws on my own activist experience during the strike. I was located in Toronto at the time and attended all the rallies and visited picket lines daily. I wrote up my experience for the December 1997 issue of *Labor Notes.*
3. Student non-passivity is a central part of the educational system. The general importance of understanding student activity (as opposed to passivity) is discussed in Apple (1995:12-13), Giroux (1985), Anyon (1985:76-77), and Osborne (1988:1-2).
4. Jameson's (1998) fascinating book begins with a discussion of Brecht's "usefulness."

# Bibliography

Abbate, Gay. 2001. "Challenge to Ontario Squeegee Law Delayed." *The Globe and Mail* 29 January 2001: A16.

Abramowitz, Mimi. 1992. "Poor Women in a Bind: Social Reproduction Without Social Supports." *Affilia* 72: 23-43.

Abrams, Philip. 1982. *Historical Sociology*. Shepton Mallet. Somerset: Open Books.

—— 1968. *The Origins of British Sociology*. Chicago: University of Chicago Press.

Adams, Mary Louise. 1997. *The Trouble with Normal: Postwar Youth and the Making of Heterosexuality*. Toronto: University of Toronto Press.

Aglietta, Michel. 1979. *A Theory of Capitalist Regulation*. London: New Left Books.

Allen, Lillian. 1993. *Women Do This Everyday: Selected Poems of Lillian Allen* Toronto: Women's Press.

—— 1992. *First steps on the Road to Cultural and Racial Equity: From Multiculturalism to Access*. Toronto: Ministry of Culture and Communications.

Anderson, Benedict. 1983. *Imagined Communities: Reflections on the Origin and Spread of Nationalism*. London:Verso.

Anderson, Perry. 1998. *The Origins of Postmodernity*. London: Verso.

Anderson, Scott. 1997. "Boot Camp Honchos Defend U.S. Record." *Now*, 14–20 August: 26, 29.

Anyon, Jean. 1985. "Social Class and The Hidden Curriculum of Work." *Journal of Education* 162:1, 67–92.

Apetekar, Louis and A. Beehailu Abebe. 1997. "Conflict in the Neighbourhood: Street and Working Children in the Public Space." *Childhood* :44, 477<-490.

Apple, Michael. 1996. *Cultural Politics and Education*. (New York: Teachers' College Press).

—— 1995. *Education and Power*. Second Edition. New York: Routledge.

Arenson, Karen. 1999. "Mayor's Task force Says CUNY Is Adrift and Needs an Overhaul." *New York Times*, 6 June 1999: 1, 44.

Ariès, Philippe.1962. *Centuries of Childhood*. London: Cape.

Armstrong, Jane. 1997. "Boot Camps to Get Even Tougher." *Toronto Star*, 4 September 1997: A1, A36.

Armstrong, Pat. 1996. "The Feminization of the Labour Force" in Isabella Bakker ed. *Rethinking Restructuring: Gender and Change in Canada*. Toronto: University of Toronto Press.

—— 1995 "The Feminization of the Labour Force" in Karen Messing, Barbara Neis and Lucie Dumais eds, *Invisible: Issues in Women's Occupational Health*. Charlottetown: Gynergy, 1995, pp.368-92.

Armstrong, Pat and Hugh Armstrong. 1996. *Wasting Away: The Undermining of Canadian Health Care*. Toronto: Oxford.

—— 1990. *Theorizing Women's Work*. Toronto, Ont.: Garamond Press.

Arnold, Michael. 1996. "The High-Tech, Post-Fordist School." *Interchange*, 273, 274:225<-50.

Aronowitz, Stanley and Henry Giroux. 1985. *Education under Siege : the Conservative, Liberal, and Radical Debate over Schooling*. South Hadley, Mass.: Bergin & Garvey.

Ashworth, Mary. 1979. *The Forces Which Shaped Them*. Vancouver: New Star Books.

Aumeeruddy, Aboo T., Bruno Lautier and Ramon G. Tortjada. 1978. "Labour Power and the State." *Capital and Class*,. 6:42-66.

Avery, Donald. 1995. *Reluctant Host: Canada's Response to Immigrant Workers, 1896–1994* Toronto: McClelland and Stewart.

Avis, James. 1996a. "The Enemy Within: Quality and Managerialism in Education" in James Avis, Martin Bloomer, Geoff Esland, Denis Glesson and Phil Hodkinson. *Knowledge and Nationhood: Education, Politics and Work* (London:Cassell, 1996), pp.105-20.

────── 1996b. "The Myth of the Post-Fordist Society" in James Avis, Martin Bloomer, Geoff Esland, Denis Glesson and Phil Hodkinson. *Knowledge and Nationhood: Education, Politics and Work* (London:Cassell, 1996), pp.71-83.
────── 1991 "The Strange Fate of Progressive Education" in Education Group II, Dept of Cultural Studies, *Education Limited* (London:Unwin Hyman, 1991),pp. 31-86, 114-39.
Axelrod, Paul. 2002. *Values in Conflict: The University, the Marketplace and the Trials of Liberal Education*. Kingston/Montreal: McGill/Queen's University Press.
────── 1982. *Scholars and Dollars: Politics, Economics and the Universities of Ontario 1945-80* Toronto: University of Toronto Press.
Bacchi, Carole 1983. *Liberation Deferred?*. Toronto: University of Toronto Press.
Baeker, Greg. 2000. *Cultural Policy and Cultural Diversity in Canada*: Prepared for the Council of Europe Study on Cultural Policy and Cultural Diversity. Ottawa/Hull: Strategic Research and Analysis, Strategic Planning and Policy Coordination, Department of Canadian Heritage.
Balibar, Etienne. 1991 "Citizen Subject" in Jean-Luc Nancy ed., *Who Cares After The Subject?* (New York:Routledge, 1991), pp.33-57.
Baldwin, Shauna Singh. 2000. *What the Body Remembers*. Toronto: Vintage Canada.
Bannerji, Himani. 2000. *The Dark Side of the Nation: Essays on Multiculturalism, Nationalism and Gender*. Toronto: Canadian Scholars Press.
────── 1995 *Thinking Through: Essays on Feminism, Marxism and Anti-Racism* Toronto: Women's Press.
Barlow, Maude and Heather-jane Robertson. 1994. *Class Warfare: The Assault on Canada's Schools*. Toronto: Key Porter.
Basok, Tanya. 1996. "Refugees and State Power." *Studies in Political Economy*, 50, Summer 1996, pp.133-66.
Battagello, Dave. 1998. "Adult Ed Business Program Facing Axe." *Windsor Star*, 10 May 1996, A3.
Beatty, Paul. 1996. *The White Boy Shuffle*. New York: Owl-Henry Holt.
Benjamin, Walter 1999a *The Arcades Project* Translated by Howard Eiland and Kevin McLaughlinCambridge, Mass: Belknap Press.
────── 1999b "Programme for a Proletarian Children's Theater" in M.W. Jennings, H. Eiland and G. Smith eds, *Selected Writings Volume 2 1927-34* (Cambridge: The Belknap Press of Harvard University Press), pp.201-6.
Bernstein, Basil. 1971. *Class, codes and control*. London : Routledge and Kegan Paul.
Berry, Mike. 1989. "Industrialization and Uneven Development: The Case of the Pacific Rim" in M. Gottdiener and Nicos Komninos eds, *Capitalist Development and Crisis Theory: Accumulation, Regulation and Spatial Restructuring* (New York: St. Martin's Press, 1989), pp.174-216.
Birney, Earle. 1975. *Down the Long Table*. Toronto: McClelland and Stewart.
Bissell, Claude T. (ed.). 1956. *Canada's Crisis in Higher Education: Proceedings of a Conference Held by the National Conference of Canadian Universities*. Toronto: University of Toronto Press.
Bourdieu, Pierre. 1984 *Distinction: A Social Critique of the Judgement of Taste*. London: Routledge Kegan Paul.
Bourdieu, Pierre and Passeron, Jean Claude. 1990. *Reproduction in Education, Society, and Culture*. London and Newbury Park, Calif.: Sage.
Bowe, Richard and Stephen J. Ball with Anne Gold .1992. *Reforming Education and Changing Schools: Case Studies in Policy Sociology*. London: Routledge.
Bowe, Richard, Stephen Ball and Sharon Gerwittz. 1994. "Parental 'Choice,' Consumption and Sociall Theory: The Operation of Micro-Markets in Education," *British Journal of Education Studies*, 42 (1), pp.38-52.
Bowles, Samuel and Herbert Gintis. 1976. *Schooling in Capitalist America: Educational Reform and the Contradictions of Economic Life*. New York: Basic.
Boyd, Monica and Doug Norris. 1999. "The Crowded Nest: Young adults at home." *Canadian Social Trends*, 52, Spring 1999.
Bradbury, Bettina. 1993. *Working families : age, gender, and daily survival in industrializing Montreal*. Toronto: McClelland & Stewart.
Braithwaite, Wendy. 1996. "Reflections on Arts Education and Youth Culture" in K. Braithwaite and C. James eds, *The Education of African-Canadians* (Toronto: OurSchools/Our Selves and James Lorimer and Company, 1996), pp.199-202.

Brand, Dionne. 1998. *Bread Out of Stone* Toronto: Vintage Canada.
Braverman, Harry. 1974. *Labour and Monopoly Capital.* New York: Monthly Review Press.
Brecht, Bertolt. 1997. *The Mother, The Decision, Lindbergh's Flight, The Baden-Baden Lesson on Consent, He who Said Yes/He Who Said No.* London: Methuen.
—— 1980. *Life of Galileo.* London: Methuen.
—— 1976. *Poems.* Edited and translated by John Willet and Ralph Mannheim. London: Methuen.
—— 1972. *The Tutor.* London: Methuen.
—— 1964. *Brecht on Theatre.* Edited and translated by John Willet. London: Methuen.
Brehl, Robert. 1996. "Virtual University." *Toronto Star,* 15 June 1996, E1 & E8.
Brennan, Richard. 2000. "September Deadline Set for Schools on Calling Police." *Toronto Star,* 9 December 2000. A25.
Brenner, Robert and Mark Glick "The Regulation Approach: Theory and History." *The New Left Review,* 188 (1991), pp.44-119.
Briskin, Linda and Newson, Janice. 1999. "Making Equity a Priority: Anatomy of the T=York Strike of 1997." *Feminist Studies,* 25 1, pp.105-18.
Broad, Dave and Wayne Antony (eds). 1999. *Citizens or Consumers?: Social Policy in a Market Society.* Halifax: Fernwood.
Brodie, M. Janine. 1995. *Politics on the Margins : Restructuring and the Canadian Women's Movement.* Halifax, N.S.: Fernwood.
Bromley, Hank. 1997. "The social Chicken and the Technological Egg: Educational Computing and the Technology/Society Divide." *Educational Theory,* 471, pp.51-56.
Brosio, Richard A. 1991. "Capital's Domination of the Quotidian." *Discourse,* 121, pp.85-99.
Burrows, Roger, Nigel Gilbert and Anna Pollert. 1992. "Introduction: Fordism, Post-Fordism and Economic Flexibility" in Nigel Gilbert, Robert Burrows and Anna Pollert (eds) *Fordism and Flexibility: Divisions and Change* (New York: St. Martin's, 1992), pp.1-12.
Callinicos, Alex. 1995. *Theories and Narratives: Reflections on the Philosophy of History.* Durham: Duke University Press.
Calliste, Agnes. 1996. "African Canadians Organizing for Educational Change" in K. Braithwaite and C. James (eds) *The Education of African-Canadians* (Toronto: OurSchools/Our Selves and James Lorimer and Company, 1996), pp.87-106.
Campbell, G. 1971. "Genesis and Growth of the Canadian Community College," in F.C. Theimann (ed) *Environments and Paradigms: Factors Affecting the Establishment of a Canadian Association of Community Colleges and Patterns of Resolution* (Edmonton: Department of Educational Administration, University of Alberta, 1971), pp.4-25.
Campbell, Murray. 1999. "Harris Clings to Slim Lead." *The Globe and Mail,* 15 May 1999, A13.
Canada News Wire. 1998. "Board of Trade Releases Framework for Change in Postsecondary Education." *Canada News Wire,* 9 February 1998.
Canadian Chamber of Commerce Task Force on Education and Training (TEFT). 1989. *Putting Business into Training: A Guide to Investing in People.* Ottawa: Canadian Chamber of Commerce.
Canadian Council on Social Development (CCSD). 1999. *The Progress of Canada's Children into the Millennium 1999<-2000.* Ottawa:Canadian Council on Social Development.
Canadian Education Statistics Council. 1996. A Statistical Portrait of Education at the University Level in Canada. Ottawa: Statistics Canada.
Canadian Federation of Independent Business (CFIB). 1996. *On Hire Ground.* Toronto: CFIB.
Caputo, T.C. 1987. "The Young Offenders Act: Children's rights, children's wrongs." *Canadian Public Policy 132,* pp.125-43.
Carby, Hazel. 1983. "Schooling in Babylon." *The Empire Strikes Back: Race and Racism in 70s Britain.* London:Hutchinson, pp.183-212.
Carnoy, Martin and Henry M. Levin. 1985. *Schooling and Work in the Democratic State.* Stanford: Stanford University Press.
Castellena, Marisa. 1997. "'It's not your skills, It's the Test': Gatekeepers for Women in the Skilled Trades," in G. Hull *Changing Work; Changing Workers: Critical Perspectives on Language, Literacy and Skills.* (New York: State University of New York Press 1997), pp.189-213.

Centre for Contemporary Cultural Studies (CCCS). 1981. *Unpopular Education:Schooling and Social Democracy in England Since 1944*. London: Hutchinson.
Chamberlin, J. Edward. 1993. *Come Back to Me My Language: Poetry and the West Indies*. Toronto: McLelland & Stewart.
Chapman, Rowena. 1988. "The Great Pretender: Variations on the New Man Theme," in Rowena Chapman and Jonathan Rutherford(eds) *Male Order:Unwrapping Masculinity* (London:Lawrence and Wishart, 1988), pp.225-48.
Clarke, John. 1980. "Social Democratic Delinquents and Fabian Families" in National Deviancy Conference (ed), *Permissiveness and Control: The Fate of the Sixties Legislation* (New York: Barnes and Noble, 1980).
Clarke, John and Chas Critcher. 1985. *The Devil Makes Work: Leisure in Capitalist Britain*. London: MacMillan.
Clarke, Simon. 1992. "What in the F—'s Name is Fordism" in Nigel Gilbert, Robert Burrows and Anna Pollert, *Fordism and Flexibility: Divisions and Change* (New York: St. Martin's, 1992), pp.13-30.
——— 1983. "State, Class Struggle and the Reproduction of Capital." *Kapitalistate*, 10/11, pp.113-30.
Clarke, Tony. 1997. "The Transnational Corporate Agenda behind the Harris Regime" in Diana Ralph, Andre Regimbald and Neree St-Amand (eds), *Open for Business, Closed to People* (Halifax:Fernwood, 1997), pp.28-36.
Clarricoates, Katherine. 1980. "The Importance of Being Earnest.. Emma ... Tom ...Jane: The Perception and Categorization of Gender Conformity VS Gender Deviation in Primary Schools" in R. Deem (ed), *Schooling for Women's Work* (London: Routledge Kegan Paul, 1980), pp.26-41.
Cleaver, Harry. 1979. *Reading Capital Politically*. Brighton: Harvester Press.
Clement, Wallace and John Myles. 1994. *Relations of Ruling*. Montreal and Kingston: McGill-Queen's University Press.
Cohen, Lizabeth. 1990. *Making a New Deal: Industrial Workers in Chicago 1919<-1939* Cambridge: Cambridge University Press.
Committee on Religious Education in the Public Schools of the Province of Ontario. 1969. *Religious Information and Moral Development: Report of the Committee on Religious Education in the Public Schools of the Province of Ontario*. Toronto: Ontario Department of Education.
Committee on the Status of Women in Ontario Universities. 1988. *Attracting and Retaining Women for Science and Engineering*. Toronto: Council of Ontario Universities.
Connell, R.W. 1995. *Masculinities*. Berkeley: University of California Press.
——— 1993. *Schools and Social Justice*. Philadelphia: Temple University Press.
——— 1989. "Cool guys, swots and wimps: the interplay of masculinity and education." *Oxford Review of Education*, v. 15, n. 3, pp.291-303.
Connelly, M. Patricia and Martha MacDonald. 1996. "The Labour Market, the State and the Reorganization of Work: Policy Impacts," in Isabella Bakker (ed), *Rethinking Restructuring: Gender and Change in Canada* (Toronto: University of Toronto, 1996), pp.82-91.
Coontz, Stephanie. 1992. *The Way We Never Were : American Families and the Nostalgia Trap* New York: BasicBooks.
——— 1988 *The Socials Origins of Private Life: A History of American Families 1600<-1900*. London: Verso.
Corrigan, Paul. 1988. "Gerbil: The Education Reform Bill," *Capital and Class*, 35, pp.29-33.
——— 1979. *Schooling the Smash Street Kids*. London:MacMillan.
Corrigan, Phillip. 1977 "State Formation and Moral Regulation in Nineteenth-Century Britain: Sociological Investigations." PhD Thesis, University of Durham.
Corrigan, Philip, Harvie Ramsey and Derek Sayer. 1980. "The State as Relation of Production," in p.Corrigan (ed), *Capitalism, State Formation and Marxist Theory* (London: Quartet, 1980), pp 1-26.
Corrigan, Philip and Derek Sayer. 1985. *The Great Arch*. Oxford: Basil Blackwell.
Council of Ontario Universities. 2000. *Access to Excellence*. Toronto: Council of Ontario Universities.
Coyle, Jim. 2000. "Rescued From Sure Classroom Anarchy," *Toronto Star*, 20 May 2000, A6.

Cross, Gary. 1997. "Consumer History and the Dilemmas of Working-Class History," *Labor History Review* 623. Winter 1997, pp.261-74.
—— 1993. *Time and Money: The Making of Consumer Culture*.New York: Routledge.
Curtis, Bruce. 1992. *True Government by Choice Men? Inspection, Education and State Formation in Canada West*. Toronto: University of Toronto Press.
—— 1988. *Building the Educational State: Canada West 1836-71*. London:Althouse Press.
Curtis, Bruce, D.W. Livingstone and Harry Smaller. 1992. *Stacking the Deck: The Streaming of Working-Class Kids in Ontario Schools*. Toronto: OS/OS.
Danylewycz, Marta. 1991. "Domestic Science Education in Ontario: 1900<-1940," in Ruby Heap and Alison Prentice, *Gender and Education in Ontario: An Historical Reader* (Toronto: Canadian Scholars Press, 1991), pp.127-46.
Danylewycz, Marta, Beth Light and Alison Prentice. 1987. "The Evaluation of the sexual Division of Labour in Teaching: A Nineteenth Century Ontario and Quebec Case Study" in J. Gaskell and A McLaren (eds) *Women and Education: A Canadian Perspective* (Calgary:Detselig, 1987).
Darrah, Charles. 1997. "Complicating the Concept of Skills Requirements: Scenes from a Workplace," in G. Hull, *Changing Work; Changing Workers: Critical Perspectives on Language, Literacy and Skills* (New York: State University of New York Press, 1997), pp.249-72.
David, Miriam. 1980. *The State, The Family and Education*. London: Routledge Kegan Paul.
Davies, Bernard. 1986. *Threatening youth: Towards a National Youth Policy*. Milton Keynes: Open University Press.
Davin, Anna. 1978. "Imperialism and Motherhood,." *History Workshop Journal* 5.
Davis, Bob. 1995. "Whatever Happened to High School History? Burying the Political Memory of youth: Ontario 1945-1995," *Our Schools/Our Selves*, 40/41.
Davis, Mike. 1992. *City of Quartz: Excavating the Future of Los Angeles*. New York: Vintage.
Day, Richard J.F. 2000. *Multiculturalism and the History of Canadian Diversity*. Toronto: University of Toronto Press.
Deem, Rosemary. 1994. "Free Marketeers or Good Citizens? Education Policy and Lay Participation in the Administration of Schools," *British Journal of Education Studies*, 421, pp.23-37.
Dei, George J. Sefa. 1996. *Anti-Racism Education: Theory and Practice*. Halifax: Fernwood.
Dei, George J. Sefa, Budd L. Hall and Dorothy Goldin Rosenberg. 2000. *Indigenous Knowledges in Global Contexts: Multiple Readings of Our World*. Toronto: An OISE/UT Book in conjunction with University of Toronto Press.
Dei, George J. Sefa., Josephine Mazzuca, Elizabeth McIsaac, Jasmin Zine. 1997. *Reconstructing "drop-out"': A Critical Ethnography of the Dynamics of Black Students' Disengagement from School*. Toronto: University of Toronto Press.
Delamont, Sara. 1996. *A Woman's Place in Education: Historical and Social Perspectives on Gender and Education*. Aldershot: Avebury.
Delap. Leanne. 1999. "Fashion Designers Thank Heaven for Little Girls" *The Globe and Mail*,, 15 April 1999, C1, C3.
Delhi, Kari. 1995. "Ontario's Royal Commission on Learning: Constructing a 'Public Good' for the Incoming Tories?" *Our Schools/ Our Selves*, 71, pp.106-20.
D'Emilio, John and Freedman, Estelle. 1988. *Intimate Matters: A History of Sexuality in America*. New York: Harper and Row.
Denby, David. 1999. "High School Confidential: Notes on Teen Movies" *The New Yorker*, LXXV, No.13, 31 May 1999.
Dennehy, Katherine and Jeylon Mortimer. 1993. "Work and Family Aspirations of Contemporary Adolescent Boys and Girls," in Jane C. Hood (ed), *Men, Work and Family* (Newbury Park: Sage,1993), pp.87-107.
Denning, Michael. 1996. *The Cultural Front: The Laboring of American Culture in the Twentieth Century*. London:Verso.
Dickson, Harley D. 1991. "The Three 'D's' of Vocational Training: Deskilling, Disempowerment and Devaluation, in T. Wotherspoon (ed), *Hitting the Books: The Politics of Educational Retrenchment* (Toronto:Garamond Press, 1991), pp.101-18.

Dobbin, Murray. 1997. "Charting a Course to Social Division: The Charter School Threat to Public Education in Canada," *Our Schools/Our Selves*, 83, pp.48-82.
Dominelli, Lena and Ankie Hoogvelt, 1996, "Globalization, Contract Government and the Taylorization of Intellectual Labour in Academia," *Studies in Political Economy*, 49, pp.71-100.
Donzelot, Jacques. 1979. *The Policing of Families*. New York: Pantheon.
Duberman, Martin Bauml, Martha Vicinus and George Chauncey Jr. 1989. *Hidden from History: Reclaiming the Lesbian and Gay Past,*. New York: Penguin.
Du Bois, W.E.B. 1986a. "The Talented Tenth" in W.E.B. Du Bois, *Writings* (New York: Library of America, 1986), pp.842-61.
—— 1986b. "The Souls of Black Folk" in W.E.B. Du Bois, *Writings* (New York: Library of America, 1986), pp.357-548.
—— 1986c. "The Damnation of Women" in W.E.B. Du Bois, *Writings* (New York: Library of America, 1086), pp.952-68.
—— 1986d "The Dusk of Dawn" in W.E.B. Du Bois, *Writings* (New York: Library of America, 1986), pp.549-802.
—— (1986e). "The Acquittal" in W.E.B. Du Bois, *Writings* (New York: Library of America, 1986), pp.1093-1109.
—— 1973. *The Education of Black People: Ten critiques, 1906<-1960*. Edited by Herbert Aptheker. Amherst : University of Massachusetts Press.
Dunk, Thomas, Stephen McBride and Randle W. Nelson. 1996. "Introduction" in T. Dunk, S. McBride and R.W. Nelson (eds), *The Training Trap: Ideology, Training and the Labour Market. Socialist Studies, Volume 11*. Winnipeg/Halifax: Society for Socialist Studies/Fernwood, pp 1-12.
Dussel, Enrique. 1998. "Beyond Eurocentrism: The World System and the Limits of Modernity" in F. Jameson and M. Miyoshi, *The Cultures of Globalization* (Durham: Duke University Press, 1998)..
Dyer-Witherford, Nick. 1999. *Cyber-Marx: Cycles and Circuits of Struggle in High-Technology Capitalism*. Urbana and Chicago: University of Illinois Press.
Eagleton, Terry. 1996. *The Illusions of Postmodernism*. Oxford: Blackwell.
—— 1991 *Ideology: An introduction*. London; New York: Verso.
Economic Council of Canada. 1992. *A Lot To Learn: Education and Training in Canada*. Ottawa: Ministry of Supply and Services.
—— 1990. *Good Jobs, Bad Jobs: Employment in the Service Economy*. Ottawa: Ministry of Supply and Services.
Education Improvement Commission. 1997. *The Road Ahead: A Report on Learning, Class Size and Staffing*. Toronto: Education Improvement Commission.
Ehrenreich, Barbara. 1983. *The Hearts of Men*. Garden City, New York: Anchor Press.
Ehrenreich, Barbara and English, Deirdre. 1978. *For Her Own Good : 150 Years of the Experts' Advice to Women*. Garden City, New York: Anchor Press.
Elger, Tony. 1982. "Braverman, Capital Accumulation and Deskilling," in Stephen Wood(ed), *The Degradation of Work?* (London: Hutchinson, 1982), pp.23-53.
Elger, Tony and Chris Smith. 1994. "Global Japanization? Convergence and Competition in the Organization of the Labour Process" in Tony Elger and Chris Smith (eds) *Global Japanization? The Transnational Transformation of the Labour Process* (London and New York: Routledge 1994).
Elger, Tony and Peter Fairbrother. 1992. "Inflexible Flexibility: A Case Study of Modularisation" in Nigel Gilbert, Robert Burrows and Anna Pollert (eds), *Fordism and Flexibility: Divisions and Change* (New York: St. Martin's Press, 1992), pp.89-106.
Engell, James and Dangerfiled, Anthony. 1998. "Humanities in the Age of Money: The Market-Model University," *Harvard Magazine*, May-June 1998, pp.48-55, 111.
Esland, Geoff. 1996. "Knowledge and Nationhood: The New Right, Education and the Global Market," in James Avis, Martin Bloomer, Geoff Esland, Denis Glesson and Phil Hodkinson, *Knowledge and Nationhood: Education, Politics and Work* (London:Cassell, 1996), pp.11-39.
Esping-Andersen, Gosta. 1989. "The Thee Political Economies of the Welfare State," *Canadian Review of Sociology and Anthropology* 261.
Eves, Ernie. 1999. *1999 Ontario Budget, Budget Speech: Foundations for Prosperity* Toronto: Queen's Printer.

## BIBLIOGRAPHY

Faderman, Lillian.1991. *Odd Girls And Twilight Lovers : A History Of Lesbian Life In Twentieth-Century America* New York: Columbia University Press.
Fanon, Frantz. 1967. *Black Skin, White Masks*. New York: Weidenfeld.
Featherstone, Mike. 1991. *Consumer Culture and Postmodernism*. London: Sage.
Field, Norma. 1995. "The Child as Laborer and Consumer: The Disappearance of Childhood in Contemporary Japan" in S. Stephens (ed), *Children and the Politics of Culture* (Princeton: Princeton University Press), pp.51-78.
Fine, Sean. 2000. "Private Tutoring Stirs Grade Expectations," *The Globe and Mail*, 9 October 2000, A3.
Fiorino, Albert. 1978. "Historical Overview," *Information Bulletin No. 3, Commission on Declining Enrollment in Ontario*. Toronto: Commission on Declining Enrollment in Ontario CODE.
Fleming, W.G. 1971a. *The Expansion of the Educational System: Ontario's Educative Society, V.1*. Toronto: University of Toronto Press.
—— 1971b. *Schools, Pupils and Teachers: Ontario's Educative Society, V.3*. Toronto: University of Toronto Press.
—— 1971c. *Post- Secondary and Adult Education: Ontario's Educative Society, V.4*.Toronto: University of Toronto Press.
Foucault, Michel. 1979. "Governmentality" in *Ideology and Consciousness,* 6, pp.5-21.
—— 1977 *Discipline And Punish : The Birth Of The Prison*. New York: Pantheon Books.
Fox, Bonnie. 1997. "Reproducing Difference: Changes in the Lives of Partners Becoming Parents" in Meg Luxton (ed), *Feminism And Families : Critical Policies And Changing Practices* (Halifax, N.S. : Fernwood, 1997), pp.142-61.
Frank, Blye. 1994. "Queer Selves, Queer in Schools: Young Men and Sexualities" in Susan Prentice (ed), *Sex in Schools Canadian Education and Sexual Regulation* (Toronto: Our Schools/ Our Selves Foundation, 1994).
Fraser, Nancy. 1989. "Women, Welfare and the Politics of Need Interpretation," in N. Fraser, *Unruly Practices: Power, Discourse and Gender in Contemporary Social Theory* (Minneapolis: University of Minnesota 1989), pp.149-52.
Freire, Paolo. 1972. *Pedagogy of the Oppressed*. New York: Herder and Herder.
Friese-German, Bernie. 1999. "The 'Computers in Schools' Express - All Aboard?" *Our Schools/ Our Selves*, 95, pp.42-63.
Fukuyama, Francis. 1992. *The End of History and the Last Man*. New York: The Free Press.
Galt, Virginia .2000a. "Daily Pledge," *The Globe and Mail*, 27 April 2000, A1, A6.
—— 2000b. "Public Schools Go With the Private Look," *The Globe and Mail*, 21 January 2000, A14.
—— 2000c. "Ontario students to study e-commerce," *The Globe and Mail*, 3 June 2000, A9.
—— 2000d "The Rise of the 'Dead End Class'," *The Globe and Mail*, 3 June 2000, A15.
—— 1999. "Ontario Stops Funding for Expelled Students," *The Globe and Mail*, 29 September 1999,. A10.
—— 1998a. "Killing of teen shocks two high schools," *The Globe and Mail* 19 May 1998, A10.
—— 1998b. "Science joins 3 Rs in junior grades," *The Globe and Mail* 31 March 1998, A1, A19.
—— 1998c. "Schools, Parents Battle 'Classism'" *The Globe and Mail* 17 February 1998,. A1, A8.
—— 1998d. "Grade 3 Test Prompts Parental Boycott," *The Globe and Mail,* 22 May 1998, A1/A10.
—— 1996a. "Use of Workfare in Schools Proposed," *The Globe and Mail* 21 June 1996, A6.
—— 1996b. "'Prep Time' needed, teachers say," *The Globe and Mail*, 22 January 1996, A5.
Gamble, Andrew. 1988. *The Free Economy and the Strong State: The Politics of Thatcherism*. Durham: Duke University Press.
Garrahan, Philip and Paul Stewart. 1992. *The Nissan Enigma: Flexibility and Work in a Local Economy*. London: Mansell.
Gaskell, Jane, Arlene McLaren and Myra Novogrodsky. 1989. *Claiming an Education: Feminism and Canadian Schools*. Toronto: Our Schools/Our Selves Education Foundation.
Gershuny, J.I. and I.D. Miles. 1983. *The New Service Economy*. Praeger: New York.

Gibbons, Michael, Camille Limoges, Helga Nowotny, Simon Schwartrzman, Peter Scott and Martin Trow. 1994. *The New Production of Knowledge: The Dynamics of Science and Research in Contemporary Societies*. London/Thousand Oaks/ New Delhi: Sage.

Gidney, R.D. 1999. *From Hope to Harris : the reshaping of Ontario's schools*. Toronto: University of Toronto Press.

—— 1996. "Instructive Parallels:Looking Back to Hall-Dennis," in G. Milburn (ed), *"Ring Some Alarm Bells in Ontario": Reactions to the Report of the Royal Commission on Learning* (London: The Althouse Press, 1996), pp 25-40.

Gilbert, B.B. 1976. *The Evolution of National Insurance in Great Britain*. London: Michael Joseph.

Gilbert, Sid. 1994. "The Search for Educational Indicators," *Education Quarterly Review*, 94, pp.44-53.

Gilroy, Paul. 1987. *There Ain't No Black in the Union Jack*. Chicago: University of Chicago.

Giroux, Henry. 1993. *Living Dangerously: Mulitculturalism and the Politics of Difference*. New York: Peter Lang.

—— 1985. "Theories of Reproduction and Resistance in the New Sociology of Education: A Critical Analysis," *Harvard Education Review*, 533, pp.257-93.

—— 1981. *Ideology, Culture & the Process of Schooling*. Philadelphia : Temple University Press and London: Falmer Press.

Glickman, Lawrence. 1997. *A Living Wage: American Workers and the Making of Consumer Society*. New York: Cornell University Press.

*Globe and Mail, The*. 1999. "Teacher's Support Grew: Polls," *The Globe and Mail*, 25 January 1999, A7.

—— 1998a. "CHA Tells of Hidden Abuse," *The Globe and Mail*, 19 May 1998, S2.

—— 1998b. "Teachers Not So Busy, Harris Says," *The Globe and Mail*, 18 February 1998, A5.

Godbout, Arthur. 1979. *Historique de l'enseignement français dans l'Ontario 1676<-1976*. Ottawa: Centre Franco-Ontarien de ressources pédagogique..

Goldberg, Theo. 1994. "Introduction:Mutlicultural Conditions." in T. Goldberg (ed), *Mulitculturalism: A Critical Reader* (Oxford: Blackwell, 1994).

Goldin, Claudia. 1990. *Understanding the Gender Gap: An Economic History of American Women*. New York: Oxford Universitiy Press.

Goodall, Alan. 1994. "Two Decades of Change: College Postsecondary Enrolment 1971-1991," *Education Quarterly Review*, 1994, pp.41-56.

Gordon, Lewis R. 1995. *Fanon and the Crisis of European Man*. New York: Routledge.

Gordon, Linda. 1990. "The Welfare State: towards a Socialist-Feminist Perspective," *Socialist Register*, 1990, pp 171-200.

Gough, Jamie. 1992. "Where's the Value in `Post-Fordism'?" in Nigel Gilbert, Robert Burrows and Anna Pollert (eds), *Fordism and Flexibility: Divisions and Change* (New York: St. Martin's Press, 1992), pp.31-48.

Gould, Stephen Jay.1981. *Mismeasure of Man*. New York: Norton.

Gramsci, Antonio. 1971. *Selections for the Prison Notebooks*. Edited by Quentin Hoare and Geoffrey Nowell Smith. New York: International Publishers.

Granatstein, Jack L. 1999. *Who Killed Canadian History?* Toronto: HarperCollins.

Gray, John. 2000. "Teenage Breakdown?" *The Globe and Mail*, 3 June 2000, A14-15.

de Grazia, Victoria. 1996. "Introduction" in V.de Grazia and E. Furlough, *The Sex of Things: Gender and Consumption in Historical Perspective* (Berkeley: University of California Press, 1996).

—— 1993 "Beyond Time and Money," *International Labor and Working-Class History*, 43, pp.24-30.

Grossmann, Atina. 1995. *Reforming Sex: The German Movement for Birth Control and Abortion Reform, 1920<-1950*. New York, Oxford: Oxford University Press.

Guest, Dennis. 1980. *The Emergence of Social Security in Canada*. Vancouver: University of British Columbia Press.

Guy, Kathleen A. 1997. *Our Promise to Children*. Ottawa: Canadian Institute of Child Health.

Hahn, Russell. 1976. "Brainworkers and the Knights of Labor: E.E. Shepherd, Philip Thompson and the Toronto News, 1883<-87," in G.S. Kealey and p.Warrian (eds), *Essays in Canadian Working Class History* (Toronto: McClelland and Stewart ).

Hall, Stuart, C. Critcher, T. Jefferson, J Clarke and B. Robert. 1978. *Policing the Crisis.* London: MacMillan.
Hall, Stuart. 1996. "Who is this 'black' in black popular culture?" in David Morley and Kuan-Hsing Chen (eds), *Stuart Hall: Critical Dialogues in Cultural Studies* (London/New York: Routledge, 1996), pp 465-83.
Haraway, Donna. 1991. *Simians, Cyborgs, and Women: The Reinvention of Nature.* New York: Routledge.
Harding, Sandra. 1998. *Is Science Multicultural? Postcolonialisms, Feminisms and Epistemologies.* Bloomington: Indiana University Press.
Hardyment, Christine. 1983. *Dream Babies: Child Care from Locke to Spock.* London: Jonathan Cape.
Harris, Mike. 1997. "Notes for remarks by The Honourable Mike Harris, MPP, Premier of Ontario, Council of Ontario Universities Summit," Toronto: Office of the Premier.
Harris, Nigel 1995. *The New Untouchables: Immigration and the New World Worker.* Harmondsworth: Penguin.
—— 1986. *End of the Third World: Newly industrializing countries and the decline of an ideology.* London: I. B. Tauris.
—— 1968. *Beliefs in Society.* London: Pelican.
Hart, Bill. 1996. "The Quality Managers," *Our Schools/Our Selves,* 81, pp.35-55.
Harvey, David. 1989a. *The Condition of Postmodernity.* Oxford, Basil Blackwell.
—— 1989b. *The Urban Experience.* Baltimore: Johns Hopkins University Press.
—— 1985. *The Urbanization of Capital.* Oxford: Oxford University Press.
Harvey, Edward. 1974. *Education systems and the Labour Market.* Toronto: Longman.
Hatcher, Richard and Troyna, Barry. 1993. "Racialization and Children" in Cameron McCarthy and Warren Crichlow (eds), *Race, Identity and Representation in Education* (New York and London: Routledge, 1993), pp.109-24.
Hayden, Dolores. 1981. *The Grand Domestic Revolution.* Cambridge: MIT Press.
Heath, Jamie. 1999. "The Attack on Our Schools: Staff and Students Fight Back," *Our Schools/Our Selves,* 95 pp.21-33.
Hennesey, Rosemary. 2000. *Profit and Pleasure: Sexual Identities in Late Capitalism.* New York: Routledge.
Hernstein, Richard J. and Charles Murray. 1994. *The Bell Curve: Intelligence and class structure in American life.* New York: Free Press.
Heron, Craig. 1995. "The High School and the Household Economy in Working-Class Hamilton 1890-1940," *Historical Studies in Education,* 72, pp.217-59.
Hill, Paul, Lawrence Pierce and James Guthrie. 1997. *Reinventing Public Education: How Contracting Can Transform America's Schools.* Chicago: University of Chicago Press.
Highway, Thomson. 1998. *Kiss of the Fur Queen.* Toronto: Doubleday Canada.
Hirsch, Joachim. 1997. "Globalization of Capital, Nation-States and Democracy," *Studies in Political Economy,* 54, pp.39-58.
Hobsbawm, Eric. 1983. "Mass Producing Traditions: Europe 1870-1914," in E Hobsbawm and T Ranger (eds), *The Invention of Tradition* (Cambridge: Cambridge University Press, 1983).
Hoddinott, Susan and Jim Overton. 1996. "Dismantling Public Provision of Adult Basic Education: The Anti-Literacy Politics of Newfoundland's Literacy Campaign," in Thomas Dunk, Stephen McBride and Randle Nelsen, "The Training Trap: Ideology, Training and the Labour Market," *Socialist Studies, Volume 11* (Winnipeg: Society for Socialist Studies).
Hodkinson, Phil. 1996. "Careership: The Individual, Choices and Markets in the Transition into Work," in James Avis, Martin Bloomer, Geoff Esland, Denis Glesson and Phil Hodkinson, *Knowledge and Nationhood: Education, Politics and Work* (London:Cassell, 1996), pp.121-39.
Høeg, Peter 1994. *Borderliners.* Toronto: Seal.
Holland, Janet, Caroline Ramazanoglu; Sue Sharpe and Rachel Thompson. 1994. "Power and Desire: The Embodiment of Female Sexuality," *Feminist Review 46,* pp.21-38.
Holland, John. 1976. "Education, Public Policy and Personal Choice" in Garnet McDiarmid (ed), *From Quantitative to Qualitative Change in Ontario Education.* (Toronto: OISE, 1976).
Holmes, John. 1997. "In Search of Competitive Efficiency: Labour Process Flex in Canadian Newsprint Mills." *Canadian Geographer,* 411 pp.7-25.

Holmes, Mark. 1998. *The Reformation of Canada's Schools*. Montreal/Kingston: McGill-Queens University Press.

Holzman, Michael. 1986. "The Social Context of Literacy," *College English*, 481, pp.27-33.

hooks, bell. 1994. *Teaching to Transgress: Education as the Practice of Freedom.* New York-London: Routledge.

—— 1989. *Talking back: Thinking Feminist, Thinking Black.* Boston: South End Press.

Horkheimer, Max and Adorno, Theodor W.1972. *Dialectic of Enlightenment.* Translated by John Cumming. New York: Herder and Herder.

Hull, Glynda. 1997. "Hearing Other Voices: A Critical Assessment of Popular Views on Literacy and Work," in G. Hull, *Changing Work; Changing Workers: Critical Perspectives on Language, Literacy and Skills* (New York: State University of New York Press, 1997), pp.3-39.

Hunter, Ian. 1990. "Personality as Vocation: The Political Rationality of the Humanities," *Economy and Society*, 194, pp.153-92.

—— 1988. *Culture and Government: The Emergence of Literary Education.* London: MacMillan.

Hyslop, Jonathon. 1999. "The Imperial Working Class Makes Itself 'White': White Labourism in Britain, Australia and South Africa Before the First World War," *Journal of Historical Sociology*, 124, pp.398-421.

Ibbitson, John. 2001. "Okay Mr. Tough Guy Harris, Can You Go the Distance?" *The Globe and Mail*, 6 January 2001.

—— 2000a. "Universities Face Funding Crapshoot," *The Globe and Mail*, 30 March 2000, A9.

—— 2000b. "Universities and Colleges to Enjoy Big Expansion," *The Globe and Mail* 23 February 2000, A1/A7.

—— 1999. "Higher Education Next Tory Target," *National Post*, Monday 26 April 1999.

Jackson, Nancy. 1992. "Training Needs: An Objective Science?" in Nancy Jackson (ed), *Training for What? Labour Perspectives on Skill Training.* (Toronto: Our Schools/Our Selves Foundation, 1992).

—— 1987. "Skill Training in Transition: Implications for Women," in J. Gaskell and A McLaren (eds), *Women and Education: A Canadian Perspective* (Calgary:Detselig, 1987).

Jackson, Nancy and Jane S. Gaskell. 1991. "White Collar Vocationalism: The Rise of Commercial Education in Ontario and B.C. 1870-1920," in Ruby Heap and Alison Prentice, *Gender and Education in Ontario: An Historical Reader* (Toronto: Canadian Scholars Press, 1991), pp.165-94.

Jacoby, Russell. 1987. *The Last Intellectuals: American Culture in the Age of Academe.* New York: Basic Books.

James, Carl E. and Karen Braithwaite. 1996. "The Education of African-Canadians: Issues, Contexts, Expectations." in K. Braithwaite and C. James (eds), *The Education of African-Canadians* (Toronto:OurSchools/Our Selves and James Lorimer and Company, 1996), pp.13-31.

James, C.L.R. 1993. *American Civilization.* Oxford: Blackwell.

James, Joy. 1997. *Transcending the Talented Tenth: Black Leaders and American Intellectuals.* New York: Routledge.

Jameson, Frederic. 1998. *Brecht on Method.* London: Verso.

—— 1991. *Postmodernism, or, The Cultural Logic of Late Capitalism.* Durham: Duke University Press.

—— 1981. *Political Unconscious : Narrative as a Socially Symbolic Act.* Ithaca, N.Y.: Cornell University Press.

Jeffrey, Steve. 1996. "France 1995: The Backward March of Labour Halted?" *Capital and Class*, 59, pp.7-22. .

Jenson, Jane. 1989. "'Different' but not 'Exceptional': Canada's Permeable Fordism," *Canadian Review of Sociology and Anthropology*, 261, pp.69-94.

Jessop, Bob. 1991. "The Welfare State in the Transition from Fordism to Post-Fordism," in Bob Jessop, Hans Kastendick, Klaus Neilsen and Ove. K. Pedersen (eds), *The Politics of Flexibility: Restructuring State and Industry in Britain, Germany and Scandinavia* (Aldershot: Edward Elgar, 1991), pp.82-105.

John, Mary. 1995. "Children's Rights in a Free-Market Culture" in Sharon Stephens (ed), *Children and the Politics of Culture* (Princeton: Princeton University Press, 1995), pp.105-37.

Johnson, Richard. 1991. "A New Road to Serfdom? A Critical History of the 1988 Act," in Education Group II, Dept of Cultural Studies, *Education Limited* (London:Unwin Hyman, 1991), pp. 31-86.
Johnston, Basil. 1988. *Indian School Days*. Toronto : Key Porter Books.
Jones, Ken and Richard Hatcher. 1994. "Educational Progress and Economic Change: Notes on Some Recent Proposals," *British Journal of Education Studies,* 423, 245-60.
Joseph, Peniel. 1996. "In the Post-Civil Rights Era," *New Politics,* 54, pp.52-54.
Katz, Cindi. 1998. "Disintegrating Developments: Global Economic Restructuring and the Eroding Ecologies of Youth" in T. Skelton and G. Valentine (eds), *Cool Places: Geographies of Youth Cultures* (London and New York: Routledge, 1998), pp.130-44.
Katz, Jonathan Ned. 1995. *The Invention of Heterosexuality.* New York: Plume.
Katznelson, Ira, Kathleen Gille and Margaret Weir. 1982. "Public Schooling and Working Class Formation: The Case of the United States," *American Journal of Education,* 902, pp.111-43.
Kaufman, Michael. 1992. "The Construction of Masculinity and the Triad of Men's Violence," in Michael S. Kimmel and Michael S. Messner (eds), *Men's Lives.* Second edition (New York: MacMillan).
Kay, Geoffrey and James Mott. 1982. *Political Order and the Law of Labour.* Lon:MacMillan.
Kazolana, Kirsten. 1996. "Will You Walk Into My Parlour? Said a Spider to a Fly: Parent Participation and School Councils," *Our Schools/Our Selves,* 74, pp.99-111.
Keenan, James. 1996. "Magna Wins Major Contract from Ford," *The Globe and Mail,* 18 June 1996, B1, B13.
Kelley, Robin D.G. 1997. *Yo' Mama's DisFunktional: Fighting the Culture Wars in Urban America.* Boston: Beacon Press.
—— 1996. *Race Rebels : Culture, Politics, And The Black Working Class.* New York: Free Press.
Kidder, Annie. 2001. "When Will Ontario Learn?" *The Globe and Mail,* 23 April 2000, A19.
Kinsman, Gary. 1996. *The Regulation of Desire.* Revised Edition. Montreal: Black Rose.
Kinsman, Gary and Patrizia Gentile.1998. *"In the Interests of the State": The Anti-gay, Anti-lesbian National Security Campaign in Canada.* Sudbury:Laurentian University
Krishnan, Raghu. 1996. "December 1995 'The First revolt Against Globalization,'" *Monthly Review,* 481, May 1996, pp.1-22.
Kuehn, Larry. 1995a. "'Everybody is trying to fix me up.' Technology and the Control of Work in the Public Schools," *Our Schools, Our Selves,* 72, #44, pp.54-68.
——1995b "Education Roundup," *Our Schools, Our Selves,* 72, #44, pp.9-15.
Kuhn, Thomas. 1970 (1962). Second edition. *The Structure of Scientific Revolutions.* Chicago: University of Chicago Press.
Lacis, Asja. 1973. "A Memoir," *Performance.* 15, pp.24-27.
Lareau, Annette. 2000. "Social Class and the Daily Life of Children: A Study from the United States," *Childhood,* 72, 155-71.
Larkin, June. 1994. *Sexual Harassment: High School Girls Speak Out.*Toronto: Second Story Press.
Law, Marc. 1997. "Ontario Takes Aim at Education Bureaucracy," Fraser Forums, September 1997 .
Lawlor, Allison. 2001. "Swimmers Fear They Will Be Left To Dry If 85 School Pools Close," *The Globe and Mail,* 18 June 2001, A19.
Laxer, Gordon. 1995. "The Privatization of Public Life," in G. Laxer and T. Harrison (eds), *Trojan Horse* (Black Rose: Montreal, 1995), pp.101-17.
Lazarus, Neil. 1999a. "The Prose of Insurgency: Sivanandan and Marxist Theory," *Race and Class,* 41, 1&2, pp.35-47.
—— 1999b. *Nationalism and Cultural Practice in the Postcolonial World.* Cambridge: Cambridge Universitiy Press.
Leach, Belinda. 1993. "'Flexible' Work, Precarious Future: Some Lessons from the Canadian Clothing Industry," *Canadian Review of Sociology and Anthropology,* 301, pp 64-82.
Lebowitz, Michael. 1995. "Situating the Capitalist State," in A. Callari, S. Cullenberg and C. Biewener (eds), *Marxism in the Postmodern Age* (New York: The Guilford Press 1995).
—— 1992. *Beyond Capital.* New York: St Martin's.
Lewchuk, Wayne. 1993. "Men and Monotony: Fraternalism as a Managerial Strategy at the Ford Motor Company," *Journal of Economic History,* 534, pp.824-56 .

Lewchuk, Wayne and David Robertson. 1997. "Working Conditions Under Lean Production: A Worker-Based Benchmarking Study" in Paul Stewart (ed), *Beyond Japanese Management: The End of Modern Times?* (London:Frank Cass), pp.60-81.
Lewington, Jennifer. 1998. "Going to Bat for Adult Education," *The Globe and Mail*, 12 March 1998, p.A8.
—— 1997. "Ontario to Curb Teacher's Powers," *The Globe and Mail*, 23 September 1997, A1/A4.
Li, Peter S.1998. *The Chinese in Canada*. Toronto: Oxford University Press.
Lipsitz, George. 1994. *Rainbow at Midnight: Labour and Culture in the 1940s*. Urbana: University of Illinois.
Little, Don. 1997. "Financing Universities: Why Are Students Paying More?" *Education Quarterly Review*, 42, pp.10-26.
Little, Doug. 1996. "Ontario Teachers Try Their Luck with the Class Struggle," *Our Schools/Our Selves*, 74, pp.17-23.
Livesay, Dorothy. 1977. *Right Hand, Left Hand*. Erin, Ont.: Press Porcepic.
Livingstone, David. 1999. *The Education-Jobs Gap:Underemployment or Economic Democracy*. Toronto:Garamond Press.
—— 1996. "Wasted Education and Withered Work: Reversing the 'Postindustrial' Education-Jobs Optic," in Thomas Dunk, Stephen McBride and Randle W. Nelson (eds), *The Training Trap:Ideology, Training and the Labour Market. Socialist Studies, Volume 11* (Winnipeg/Halifax: Society for Socialist Studies/Fernwood).
—— 1995a, "The Uses of Computer Literacy," *Orbit*, 262, pp.36-40.
—— 1995b, "For Whom the Bell Curve Tolls," *Alberta Journal of Educational Research*, Vol. XLI, No. 3, Sept 1995, pp.335-41.
Livingstone, David and Elizabeth Asner. 1996. "Feet in Both Camps: Household Classes, Divisions of Labour and Group Consciousness," in D.W. Livingstone and J. Marshall Magnan, *Recast Dreams: Class And Gender Consciousness In Steeltown*. (Toronto : Garamond Press, 1996), pp.72-99.
Livingstone, David and Meg Luxton. 1996. "Gender Consciousness at Work: Modification of the Male Breadwinner Norm," in D.W. Livingstone and J. Marshall Magnan, *Recast Dreams: Class And Gender Consciousness In Steeltown* (Toronto: Garamond Press, 1996), pp.100-29.
Lloyd, David and Paul Thomas. 1998. *Culture and the State*. London:Routledge.
Lukács, Georg. 1971. *History and Class Consciousness*. Translated by Rodney Livingstone. London: Merlin.
Luke, Paul. 2000. "An ability to learn: As Canada's high-tech sector matures, it is in need of people able to grasp the bigger picture," *The Province*, Wednesday 4 October 2000, C1.
Luxton, Meg. 1997. "Feminism and Families: The Challenge of Neo-Conservatism" in M. Luxton (ed), *Feminism and Families : Critical Policies and Changing Practices* (Halifax, N.S.: Fernwood, 1997).
—— 1981. *More Than a Labour of Love : Three Generations of Women's Work in the Home*. Toronto: Women's Educational Press.
McBride, Stephen. 1992. *Not Working: State, Unemployment and Neo-conservatism in Canada*. Toronto: University of Toronto Press.
McBride, Stephen and John Shields. 1993. *Dismantling a Nation: Canada and the New World Order*. Halifax: Fernwood.
McCarthy, Cameron and Warren Crichlow. 1993. *Race, Identity and Representation in Education*. New York and London: Routledge.
McCaskell, Tim. 1995. "Anti-Racist Education and Practice in the Public School System" in Stephen Richer and Lorna Weir, *Beyond Political Correctness:Toward the Inclusive University* (Toronto: University of Toronto Press, 1995).
McDiarmid, Garnet. 1976. "Trends in Society, Trends in Curriculum" in Garnet McDiarmid (ed), *From Quantitative to Qualitative Change in Ontario Education*. (Toronto: OISE, 1976), pp.149-90.
MacDonald, Madeleine. 1980. "Socio-Cultural Reproduction and Women's Education." in R. Deem (ed), *Schooling for Women's Work* (London: Routledge Kegan Paul, 1980).
Mackenzie, Hugh. 1999. "Education Funding in Ontario," *Our Schools/Our Selves*, 95 pp.97-126.

McIlroy, Anne. 2001. "Last Place for Quality, Accessibility Goes to Universities in Ontario," *The Globe and Mail,* 10 January 2001, A7.
Mackie, Richard. 2001. "Ontario Plans Report Cards to Help Parents Choose Schools." *The Globe and Mail,* 11 April 2001, A1/A9.
—— 2000 "Ontario Colleges Get More Cash to Cope with Growing Enrolment," *The Globe and Mail,* 22 February 2000, A7.
McKillop, A.B. 1994. *Matters of the Mind: The University in Ontario 1797<-1951.* Toronto: Ontario Historical Studies Series/University of Toronto Press.
MacLeod, Linda. 1988. *Progress as Paradox: A Profile of Women Teachers.* Ottawa: Canadian Teachers Federation.
McNally, David. 2001. *Bodies of Meaning: Studies on Language, Labor and Liberation.* Albany: State University of New York Press.
—— 1998. "Marxism in the Age of Information," *New Politics,* 24, Winter 1998, pp.99-106.
—— 1993 *Against the Market.* London:Verso.
McRobbie, Angela. 1996. "Looking Back at New times and Its Critics," in David Morley and Kuan-Hsing Chen, *Stuart Hall: Critical Dialogues in Cultural Studies* (London: Routledge,1996), pp 238-61.
—— 1978 "Working Class Girls and the Culture of Femininity" in Women's Studies Group, Centre for Contemporary Cultural Studies (eds), *Women Take Issue: Aspects of Women's Subordination* (London: Hutchinson, 1978), pp.96-108.
Marable, Manning. 1995. "Black Intellectuals in Conflict," *New Politics,* 53, pp.35-40 .
Marowits, Ross. 2001. "Standardized tests to count for 20% of final grade," *The Globe and Mail,* 25 June 2001, A6.
Marshall, T.H. 1950. *Citizenship and Social Class.* Cambridge: Cambridge University Press.
Martell, George. 1995. *A New Education Politics: Bo Rae's Legacy and the Response of the OSSTF.* Toronto: James Lorimer and Our Schools Our Selves.
—— 1974. "The Schools, the State and the Corporations," in George Martell, *The Politics of the Canadian Public School* (Toronto:James Lewis & Samuel, 1974), pp.3-36.
Martin, Emily. 1994. *Flexible Bodies: Tracking Immunity in American Culture: From the Days of Polio to the Age of AIDS.* Boston: Beacon Press.
Marx, Karl. 1954. *Capital, V.1.* Moscow: Progress.
—— 1969. "The Eighteenth Brumaire of Louis Bonaparte" in Marx and Engels, *Selected Works* V.1 (Moscow: Progress, 1969), pp 398-487.
Marx, Karl and Engels, Frederick. 1969. "Manifesto of the Communist Party" in *Selected Works* V.1 (Moscow: Progress, 1969), pp.108-137.
Meaghan, Diane and François Cassis. 1995. "Quality Education and Other Myths," *Our Schools/ Our Selves,* 71, pp.37-53.
Milloy, John S. 1999, *A National Crime: The Canadian Government And The Residential School System, 1879<-1986* Winnipeg : University of Manitoba Press.
Mittelstaedt, Martin. 1996. "Ontario to Overhaul Labour Legislation," *The Globe and Mail,* 16 April 1996, B1/B14.
—— 1995. "Changes in Ontario Labour Law Formalized," *The Globe and Mail,* 10 November 1995, A5.
Mishel, Lawrence and Ruy A. Teixeira. 1991. *The Myth of the Coming Labor Shortage: Jobs, Skills and Incomes of America's Workforce 2000.* Washington:Economic Policy Institute.
Mishra, Ramesh. 1990. *The Welfare State in Capitalist Society.* Toronto: University of Toronto Press 1990.
Moody, Kim. 1997. *Workers in a Lean World.* London:Verso.
Morisette, René, John Myles, Garnett Picot. 1995. "Earnings Polarization in Canada, 1969-1991" in Keith G. Banting and Charles M. Beach (eds), *Labour Market Polarization and Social Policy Reform* (Kingston: School of Policy Studies, Queen's University, 1995), pp.23-50.
Mort, Frank. 1996. *Masculinities and Social Space in Late Twentieth-Century Britain.* London/New York: Routledge.
Moscovitch, Allan. 1997. "Social Assistance in the New Ontario," in Diana Ralph, André Regimbald and Neree St-Amand (eds), *Open for Business, Closed to People* (Halifax: Fernwood 1997), pp.80-91.

Munro, Marcella. 1997. "Ontario's 'Days of Action' and Strategic Choices for the Left in Canada," *Studies in Political Economy*, 53, pp 125-40.
Murphy, J.T. 1972. *Preparing for Power*. Pluto: London.
*National Post*. 2000. Canadian Education Industry Summit 2000 Conference Website <http://www.nationalpost.com/npevents/conferences.html>.
Neary, Mike and Graham Taylor. 1998. "From the Law of Insurance to the Law of Lottery: An Exploration of the Changing Composition of the British State," *Capital and Class*, 65, pp.55-72.
Neilsen, Klaus. 1991. "Towards a Flexible Future — Theories and Politics," in Bob Jessop, Hans Kastendick, Klaus Neilsen and Ove. K. Pedersen, *The Politics of Flexibility: Restructuring State and Industry in Britain, Germany and Scandinavia* (Aldershot: Edward Elgar, 1991), pp.3-32.
Nelson, Marissa. 2001. "Students Take Special Pride in Prom Night," *The Globe and Mail* Saturday 25 June 2001, A16.
Neocleous, Mark. 1996. *Administering Civil Society: Towards a Theory of State Power*. New York: St Martin's Press.
Ng, Roxanna. 1995. "Multiculturalism as Ideology: A Textual Analysis" in M. Campbell and A. Manicom (eds), *Knowledge, Experience and Ruling Relations: Studies in the Social Organization of Knowledge* (Toronto: University of Toronto Press, 1995), pp.35-48.
—— 1993. "Racism, Sexism and Nation-Building in Canada: in C. McCarthy and W. Crichlow, *Race, Identity and Representation in Education* (New York and London: Routledge, 1993).
Oates, Joyce Carol. 1969. *Them*. Greenwich, Conn.: Fawcett Crest.
Omi, Michael and Howard Winant. 1993. "On the Theoretical Concept of Race." in C. McCarthy and W. Crichlow (eds), *Race, Identity and Representation in Education* (New York and London: Routledge, 1993), pp.3-10.
Ontario, Government of. 2001. *21 Steps in to the 21st Century*. Toronto: Government of Ontario.
—— 1996. *Doing Better for Less: Introducing Ontario's Business Plans*. Toronto: Government of Ontario.
Ontario Department of Education 1964, *Report of the Grade 13 Study Committee, 1964*. Grade 13 Study Committee.Toronto: Ontario Department of Education.
—— 1966. *Annual Report of the Department of Education*. Toronto: Ontario Department of Education.
—— 1911 *Education for Industrial Purposes. A Report By John Seath*. Toronto: King's Printer.
Ontario Education Alliance. [n.d.] 1997. *Every Day We Put Our Trust in Teachers to Look After Our Children*. Toronto: Ontario Education Alliance.
Ontario Federation of Labour. 1996. *Fight Back News*. 16 January 1996.
Ontario Jobs and Investment Board. 1999. *A Road Map to Prosperity: An Economic Plan for Jobs in the 21st Century*. Toronto: Ontario Jobs and Investment Board.
—— 1998a. Creating an Innovation Culture. Toronto: Ontario Jobs and Investment Board.
—— 1998b. *Preparing People for Tomorrow's Jobs*. Toronto: Ontario Jobs and Investment Board.
Ontario Legislative Assembly. Select Committee on Manpower Training 1963 *Report of the Select Committee on Manpower Training* Toronto: Ontario Legislative Assembly.
Ontario Ministry of the Attorney-General 2000 "Fact Sheet: The Parental Responsibility Act 2000." New Release, 15August 2000.
Ontario Ministry of Education and Training. 2001. "Backgrounder: Strict Discipline Programs." Toronto: Ontario Ministry of Education and Training. 23May 2001.
—— 2000a. "Ontario Schools Code of Conduct." Toronto: Ontario Ministry of Education and Training.
—— 2000b. "New government policy will allow majority of parents to set student dress codes" News Release. Toronto Ontario Ministry of Education and Training. February 2000.
—— 1999a. " Science: The Ontario Curriculum for Grades 9 and 10." Toronto: Ontario Ministry of Education and Training.
—— 1999b."Ontario's new high school curriculum increases emphasis on math, science, English." News Release. Toronto: Ministry of Education and Training, 4 March 1999.

―― 1999c. "English: The Ontario Curriculum Grades 9-10." Toronto: Ontario Ministry of Education and Training.
―― 1999d. "Ontario Secondary Schools, Grades 9-12 Program and Diploma Requirements." Toronto: Ontario Ministry of Education and Training.
―― 1998a. "Backgrounder: Access to Opportunities." Toronto: Ministry of Education and Training, 29 May 1998.
―― 1998b. "Excellence in Science and Technology to Be Recognized." News Release. Toronto: Ministry of Education and Training, 2 September 1998.
―― 1998c. "Science curriculum passport to jobs and opportunity, Johnson says." Ministry of Education and Training News Release, 30 March 1998.
―― 1998d. "Backgrounder: Highlights of the New High School Program." Toronto: Ontario Ministry of Education and Training.
―― 1996a. "Excellence in Education: High School Reform." Toronto: Ontario Ministry of Education and Training.
―― 1996b. "Excellence, Accessibility, Responsibility: Report of the Advisory Panel on Future Direction for Postsecondary Education." Toronto: Ontario Ministry of Education and Training.
―― 1996c. "Curriculum for Ontario Secondary Schools." Toronto: Ontario Ministry of Education and Training.
―― 1996d. "Choices into Action: Guidance and Career Education Policy Grades 1 to 12." 1998 Detailed Discussion Document. Toronto:Ontario Ministry of Education and Training.
―― 1993. "Key Statistics: Elementary and Secondary Education in Ontario." Toronto: Ontario Ministry of Education and Training.
Oates, Joyce Carol. 1969. *Them.* New York: Fawcett.
OECD. 1995. *Governance in Transition: Public Management Reforms in OECD Countries.* Paris: OECD.
―― 1993. *Higher Education and Employment: The Case of Humanities and Social Sciences.* Paris:OECD.
Oosthoek, Sharon. 2000. "Students Irked by Limits on Piercings," *Windsor Star*, 2 September 2000, E3.
Ornstein, Michael, Penni Steward and Janice Drakich. 1998. "Status of Women Faculty in Canadian Universities," *Education Quarterly Review*, 52.
Osborne, Ken. 1999.*Education : a guide to Canadian school debate, or, who wants what and why.*Toronto: Penguin.
―― 1988. *Educating Citizens: A Democratic Socialist Agenda for Canadian Education.* Toronto: Our Schools/Our Selves Foundation.
Owens, Robert E. 1998. *Queer Kids : The Challenges And Promise For Lesbian, Gay, And Bisexual Youth.* New York : Haworth Press.
Provincial Committee on Aims and Objectives of Education in the Schools of Ontario (PCAOESO). 1968. *Report.* Toronto:Ont Dept of Ed [Hall-Dennis].
Palmer, Bryan D. 1999. "Of Silences and Tranches: A Dissident's View of Granatstein's Meaning," *Canadian Historical Review,* 804, pp.676-86.
―― 1992. *Working Class Experience: Rethinking the History of Canadian Labour 1800<-1990.* Toronto: McClelland and Stewart.
Panitch, Leo and Donald Swartz. 1993. *The Assault on Trade Union Freedoms.* Toronto: Garamond Press.
Parker, Mike and Slaughter, Jane.1994. *Working Smart: A Union Guide to Participation Programs and Reengineering.* Detroit: Labor Notes .
Parr, Joy. 1999. *Domestic Goods: The Material, The Moral and the Economic in the Postwar Years.* Toronto: University of Toronto Press.
―― 1990. *The Gender of Breadwinners: Women, Men and Change in Two Industrial Towns 1880-1950.* Toronto:University of Toronto Press.
Pevere, Geoff and Dymond, Greig. 1996. *Mondo Canuck: A Canadian Pop Culture Odyssey.* Toronto: Prentice-Hall Canada.
Phillips, Paul and Erin Phillips. 1993. *Women and Work: Inequality in the Canadian Labour Market.* Toronto: James Lorimer.
Postman, Neil. 1995. "Education and Technology: Virtual Students, Digital Classroom," *Our Schools, Our selves,* 72, pp.69-79.
―― 1982. *Disappearance of Childhood.* New York: Delacorte Press.

Prentice, Alison. 1977. *The School Promoters: Education and Social Class in Mid-Nineteenth Century Upper Canada.* Toronto: McClelland and Stewart.
Purich, Donald. 1986. *Our Land.* Toronto: Lorimer.
Radforth, Ian and Joan Sangster. 1981. "A Link Between Labour and Learning: The Workers' Education Association in Ontario, 1917-51," *Labour/Le Travail,* 8/9, pp.41-78.
Rainnie, Al and David Kraithman, 1992. "Labour Market change and the Organisation of Work," in Nigel Gilbert, Robert Burrows and Anna Pollert, *Fordism and Flexibility: Divisions and Change* (New York: St. Martin's Press, 1992), pp.49-65.
Readings, Bill. 1996. *The University in Ruins.* Cambridge, Mass.: Harvard University Press.
Reed, Adolph Jr. 1997. *W.E.B. Du Bois and American Political Thought: Fabianism and the Colour Line.* New York and Oxford: Oxford University Press.
Reed, Julia. 1999. "Can B. Smith Be Martha?" *New York Times Magazine,* 22 August1999, pp.26-29.
Renzetti, Elizabeth. 1999. "Little Girls: Signed, Sealed and Delivered to the Label Marketers," *The Globe and Mail,* 9 September 1999, C5.
Repo, Satu. 1999. "Education Notes: Computers in Schools, A Solution in Search of the Problems?" *Our Schools/Our Selves,* pp.14-20.
Reynolds, Cecilia. 1989. "Man's World/ Woman's World: Women's Role in Schools," *Women's Educatio/Education des femmes,* 73, pp.29-33.
Rinehart, James, Christopher Huxley and David Robertson. 1997. *Just Another Car Factory? Lean Production and Its Discontents.* Ithaca, N.Y.:ILR Press.
Rinehart, James, David Robertson, Christopher Huxley and Jeff Wareham. 1994. "Reunifying conception and Execution of work under Japanese Prod Management" in Tony Elger and Chris Smith (eds), *Global Japanization? The Transnational Transformation of the Labour Process* (London and New York: Routledge, 1994).
Roberts, Harry V. 1995. "Introduction" in H.V. Roberts (ed), *Academic Initiatives in Total Quality for Higher Education.* Milwaukee: ASQC Quality Press.
Robertson, David, James Rinehart, Christopher Huxley and the CAW Research Group on CAMI. 1992. "Team Concept and Kaizen: Japanese Production in a Unionized Canadian Plant," *Studies in Political Economy,* 39, Autumn 1992, pp.77-107.
Robertson, Heather-jane. 1998. *No more teachers, no more books : the commercialization of Canada's schools.* Toronto: McClelland and Stewart.
—— 1995. "Hyenas at the Oasis: Corporate Marketing to Captive Students," *Our Schools, our Selves,* 72 #44, pp.16-39.
—— 1993. *Progress Revisited: The Quality of Work Life of Women Teachers.* Ottawa: Canadian Teachers Federation.
Robertson, Susan, Victor Soucek, Raj Pannu and Daniel Schugurensky. 1995. "'Chartering' New Waters: The Klein Revolution and the Privatization of Education in Alberta," Our Schools/ Our Selves, 72, pp.80-106.
Roche, Jeremy. 1999. "Children's Rights, Participation and Citizenship," *Childhood,* 64, pp.475-93.
Rowbotham, Sheila. 1973. *Hidden from History: 300 Years of Women's Oppression and the Fight Against It.* London: Pluto.
Roy, Richard, Harold Henson and Claude Lavoie. 1996. "A Primer on Skill Shortages in Canada." Ottawa: Applied Research Branch, Strategic Policy, Human Resources Development Canada. R-96-8E .
Royal Commission on Education in Ontario. 1950. *Report of the Royal Commission on Education in Ontario.* Hope Commission Toronto: King's Printer.
Royal Commission on Learning. 1994. *For the Love of Learning.* Toronto: Queen's Printer for Ontario.
Royal Commission on the National Development in the Arts, Letters and Sciences (RCNDALS) 1949<-51. 1951. *Report of the Royal Commission on the National Development in the Arts, Letters and Sciences.* Ottawa: King's Printer.
Rutherford, Jonathan. 1997. *Forever England: Reflections on Masculinity and Empire.* London: Lawrence and Wishart.
—— 1988. "Who's That Man?" in Rowena Chapman and Jonathan Rutherford (eds), *Male Order:Unwrapping Masculinity* (London: Lawrence and Wishart, 1988), pp.21-67.
Ryan, Toby Gordon. 1981. *Stage Left: Canadian Theatre in the 30s: A Memoir.* Toronto: CTR Publications.

Sadker, Myra, Sadker, David and Sharon Steindam. 1989. "Gender Equity and Education Reform," *Education Leadership*, 46 6, pp.44-47.

Sallot, Jeff. 1998. "Baril Vows to Fight Sexism in Military," *The Globe and Mail* 20 May 1998, A6.

Sangster, Joan. 1995. *Earning respect : the lives of working women in "small-town" Ontario, 1920<-1960*. Toronto: University of Toronto Press.

Sarick, Lila. 1996. "Metro Panel Approves Fingerprint Plan," *The Globe and Mail*, 15 May 1996, A5.

Schellenberg, E. Glenn, Jessie Hirt and Alan Sears. 1999. "Attitudes Toward Homosexuals Among Students at a Canadian University," *Sex Roles*, 401/2, 137-150.

Schissel, Bernard. 1997. *Blaming Children : Youth Crime, Moral Panics And The Politics Of Hate*. Halifax, N.S.: Fernwood.

Scott, Donna. 2000. "Why I Quit: Ontario Arts Council Boss Donna Scott Tells the Province's Cultural Priorities Shortchange Artists," *The Globe and Mail*, 4 Monday, December 2000, A17.

Scott, James C. 1998. *Seeing Like A State: How Certain Schemes To Improve The Human Condition Have Failed*. New Haven: Yale University Press.

Scott, Katherine. 1996. "The Dilemma of Liberal Citizenship: Women and Social Assistance Reform in the 1990s," *Studies in Political Economy*, 50, pp.7-36.

Sears, Alan. 1999. "The 'Lean' State and Capitalist Restructuring: Towards a Theoretical Account," *Studies in Political Economy*, 59, pp.91-114.

―――― 1997 Ontario Teachers Strike, *Labor Notes*, December 1997.

―――― 1995. "Before the Welfare State: Social Policy and Social Theory," *Canadian Review of Sociology and Anthropology*, 322, pp.169-88.

―――― 1990. "Immigration Controls As Social Policy: The Case of Canada 1900<-20," *Studies in Political Economy*, 33: pp.91-112.

Seccombe, Wally. 1993. *Weathering the Storm: Working Class Families from the Industrial Revolution to the Fertility Decline*. London: Verso.

Segal, Lynne. 1994. *Straight Sex : Rethinking the Politics of Pleasure*. Berkeley: University of California Press.

Semmel, B.1960. *Imperialism and Social Reform*. London: George Allen and Unwin.

Sgritta, Giovanni. 1997. "Inconsistencies: Childhood on the Economic and Political Agenda," *Childhood*, 44, pp.375-404.

Shaw, Martin and Ian Miles. 1979. "The Social Roots of Statistical Knowledge" in J. Irvine, I. Miles and J. Evans (eds), *Demystifying Social Statistics* (London: Pluto, 1979), pp.27-38.

Shepard, Michelle. 1998. "Trustees Vote to Cut Adult Education," *Toronto Star*, 16 April 1998, A1/A26.

Shragge, Eric. 1997. "Workfare: An Overview," in E. Shragge (ed), *Workfare: Ideology for a New Under-Class*. Toronto: Garamond Press, pp.17-34.

Shephard, Michelle. 1998. "Trustees Vote to Cut Adult Education," *Toronto Star*, 16 April 1998, A1.

Shields, John. 1996. "Flexible Work, Labour Market Polarization and the Politics of Skills Training and Enhancement," in Thomas Dunk, Stephen McBride and Randle W. Nelsen (eds), *The Training Trap: Ideology, Training and the Labour Market. Socialist Studies 11* (Winnipeg/Halifax: Society for Socialist Studies/ Fernwood Publishing 1996), pp.57-58.

Shields, John and B. Mitchell Evans. 1998. *Shrinking the State: Globalization and Public Administration "Reform."* Halifax: Fernwood.

Simmons, Christina. 1993. "Modern Sexuality and the Myth of Victorian Repression" in Barbara Melosh (ed), *Gender and American history Since 1890* (London/New York: Routledge, 1993), pp.17-42.

Simpson, Mark. 1994. *Male Impersonators: Men Performing Masculinity* London: Cassell.

Sivanandan, A. 1985. "RAT and the Degradation of Black Struggle," *Race and Class*, xxvi 4, pp.1-33.

Smaller, Harry. 1995. "The Teaching Profession Act in Canada: A Critical Perspective," in Cy Gonick, Paul Phillips and Jesse Vorst (eds), *Labour Pain, Labour Gains: 50 Years of PC 1003. Socialist Studies 10* (Winnipeg/Halifax: Society for Socialist Studies/ Fernwood, 1995).

Smith, Dorothy. 1990. "Women's Experience as a Radical Critique of Sociology,"in D. Smith *The Conceptual Practices of Power* (Toronto: University of Toronto Press, 1990), pp.11-30.
—— 1987 *The Everyday Worlds as Problematic: A Feminist Sociology* Toronto: University of Toronto Press.
Smith, Murray E.G. and K.W. Taylor. 1996. "Profitability Crisis and the Erosion of Popular Prosperity: The Canadian Economy, 1947<-1991," *Studies in Political Economy*, 49, pp.101-130.
Spigel, Lynn. 1992. *Make Room for TV: Television and the Family Ideal in Postwar America*. Chicago:University of Chicago Press.
Stager, David. 1999. "Labour Market Trends and Projections for Systems Analysts and Computer Programmers in Canada." Ottawa: Applied Research Branch, Strategic Policy, Human Resources Development Canada. R-99-4E.
Statistics Canada. 1998. "The Daily," 14 April 1998.
—— 1995. "The Daily," Tuesday 19 September 1995.
—— 1978. *Historical Compendium of Education Statistics, Confederation to 1975*. Ottawa: Ministry of Industry, Trade and Commerce.
Stedman Jones, Gareth. 1971. *Outcast London*. Harmondsworth: Pelican..
Steedman, Carolyn. 1987. "Prison Houses" in Martin Lawn and Gerald Grace (eds), *Teachers: The Culture and Politics of Work*. London: Falmer Press.
—— 1982. *The Tidy House*. London: Virago.
Stephens, Sharon. 1995. "Children and the Politics of Culture in 'Late Capitalism'" in S. Stephens (ed), *Children and the Politics of Culture* (Princeton: Princeton University Press 1995), pp.3-47.
Stokes, Peter. 1989. "College Transfer Revisited" in *Vison 2000. Colleges and the Educational Spectrum: Colleges and Universities. Background Papers* (Toronto: Ontario Council of Regents), pp.1-17.
Storey, Robert 1994. , "The Struggle for Job Ownership in the Canadian Steel Industry," *Labour/ Le Travail* 33 Spring 1994, 65-106. .
Strange, Carolyn. 1995. *Toronto's Girl Problem : the Perils and Pleasures of the City, 1880-1930* Toronto: University of Toronto Press.
Stuckey, J. Elspeth. 1991. *The Violence of Literacy*. Portsmouth, N.H.:Boynton Cook.
Tackaberry, Jason. 2000. "Rave New World," *Ottawa Citizen*, Saturday 27 May 2000, A15.
Tasker, Mary and David Packham. 1994. "Changing Cultures? Government Intervention in Higher Education 1987-93," *British Journal of Education Studies*, 422, pp.150-62.
Taylor, Alison. 2001. *The Politics of Educational Reform in Alberta* .Toronto: University of Toronto Press.
Taylor, Jeffrey. 2001. *Union Learning: Canadian Labour Education in the Twentieth Century*. Toronto: Thompson.
Thane, Pat. 1982. *The Foundations of the Welfare State*. Essex: Longman.
Thomas, Alan M. 1976. "A Funny Thing Happened on the Way to Parnassus," in Garnet McDiarmid (ed), *From Quantitative to Qualitative Change in Ontario Education* (Toronto: OISE, 1976), pp.101-18.
Thompson, Audrey. 1997. "Surrogate Family Values: The Refeminization of Teaching." *Educational theory*, 472, pp.315-39.
Thompson, E.P. 1993a. "The moral Economy of the Crowd in the Eighteenth Century." in E.P. Thompson, *Customs in Common* (New York: New Press, 1993), pp.185-258.
—— 1993b "Time, Work-Discipline and Industrial Capitalism." in E.P. Thompson, *Customs in Common* (New York: New Press, 1993), pp.352-403.
—— 1968. *The Making of the English Working Class*. Harmondsworth: Penguin.
Thompson, Grahame. 1990. *The Political Economy of the New Right*. Boston: Twayne.
Thorne, Barrie. 1993. *Gender Play: Girls and Boys in School*. Buckingham: Open University Press.
—— 1987. "Revisioning Women and Social Change: Where are the Children?" *Gender and Society*, 11, pp 85-109.
Tilly, Charles. 1995. "Citizenship, Identity and Social History," *International Review of Social History* 40, Supplement 3, pp 1-17.
Tomlinson, J. 1981. *Problems of British Economic Policy*. London: Methuen.
Topalov, C. 1985. "Social Policy from Below: A Call for Comparative Historical Studies," *International Journal of Urban and Regional Research*, 92.

Traub, James. 1997. "Drive-thru U.: Higher Education for People Who Mean Business," *The New Yorker*, 20 & 27 October 1997, pp.114-23 .
Trickey, Jean. 1997. "The Racist Face of Common Sense" in D, Ralph, A Regimbald and N St-Amand (eds), *Open for Business, Closed to People: Mike Harris's Ontario* (Halifax: Fernwood, 1997), pp.113-121.
Troper, Harold. 1972. *Only Farmers Need Apply: Official Canadian Government Encouragement Of Immigration From The United States, 1896<-1911*. Toronto: Griffin House.
Tudiver, Neil. 1999. *Universities for Sale: Resisting Corporate Control over Canadian Higher Education*. Toronto: Lorimer.
Turk, James. 2000. "Introduction: What Commercialization Means for Education" in J. Turk (ed), *The Corporate Campus: Commercialization and the Dangers to Canada's Colleges and Universities* (Toronto: Lorimer, 2000).
———— 1997, "Days of Action, Challenging the Harris Corporate Agenda," in Diana Ralph, Andre Regimbald and Neree St-Amand (eds), *Open for Business, Closed to People* (Halifax: Fernwood 1997).
United Nations 1995 "The United Nations Convention on the Rights of the Child [1989]". Reprinted in S. Stephens (ed), *Children and the Politics of Culture* (Princeton: Princeton University Press, 1995), Appendix, pp.335-52.
Urquhart, Ian. 2001. "Private Schools: How They Decided," *Toronto Star* 12 May 2001, A1, A4.
Ursel, Jane. 1992. *Private Lives, Public Policy: 1000 Years of State Intervention in the Family*. Toronto: Women's Press.
Vallance, Elizabeth 1983, "Hiding the Hidden Curriculum: An Interpretation of the Language of Justification in Nineteenth-Century Educational Reform" in Henry Giroux and David Purpel (eds), *The Hidden Curriculum and Moral Education; Deception or Discovery?* (Berkeley: McCutchan Publishing, 1983), pp.9-27.
Valverde, Mariana. 1991. *The Age of Light, Soap and Water: Moral Regulation in English Canada 1885<-1925*. Toronto: McClelland and Stewart.
Vision 2000. 1990. *Vision 2000: Quality and Opportunity: A Summar.y* Toronto: Ontario Council of Regents.
Vygotsky, L.S. 1978. *Mind in Society: The Development of higher Psychological Processes*. Cambridge: Harvard University Press.
Wald, Alan. 1987. *The New York Intellectuals: The Rise and Decline of the Anti-Stalinist Left from the 1930s to the 1980s*. Chapel Hill: University of North Carolina Press.
Walker, Richard. 1989. "Machinery, Labour and Location" in Stephen G. Wood (ed), *The Transformation of Work* (London: Unwin Hymen, 1989), pp.59-90.
Walkom, Thomas. 1997. "The Truth Behind Mike Harris' Handling of Teachers," *Toronto Star*, 30 September 1997, A2.
Warburton, Rennie. 1997. "Aboriginal Status and Canadian Politics," *Studies in Political Economy*, 54.
Weber, Max. 1958. "Science as Vocation" in H.H. Gerth and C. Wright Mills (eds), *From Max Weber: Essays in Sociology* (New York: Oxford University Press, 1958), pp.129-56.
Weeks, Peter. 1995. "Current Educational Initiatives in New Brunswick," *Our Schools/ Our Selves*, 71, pp.83-102.
Welch, David. 1997. "The Franco-Ontarian Community under the Harris Counter-Revolution," in Diana Ralph, Andre Regimbald and Neree St-Amand (eds), *Open for Business, Closed to People* (Halifax: Fernwood, 1997).
Wells, Don. 1997. "From Fordist Worker Resistance to Post-Fordist Capitalist Hegemony?" *Labour/Le Travail*, 39, Spring 1997, pp.241-60.
White, Hayden. 1987. *The Content of the Form: Narrative, Discourse and Historical Representation*. Baltimore: Johns Hopkins University Press.
Wideman, Ron. 1995. "The Common Curriculum: Policies and Outcomes, Grades 1<-9," *Orbit*, 261, pp.2-5.
Williams, Raymond. 1981. *Culture*. London: Fontana.
———— 1977. *Marxism and Literature*. Oxford: Oxford University Press.
Willis, Paul. 1977. *Learning to Labour: How Working Class Kids Get Working Class Jobs*. Farnsborough: Saxon House.
Wilson, Elizabeth. 1991. *The Sphinx in the City: Urban Life, The Control of Disorder and Women*. Berkeley: University of California Press.

*Windsor Star.* 2000. "U.S. Campuses Considered," *Windsor Star,* 4 March 2000, A9.

——— 1999. "Runciman Urges Cops for Schools," *Windsor Star,* 1 May 1999, A1, A2.

Wolf, Eric. 1982. *Europe and the People Without History.* Berkeley: University of California Press.

Wolfe, David. 1989. "New Technology and Education: A Challenge for the Colleges," in Vision 2000 Study Team 2 (eds), *Vision 2000: Colleges and the Changing Economy* (Toronto: Ontario Council of Regents, 1990).

Womack, J.P., Daniel T. Jones and Daniel Roos. 1990. *The Machine that Changed the World.* New York: HarperCollins.

Wood, Ellen Meiksins. 1999. "An Interview with Ellen Meiksins Wood," *Monthly Review,* 511, pp.74-92.

——— 1998. "Class Compacts, The Welfare State and Epochal Shifts: A Response to Frances Fox Piven and Richard A. Cloward," *Monthly Review,* 498, pp.24-43.

——— 1997. "What is the Postmodern Agenda?" in Ellen Meiksins Wood and John Bellamy Foster, *In Defense of History* (New York: Monthly Review, 1997), pp.1-16.

——— 1995. *Democracy Against Capitalism.* Cambridge: Cambridge University Press.

——— 1988."Capitalism and Emancipation," *New Left Review,* 67, pp.1-21.

Wood, Stephen. 1982. "Introduction" in Stephen Wood (ed), *The Degradation of Work?* (London: Hutchinson, 1982), pp.11-23 .

Wotherspoon, Terry. 1998. *The Sociology of Education in Canada: Critical Perspectives.* Toronto: Oxford University Press .

——— 1991 "Educational Reorganization and Retrenchment," in T. Wotherspoon (ed), *Hitting the Books: The Politics of Educational Retrenchment* (Toronto:Garamond Press, 1991), pp.15-34.

Wright, Lisa. 1995. "Welfare Squad to Visit Homes," *The Toronto Star,* 24 August 1995, A1/A18.

Wrigley, Julia. 1992. "Gender and Education in the Welfare State," in J. Wrigley (ed), *Education and Gender Equality* (London: The Falmer Press, 1992).

Yates, Charlotte. 1993. *From Plant to Politics: The Autoworkers Union in Postwar Canada.* Philadelphia: Temple University Press.

Young, Iris Marion 1995 "Polity and Group difference: A Critique of the Ideal of Universal Citizenship," in Ronald Beiner (ed), *Theorizing Citizenship* (Albany: State University of New York Press, 1995), pp.175-208.

Zuboff, Shoshana. 1988. *In the Age of the Smart Machine: The Future of Work and Power.* New York: Basic Books.

# Index

aboriginal peoples
   residential school system 144
   social policy 11
Abramovitz, Mimi 165
Abramowitz, Mimi 130
Abrams, Phillip 25
Adams, Mary Louise 166, 186
Adorno, Theodor 105
adult education
   cutbacks 66
African Canadians
   disengagement from school 148
   streaming in educational system 148
Alberta
   charter schools 222
   Klein government 18
Allen, Lillian 137
Anderson, Benedict 38
Apple, Michael 24, 212
Ariès, Phillipe 192
assimilation of immigrants and ethnic minorities 96, 129, 136, 137, 143
Axelrod, Paul 101

Balibar, Etienne 34
Bannerji, Himani 24, 136, 138
Barlow, Maude 238
Beatty, Paul 147
Benjamin, Walter 257
Bernstein, Basil 24, 92
bodies
   and consumerism 173
   gendered 167
Bourdieu, Pierre 24
Bowles, Samuel 23, 87
Braithwaite, Wendy 147
Brand, Dionne 135, 136, 139
Braverman, Harry 59, 62
Brecht, Bertolt 247, 251, 252, 253, 254, 255
Brodie, Janine 171
business
   partnerships with educational institutions 118, 119, 224

Callinicos, Alex 25
Canada
   national identity 85, 96, 141, 145
Canadian Chamber of Commerce 73, 74, 156, 214
Canadian Federation of Independent Business 73, 214
Canadian Federation of Students 245
Canadian Union of Public Employees
   Local 1001 strike 244
   Local 3903 strike 234, 244

Carby, Hazel 148
career planning 80
Carnoy, Martin 23
Cassis, François 66
Chapman, Rowena 174
charter schools 222, 237
child labour 197
childhood
   as subversive 200
   child poverty 201, 202
   historical changes 192
   increasing stress 197
   play time 177, 195
citizenship 28, 32
   and children 48, 196, 202
   and education policy 10
   formation in schools 76
   inclusion and exclusion 11, 15, 17, 19, 45, 150
   social citizenship 10, 44
   university students 53
Clarke, John 104
Clarke, Simon 35
Clarricoates, Katherine 180
class and education 199
   working-class students 37
Committee on Religious Education in the Public Schools of the Province of Ontario 145
commodification
   knowledge 215
   self-commodifying individuals 210, 211
Connell, R.W. 174
consumerism 28, 229
   and parental choice ideology 222
   working class 17
Coontz, Stephanie 165
corporal punishment 40, 46, 47
Corrigan, Paul 78
Corrigan, Phillip 12, 16
Council of Ontario Universities 57
credentialism 91
Critcher, Chas 104
cultural revolution 9, 12, 119
   and neo-liberalism 10
Curtis, Bruce 39, 40, 49

D'Emilio, John 169
Davis, Bill 55
Day, Richard 142
Dei, George 135, 139
deskilling 8, 55, 59, 63
   of teaching 217
discipline
   administration of population 24, 35
   and citizenship 32
   and lean production 72

boot camps 18, 29, 200, 203
citizenship as 88
Foucault 32
labour discipline 7, 8, 73, 74, 162
market discipline 17, 18, 207, 209
self-discipline through education 54
time-discipline
    35, 38, 39, 48, 88, 177, 194, 195
Du Bois, W.E.B. 24, 124, 136
Dunk, Thomas 69
Dymond, Grieg 85

Ecker, Janet 204, 205
Economic Council of Canada 9, 68, 72, 212
education workers
    non-teaching employees 22
Ehrenreich, Barbara 161, 173
Elger, Tony 62
entitlement 14, 21, 200, 210, 231
    social policy 18
Eves, Ernie 59

Fanon, Frantz 135, 138
Field, Norma 197
Fiorino, Albert 47
Fleming, W.G. 32, 46
Fordism
    13, 16, 23, 28, 71, 105, 158, 174, 175, 179
Foucault, Michel 24, 32
Fox, Bonnie 173
francophones
    educational rights 144
    social policy 11
Frank, Blye 182
Fraser, Nancy 24
Freedman, Estelle 169
Freire, Paolo 216
Fukuyama, Francis 111, 112

Garrahan, Philip 72
Garrahan, Phillip 8
Gaskell, Jane 43
gays and lesbians
    accomodation in schools 187
    discrimination in schools 182, 185
    queering perspectives 256
    social policy 11
gender
    in classroom teaching 181
generic skills 64, 65, 67, 82, 83
Gentile, Patrizia 166
Gidney, R.D. 27
Gilroy, Paul 148
Gintis, Herb 23, 87
Giroux, Henry 24, 25, 37
Goldberg, Theo 143
Goldin. Claudia 163
Gordon, Lewis R. 134
Gordon, Linda 19, 24, 171
Grade 13 Study Committee 48
grading system
    and commodification 216
    competition 10, 90
    failure 21, 45
    gendered 180

Gramsci, Antonio 26, 58, 154
    common sense 6
    Fordism 13, 16
Granatstein, Jack 107, 109
Grossmann, Atina 19, 163
Guthrie, James 236

Hall-Dennis report
    44, 45, 50, 53, 77, 95, 96, 121
Haraway, Donna 157
Harris, Mike 1, 3, 5, 6, 19, 23
    common sense revolution 3, 6
    on PhD programmes 60
    on skills requirements 65
Harris, Nigel 85
Harvey, David 193
Hayden, Dolores 164
Heron, Craig 43, 168
heterosexuality 186
hidden curriculum 39, 181
hierarchies of knowledge 89, 92, 98, 108
Highway, Thomson 137
Hill, Paul 236
historical sociology 25, 58
history education 108, 109
Hobsbawm, Eric 107
Hoddinott, Susan 66
Hodkinson, Phil 80
Høeg, Peter 88
Holland, John 41
Holmes, John 62
Holmes, Mark 216, 221
Holzman, Michael 91
hooks, bell 136, 251
Horkheimer, Max 105
Human Resources Canada 75
Hunter, Ian 181

immigration controls 118, 150, 159
    tightening 19
information technologies
    and lean production 8
    skills shortage 60
    virtual university 15
institutional ethnography 27
invention of tradition 107

Jackson, Nancy 43
James, C.L.R. 91
Jameson, Frederic 9, 108, 110
Jessop, Bob 70
Johnson, Dave 101
Johnson, Richard 5, 151

Kay, Geoffrey 24, 33
Kelley, Robin D.G. 105, 152
Kinsman, Gary 166
Kuehn, Larry 239
Kuhn, Thomas 98, 112

labour education 93
labour market
    and changes in education 23
    and welfare state 12

# INDEX

deregulation 14
flexibility 13
part-time or temporary work 9
polarization 9
position of young people 71
Labour Party (U.K.) 70
Lacis, Asja 257
Lareau, Annette 197
Lazarus, Neil 139
Leach, Belinda 13, 175
lean production 28, 29
  and workers' knowledge 61
  cultural dimensions 17
  definition 2
  elimination of "waste" 7
  gender polarization 158
  implications for education 24, 194
  just in time 8, 9
  key principles 7
  management by stress 8, 12, 21, 68, 72, 83
  subcontracting 9
  work teams 8
  workplace organization 8
Levin, Henry 23
Lewchuk, Wayne 160, 163
liberal arts 81
  debates about relevance 51
  impact of Massey Commission 52
  shift away from 100
liberal education 28, 121, 154, 211
  and transition to post-liberal education 132
  community colleges 56
  critique 23
  expansion in the 1960s 53
  under threat 101
Lindsay, David 101, 114
literacy
  and social inequality 90
  cuts in programmes 66
  workplace requirements 63
Little, Doug 240
Livingstone, David 24, 49, 60, 69, 70, 90, 218
Lloyd, David 10, 24, 33, 39, 76, 97

MacDonald, Madeleine 181
market orientation 3
  education system 21, 78, 210, 221
  enterprise culture 79, 117, 214
  youth and children 176, 206, 207, 209, 225
Martell, George 49
Marx, Karl
  analysis of commodification 207, 208
  dynamism of capitalism 99
  value and labour time 35
masculinity 188, 189
  and consumerism 176
  at school 37
  at work 20
  breadwinner norm 160
  changes over time 20
Massey Commission 51, 52, 53, 95, 142
McBride, Steven 69
McDiarmid, Garnet 47
McKillop, A.B. 51
McNally, David 216
McRobbie, Angela 183

Meaghan, Diane 66
moral economy 12, 13, 228, 231, 232
Morisette, René 69, 71
Mott, James 24, 33
multiculturalism
  Canadian strategy 96, 133, 141, 145
  vs. monoculturalism 133, 143
Murphy, J.T. 93
Myles, John 69, 71

Nelson, Randle 69
neo-liberalism 239
  and citizenship 10
  definition 2
Neocleous, Mark 24
New Democratic Party 1, 70

Oates, Joyce Carol 45
Ontario Days of Action 22, 234, 239, 240, 241
Ontario Jobs and Investment Board 101, 103, 114
Osborne, Ken 32
Our Schools/Our Selves 27
Overton, Jim 66

Packham, David 214
Parker, Mike 8
Parr, Joy 158
Passeron, Jean-Claude 24
Pevere, Geoff 85
Picot, Garnett 69, 71
Pierce, Lawrence 236
Postman, Neil 193
privatization
  and social policy 18
  post-secondary education 82
  transportation 17

racialization
  and criminalization 19, 203
  and labour market polarization 9
  family forms 169
  ideology of standards 150, 152
  liberal education 133
  school integration and segregation 123, 144
  whiteness 142
Rand Corporation 236
Readings, Bill 24
Reed, Adolph 125, 128
Repo, Satu 213
Reynolds, Cecilia 180
Roberts, Harry V. 226
Robertson, Heather-jane 180, 224, 238
Runciman, Bob 204
Rutherford, Johnathon 174

Safe Schools Act 2000 204
Sayer, Derek 12, 16
Schissel, Bernard 203
school uniforms 154, 205, 242
Seath, John 42, 43
sexual harassment 182
sexualization of children 209
Sgritta, Giovanni 201

Sivanandan, A 146
Slaughter, Jane 8
Smaller, Harry 49
Smith, Dorothy 27, 155
Snobelen, John 3
social inequality
  increasing polarization
    2, 7, 9, 13, 14, 20, 198
social policy
  lean state 2, 13, 14, 15, 18, 19, 20, 22
  welfare state 2, 10
Spock, Benjamin 87
Stager, David 60
standardized testing 21, 56, 67, 198
  and gender 183
  and market orientation 220
  boycotts 243
  critique 66
  elimination of Grade 13 exam 49, 198
  Grade 10 literacy test 102
  I.Q. test 91, 151
Steedman, Carolyn 164, 167, 180, 199
Stephens, Sharon 193, 196
Stewart, Paul 8, 72
streaming 48, 49, 67, 68, 83, 102, 148, 152
  and labour market inequality 44
  and social inequality 123
  by gender 156, 172, 183
Stuckey, J. Elspeth 90, 94
student activism 53, 233, 242, 243, 245
student-centred learning
  47, 48, 49, 50, 67, 193, 194, 216, 217, 238, 258

Tasker, Mary 214
Taylor, Alison 26
Taylor, Jeffrey 93
Taylorism 22, 61, 160, 217
teacher training
  historical development 40
teacher unions
  and labour movement 240
  unionization in Ontario 239
teachers
  blaming 4, 235, 236
  lesbian and gay 187
  professionalism 41, 238
  strike 1997 6, 233, 234, 240
teaching
  as labour process 21, 237
  feminization of teaching 41, 179
technological change 116, 244
  and education reform 4
technological determinism 112, 116
Thatcher government, UK
  4, 5, 18, 73, 80, 117, 151, 152, 212, 220
Thomas, Paul 10, 24, 33, 39, 76, 97
Thomas, Alan 87
Thompson, E.P. 195, 231

Thompson, Grahame 17
Thorne, Barrie 167, 179, 181
Tomlinson, Jim 86
Total Quality Management 15, 226
  in education 227
trade unions
  anti-union laws 14
  public sector 15
tuition fees 223

underfunding
  universities 52, 95
University of Phoenix 82, 222
user pay
  17, 57, 107, 176, 184, 195, 206, 210, 223, 229, 244
  education system 21

Vallance, Elizabeth 39
violence in schools
  perception of increase 4, 177
Vision 2000 56
vocationalism
  and generic skills 64
  community colleges 55
  expansion of vocational streams 49
  historical development 42
  new vocationalism 68, 73, 77, 100
volunteerism
  compulsory community service 81
  labour market restructuring 16
voucher system 6, 118, 237
Vygotsky, L.S. 218

welfare state
  impact on education policy
    45, 46, 47, 48, 50, 54
Willis, Paul 182
women
  educational achievement 156
  flexible labour 13, 157
  labour market 9
  social policy 11, 19, 130
  unpaid labour
    20, 43, 157, 162, 163, 165, 168, 171, 172, 185
Wood, Ellen 131, 196
worker activism 17, 40, 42
  France 1995 15
  impact on social policy 11
Workers Education Association 93
workplace culture 8
Wotherspoon, Terry 219, 226

York University Faculty Association 243
Young, Iris Marion 24, 129

Zuboff, Shoshana 63, 160, 172

# Recently Published Titles from Garamond Press

Yildiz Atasoy & Wiliam K. Carroll eds.
**Global Shaping and its Alternatives**
1-55193-043-9

Deborah Barndt
**Tangled Routes: Women, Work and Globalization on the Tomato Trail**
1-55193-042-0

Pat Armstrong et al.
**Exposing Privatization: Women and Health Care Reform in Canada**
1-5519-037-4

Marie Campbell & Fran Gregor
**Mapping Social Relations: A Primer in Doing Institutional Ethnography**
1-55193-034-x

Robert Hackett and Richard Gruneau
**The Missing News: Filters and Blindspots in Canada's Press**
1-55193-027-7

D.W. Livingstone
**The Education-Jobs Gap: Underemployment or Economic Democracy**
1-55193-017-X

James P. Mulvale
**Reimagining Social Welfare: Beyond the Keynesian Welfare State**
1-55193-030-7

Janice Newton et al
**Voices From the Classroom: Reflections on Teaching and Learning in Higher Education**
1-55193-031-5

H. C. Northcott and Donna M. Wilson
**Dying and Death in Canada**
1-55193-023-4

Manjunath Pendakur & Roma Harris eds.
**Citizenship and Participation in the Information Age**
1-55193-035-8

Gary Teeple
**Globalization and the Decline of Social Reform: Into the 21st Century**
1-55193-026-9

Roberto Bissio ed.
**The World Guide 2003-2004 An Alternative Reference**
1-55193-046-3

Garamond Press Ltd., 63 Mahogany Court, Aurora, Ontario L4G 6M8
Tel (905) 841-1460 • Fax (905) 841-3031 • garamond@web.ca • www.garamond.ca

Quebec, Canada
2003